Selling For Dummies®, 4th Edition

Published by: **John Wiley & Sons, Inc.,** 111 River Street, Hoboken, NJ 07030-5774, www.wiley.com

Copyright © 2015 by John Wiley & Sons, Inc., Hoboken, New Jersey

Media and software compilation copyright © 2015 by John Wiley & Sons, Inc. All rights reserved.

Published simultaneously in Canada

For general information on our other products and services, please contact our Customer Care Department within the U.S. at 877-762-2974, outside the U.S. at 317-572-3993, or fax 317-572-4002. For technical support, please visit www.wiley.com/techsupport.

Wiley publishes in a variety of print and electronic formats and by print-on-demand. Some material included with standard print versions of this book may not be included in e-books or in print-on-demand. If this book refers to media such as a CD or DVD that is not included in the version you purchased, you may download this material at http://booksupport.wiley.com. For more information about Wiley products, visit www.wiley.com.

Library of Congress Control Number: 2014951025

ISBN: 978-1-118-96723-2 (pbk); ISBN: 978-1-118-96725-6 (ebk);
ISBN: 9781118967249 (ebk)   658·85

Manufactured in the United States of America

10 9 8 7 6 5 4 3 2

Contents at a Glance

Table of Contents

Part II: Doing Your Homework Before You Sell a Thing 47

Chapter 4: Understanding Your Potential Clients. 49

Introduction

∙ ∙

*W*elcome to *Selling For Dummies,* 4th Edition. Although this book is about selling products and services to businesses and consumers, it goes beyond that knowledge. This book is really about people skills. After all, knowing how to get along well with others is a vital skill — especially if your career involves persuading them toward ownership of your ideas, concepts, products, or services.

If all you want to do is discover how the masters of sales accomplish what they accomplish, you would be able to do that just by reading this book. But if you want to achieve that master's status in sales for yourself, then you have to do more than a one-time read-through. Think of this book as a reference tool — it's designed to help you discover the basic techniques of sales and establish a strong foundation of good habits on which to build a great career. So don't save a space for this book on the top shelf of your bookcase with all the other dust collectors. Keep it within easy reach so when you need to refer back to one of its pearls of wisdom for encouragement, you won't have far to go.

To be successful in sales, you must be flexible, have good listening skills, and be willing to put others' needs before your own. With the selling skills covered here in your arsenal, you'll have more happiness and satisfaction in *all* areas of your life, not just in your selling career (although your career will certainly benefit, too).

About This Book

Selling For Dummies, 4th Edition, can help you get more happiness and contentment out of your life right now by helping you gain more respect, earn more money and more recognition for the job you do. It can help you get more agreement from your friends and family, have more control in negotiations, and of course, garner more sales. Above all, this book is a reference tool, so you don't have to read it from beginning to end. Instead, you can turn to any part of the book that gives you the information you need when you need it. And you can keep coming back to the book over and over throughout your selling days.

As the original dummy in sales, I'm the perfect person to write this book. I started my selling career in real estate at age 19. Real estate may have been a great career choice, but at the time I owned neither a suit nor a car. All I had was a band uniform and a motorcycle. And believe me, selling real estate on a motorcycle wasn't easy; rather than loading up the prospective buyers in my car, I had to ask them to follow me to the properties and hope they didn't get lost along the way. When they finally came to their senses and realized that this kid couldn't possibly be for real, they'd keep going straight when I'd make a turn. (To make things even worse, wearing a woolen band uniform in Southern California's summer heat didn't allow me to present the coolest image, either.)

But I stuck it out because I knew there was big money to be made in the selling business — if I could just find out what the successful people were doing that I wasn't. I learned it all the hard way, through trial and error. Early in my career, a professional, experienced salesperson told me I had to learn how to *close,* meaning "to close the sale." I responded, "I don't have many clothes." See why I only averaged $42 a month in my first six months of selling real estate?

Needless to say, I've come a long way since then, and it thrills me to give you the chance to benefit from the mistakes I made, as well as from the subsequent success I've had. Yes, I've had successes. I achieved my goal of becoming a millionaire by the age of 30, beating my own deadline by nearly three years! At age 27, I was one of the most successful real estate agents in the whole country — a guy who started without a decent suit or a vehicle with four wheels! Just goes to show you that it doesn't matter how much of a dummy you are on this subject when you start. With this book by your side, serving as a reference for all the selling situations you encounter, you'll master the selling, persuasion, and people skills you need to really shine.

Foolish Assumptions

When writing this book, I assumed that its readers would either already be in sales careers or considering going into sales. It doesn't matter whether you're selling corporate jets or cookies, the basic selling strategies apply simply because you're selling to *people.*

I also assumed that you like people in general and that you enjoy working with them. You're not a hermit or a recluse, you don't have an extreme case of anthropophobia (a fear of people), and you aren't painfully shy.

Another assumption is that you're interested in learning and willing to experiment and apply the strategies in this book. If you're not serious about at least trying something new to get different results than you're getting now, you might as well give this book to someone else. This book contains answers, strategies, and tactics for successfully selling products and services, but they won't work until you put them to work.

Conventions Used in This Book

To help you navigate this book, I include the following conventions:

- ✔ **Boldface** highlights key words in bulleted lists and action steps that you should follow in a specific order.
- ✔ Defined terms and words I choose to emphasize are in *italics*.
- ✔ Web addresses appear in `monofont`.

When this book was printed, some of the Web addresses I reference may have needed to break across two lines of text. If that happened, rest assured that there are no extra characters (such as hyphens) to indicate the break. So, when using one of these Web addresses, just type in exactly what you see in this book, pretending as though the line break doesn't exist.

I also use some terms interchangeably in this book. For example, the people you look for to present your offering to may be called *prospects* or *buyers* in one area. In other areas, I refer to them as *potential clients,* which I believe creates a more positive, powerful mental image about who they are.

Icons Used in This Book

Icons are those little pictures in the margins throughout this book, and they're meant to draw your attention to key points that are of help to you along the way. Here's a list of the icons I use and what they signify.

When you see this icon, you can bet that stories from my years of experience in selling and from my students' experiences are nearby. And, oh, what stories I have to share. . . .

This icon highlights phrases to say to go beyond the basics and become a true champion at selling. This icon highlights sample exchanges between you and your prospective client so you can see exactly how a conversation can develop if you know just what to say.

I once had a college professor who told us that he didn't care whether we were awake or slept in his class as long as we learned the things he highlighted with red flags — because those were the areas we'd be tested on. So instead of being the typical warning that red flags usually indicate, this icon highlights the crucial pieces of information and skills you need for selling anything. When you see this flag in the margin, take notice. Great selling tips are at hand.

Some things are so important that they bear repeating. So this icon — like a string tied around your finger — is a friendly reminder of information you'll want to commit to memory and use over the long haul.

When you see this icon in the margin, the paragraph next to it contains valuable information on making the sales process easier or faster — anything from prospecting to closing and beyond.

This icon highlights things you want to avoid and common mistakes salespeople make. An important part of achieving success is simply eliminating the mistakes. And the information marked by this icon helps you do just that.

Beyond the Book

In addition to the material in the book you're reading right now, this product also comes with additional access-anywhere content on the web. You'll find more information on the free Cheat Sheet at www.dummies.com/cheatsheet/Selling. I include links to relevant articles on the parts pages of this book as well, which you should also check out at www.dummies.com/extras/Selling.

Where to Go from Here

Glance through the Table of Contents and find the part, chapter, or section that resonates with where you currently are in your selling career. That's the best place to begin.

To benefit the most from the material in this book, do a little self-analysis to see where you're the weakest. I know admitting your faults is tough, even to yourself. But reading the material that covers your weaker areas is likely to bring you the greatest amount of success.

Studies by my company, Tom Hopkins International, show that most traditional salespeople lack qualification skills. They waste a lot of time presenting to people who can't make decisions on what they're selling. If you're in traditional sales and you aren't sure whether qualification is your weakness, Chapter 9 is a great place to start.

The most successful people in life are those who continue to grow. The fact that you're reading these words now puts you into that realm — because it isn't how much you know that counts, but how much you can discover *after* you "know it all." Congratulations for believing in yourself, in your ability to change for the better, in your ability to improve your lifestyle, *and* in your ability to improve the lives of the people you help with this book's many tips on the art of selling. I wish you greatness!

Part I
Laying a Solid Foundation for Selling

getting started

with

selling

In this part . . .

- ✔ Understand what the role of selling is, what common approaches successful sales people use to convey messages, and how better selling skills can boost your career.

- ✔ See how to achieve selling goals and make clients happy in each of seven simple selling steps.

- ✔ See how getting out of your comfort zone can help you improve sales, enjoy your career, and sell what people want to buy.

Chapter 1

Selling Makes the World Go Around

Selling is happening every time two human beings communicate. It's everywhere around you. In fact, selling affects nearly every waking moment of your day. So in this chapter, I help you understand what exactly this thing called *selling* is, how it's done, and how you can use selling skills to make your life and your career better.

Understanding What Selling Is

In the strictest sense of the word, *selling* is a process of communication in which one party imparts knowledge and information to the other party in order to win the first party over to the other's ideas, concepts, products, or services. In the traditional sense of the word, *selling* is the process of moving goods and services from the hands of those who produce them into the hands of those who can benefit from their use.

Selling involves both educational and persuasive skills on the part of the person doing the selling. It's supported by print, audio, video, and online messages that sell either the particular item or the brand name as being something the buyer would want to have.

In the 1800s Robert Louis Stevenson said, "Everyone lives by selling something." Without selling, products that have been manufactured would sit in warehouses for eternity, people working for those manufacturers would become unemployed, transportation and freight services wouldn't be needed, and all of us would be living isolated lives, enjoying only the fruits of our own labors.

Look around you right now. You can probably spot hundreds, if not thousands, of items that were sold to get where they are right now. Even if you're totally naked, sitting in the woods, you had to be involved in some sort of selling process to have this book with you.

If you choose to ignore material possessions, take stock of yourself internally. What do you believe? Why do you believe what you do? Did someone — like your parents or your peers — sell you a set of values as you were growing up? Did your teachers persuade you to believe, through demonstration, that 2 + 2 = 4? Or did you figure that one out on your own? Odds are that whether you're living in a material world or you've forsaken all earthly possessions, you've been involved in selling one way or another.

The preceding paragraph should have persuaded you to at least look at selling a bit differently than you have in the past. It was done, too, without pushing facts and figures on you. Good selling isn't pushing; it's gently pulling with questions and getting people to think a bit differently than they have before.

The selling triangle

When I give seminars about mastering the fundamentals of selling, I use a triangle with equal sides, like the one here, to illustrate the three main elements of selling:

✔ On one side is product knowledge, which I cover in Chapter 5.

✔ On the other side are selling tactics and strategies — the people skills — that I cover in Part III.

✔ And on the base of the triangle are the words *attitude*, *enthusiasm*, and *goals*, which I cover in Part V.

Attitude, enthusiasm, and goals

The three sides of the selling triangle are equally important. If product knowledge was all that mattered, then technical designers, manufacturers, or assemblers of products would be the best salespeople. Of course, these folks often know the products quite literally from the inside out. But until they are trained in selling skills and understand how much of a role attitude plays in sales, their sales approach is often 99 percent description of product and 1 percent relation of the product to the needs of the individual clients — and that rarely results in a sale.

Great selling skills, without product knowledge and enthusiasm, won't get you far either. Even if you're comfortable talking with practically anyone, and you've invested a tremendous amount of time mastering the best words for creating positive pictures in the minds of your prospects, if you don't have a clear picture in your own mind of what your product, service, or idea *will do for your buyers,* how can you paint the right pictures in someone else's mind?

And if you're excited about selling, but you have little knowledge or experience with selling tactics and strategies, your enthusiasm will open the doors a crack. But you'll get your fingers slammed when you start pushing product (because *pushing product* isn't how you sell anything).

Remember: A professional who hasn't developed all three sides of the triangle is failing to reach his full potential and letting down his clients, who expect to work with a competent person. Do your best to develop all three areas of your selling life in order to reap the highest rewards.

Getting a Grip on How Selling Is Done

Although the definition of selling is fairly straightforward, the approaches to selling are virtually endless. In this section, I cover the primary ways that products and services are sold (in order from most direct contact to least amount of contact), and I give you some important tips for using each method.

Face-to-face

On an average day, many sales are concluded in a face-to-face fashion. Breakfast, lunch, and dinner are purchased in person at favorite restaurants. People physically register in hotels or check in at airport counters. Retail stores abound with sales opportunities, and millions of salespeople sit across desks, conference tables, or kitchen tables turning prospects into clients. The only retail establishment I can think of where you can make a purchase without speaking with someone is the self-checkout line at the grocery store.

The fun part about person-to-person selling is that you can read prospects' body language and speak with yours. You can hand them information. Have them handle your product or experience the service firsthand. Involve all their senses. Have them taste, touch, smell, hear, and see just how cool your widget is. (I cover methods for doing this in Chapter 10.)

Phone

With a telephone, salespeople have the potential to reach nearly any other person on the planet. And what you say when your prospective client answers the phone, if he answers at all, is critical. In some industries, you actually try to sell the product on the first call (referred to as a *one-time close*). In other industries, you're selling interest — enough interest that the person to whom you speak gets out of his home and down to your store or lets you visit him in his home or place of business. Either way, you're selling what your business is all about, leaving the person on the other end with a very distinct impression of you and your company — good or bad. And you only have a few seconds to make that connection before he reacts with a brush off or hang up.

Although telemarketing is a thriving method for reaching potential clients, many telemarketers who sell to consumers are finding it more and more challenging to reach a live person when they place their calls. If you plan to use this method of approach, be prepared to leave curiosity-building voice messages in order to make connections with potential clients. More and more people are screening their calls with caller ID features and voice mail than ever before. So unless you have your number listed in the phone book as "Sweepstakes Winner Announcement," plan on reaching a lot of answering devices. (I cover telephone strategies in more detail in Chapter 7.)

If you hear a live person say "Hello" on the other end of the line, you almost have cause for rejoicing — and you have to be prepared for that happening. Be clear about what you're selling, whether it's a product, a meeting, or simply getting permission to send the person information.

Despite the difficulty telemarketers often have in getting through to people who are willing to listen to them, selling by phone is widely accepted and recognized as a true sales profession. It requires tact, training, and the ability to articulate a compelling message in a very brief amount of time, as well as the skill of helping others recognize you as a warm, caring individual who has their needs at heart. Companies across many industries realize that gifted phone sales professionals can help bring a product or service to market in a much more efficient and cost-effective manner than face-to-face selling and reward good ones accordingly.

Email

Many companies rely primarily on email solicitations. In fact, an entire industry revolves around writing copy specific to email marketing and strategies to get your messages through the many spam filters employed by individuals and companies alike.

Even though email allows to you get your message to the person who owns the email address, it doesn't mean you're actually reaching him. Many people set up multiple email addresses. People may use one email account for personal communication, another for providing contact information on websites, and one for commercial use. Thousands of email addresses lie abandoned in cyberspace — with completely full inboxes.

Although the cost of sending email messages is minimal compared to the cost of printing a mail piece and adding the postage to it, getting through to the person you're trying to reach is getting tougher — unless you sell business-to-business (B2B) and have a business email address. Most businesses are in the habit of forwarding emails of employees who have left the company to the person who becomes responsible for their work. So, there's an advantage of email in that if a buyer or purchasing agent moves on, you don't have to look too far to connect with his replacement.

So far, business email appears to be deemed hands-off. Secretaries and receptionists may receive copies of emails, but they aren't likely to delete email messages from their bosses' computers. Home email, on the other hand, may not be thought of as quite so sacred. In fact, some couples share an email address. In that case, your message may be seen and deleted by one party when it was intended for the other, but it still has a decent chance of being seen by the person you want to reach.

To make sure that your intended recipient receives the message you're sending, I suggest putting the recipient's name in the subject line (for example, "Here's the information you asked for, Mike").

If you use email to connect with prospective clients, you can include your message in the body of the email itself, or you can send it in an attachment that looks like one of your ads or printed pieces or that contains a link to your website. Be aware that many companies set spam filters to not allow emails through that have attachments of a certain size. Some go so far as to not allow emails with any type of attachment. Some companies even ban emails that include hyperlinks to web pages. The rules keep changing and you must be ready and willing to adapt to them.

Email, when used properly, is an extraordinary vehicle for getting your message out. However, you need to be aware of the laws governing the use of email. Sending follow-up emails or proposals and presentation materials is fine, but if you're planning to use email as part of a larger sales campaign (similar to the way you would use direct mail), you must first get the permission of the recipient of the message, or what is commonly referred to as an *opt-in email list*. I discuss email lists in more depth in Chapter 7.

Social media

At the time of this writing there are no fewer than 6 types of social media and well over 50 social media platforms available for your use. It's not feasible to expect you or anyone else to be expert in all of them. What I recommend is to determine which two or maybe three platforms would be of best use to you. By that I mean, find out where the people in your client demographic participate in social media and use those platforms. Many of my students find LinkedIn to be extremely beneficial as a prospecting tool. They can find out a lot about prospective clients before ever contacting them — turning cold calls into slightly warmer calls by searching out common ground in advance of making contact.

Other students make great connections on Twitter by following and reading the Tweets posted by potential business partners or clients. Then, they can reach out to those people with a bit of knowledge of what their hot buttons are.

Some small business clients find great success by promoting their products via Instagram, Pinterest, or Facebook, all of which offer the opportunity to use visual images to sell concepts or products.

I can't tell you which social media platform is best for your particular field of sales. Speak with other successful sales pros in your company or your industry to learn how they're benefiting from social media. Then, do yourself a favor and attend a webinar, read a book, or take a class on the platform you select. Knowing the basics saves you a lot of frustration, time, and effort.

The technological revolution — and your role in it

If you plan to have a successful career in sales, you need to become somewhat computer savvy. Even if you're still selling something as simple as buggy whips, you need to track your client contacts in the most efficient manner possible to maximize your sales. You also need to have access to the phenomenal volume and quality of information available on the Internet. Not becoming familiar with the basics of computers and what they can do for you is like locking yourself outside your place of business with nothing more than a business card.

Understanding the basics of today's technology is also crucial so you can converse with clients who are in tune with it. Nothing ruins your credibility faster than pulling out your 3-x-5-inch index cards to jot down a client's contact information when he's using the latest tablet or smartphone.

Take advantage of contact management software (CMS), contact relationship management software (CRM), or sales force automation (SFA), all of which allow you to maintain customer lists, prospect information, schedules, contact information, follow-up notes, and a variety of other sales-related tasks. Talk with others in your particular field to determine which software has the features you'll benefit from the most, or see whether your company has made arrangements to use a specific program.

Online

Imagine that you're a customer, and you really, really want a new widget in a razzle-dazzle raspberry color. If you want to see it right away to be sure the color matches or complements your other widgets, what's the best solution? You can place a call to a widget manufacturer and wait for a salesperson to contact you and then send you a brochure or catalog. Or you can visit the manufacturer's website and, within a few minutes, see the actual widget in all its razzle-dazzleness. As a busy customer, what's the best use of your time? To go online and visit the website, of course. This way, you haven't wasted your time or the time of the salesperson if it turns out that the color wasn't what you had in mind.

Wouldn't your customers want to take advantage of the same opportunity? Yes, and if you don't offer your customers that opportunity, your competitors will.

Efficiency is the name of the game when it comes to technology. And you have to take advantage of every method possible to increase your efficiency while remaining easily accessible to your client base. The key is not to invest so much time in mastering the technology that you have no time remaining to do what you're paid for — and that is to sell products and services.

The Internet is like the library. You can find just about any piece of information you want there — and so can your potential clients. Not too many people invest a lot of time trotting down to their local library to look up information. They do, however, click on over to the Internet and search for information on your product or service and that of your competition. The key is to provide enough information and build enough curiosity about your product that buyers *want* to speak with you, the salesperson, in order to confirm you have what they need at a price they're willing to pay.

The people you approach to do business will likely have a great deal of knowledge about your product or service, so you better know those products and services better than they do (see Chapter 5 for more on this important topic). Look at the same resource information that your customers see. In fact, add to your repertoire a question about where they did their research on your product. Find out where your customers are going for information. If you have any impact on what's put there, make sure it's positive. If the information is incorrect, be prepared with facts, figures, and testimonials to correct it in the minds of your buyers.

Direct mail

Every piece of mail you receive, whether it's a letter of solicitation, a coupon, or a catalog, is devised for a single purpose — to build your curiosity and get you to take some type of action so that someone can sell you something. Companies play the odds that enough people will stop long enough to look at and consider their products before the direct mail hits the trash.

Believe it or not, a one-percent response rate for direct mail is considered average. That means only 1 out of 100 mail pieces generate an actual order. Ninety-nine of those mail pieces are tossed into the trash without ever generating a penny for the company that sent them. Plus, each of those mail pieces may cost a good bit to produce and distribute, especially if they contain a lot of full-color photos. So if that's the case, why is direct mail still so prevalent? The reason is simple: When you order from a company, you'll probably order something else from that company in the future. You become a customer, and good companies work very hard to keep you coming back for more. Over the long haul, a company recoups the dollars lost on tossed mail pieces with orders from the one percent who place repeat orders.

Recognizing What Selling Skills Can Do for You

Selling skills can do for you what a way with words did for William Shakespeare. They can do for you what powerful communication skills did for Abraham Lincoln, Franklin D. Roosevelt, and Martin Luther King, Jr. Selling skills can make or break you in whatever endeavor you choose. They can mean the difference between getting the promotion or job, landing the girl or guy of your dreams, or having to settle for less in life than you deserve.

If you're good at selling, you probably earn a satisfactory income and have rewarding personal relationships. If you're not completely satisfied with your income level or with the quality of your personal relationships, make the development of selling skills a priority, and you'll reap the rewards.

Having a strong set of selling skills is like having an inside track on what the next batch of winning lottery numbers will be. All you have to do is invest a bit of your time and effort to understand and apply this book's tried-and-true, proven-effective skills to your everyday life. Before you know it, they'll be such a natural part of you that no one, including yourself, will even recognize them as selling skills. People around you will just see you as a really nice, competent person instead of the stereotypical, cigar-chomping, back-slapping, plaid-coated, hand-mashing, used-car salesman that most people associate with selling. And, believe me, you'll then be in the class of people who make the world go 'round.

Salespeople are everywhere — even where you least expect them

The person who isn't selling isn't living. Think about that: At some point nearly every day, you're involved in a selling situation of some sort. You may call it by a different name or not even recognize it as an act of selling, but, all the same, selling it is. Here's just a short list of the people who sell things and whose "products" you buy:

✔ **Actors and actresses:** If you've ever watched a television show, movie, or play and been caught up in the story, you've been a part of a selling situation. The actor has given a believable performance — he's sold you on his portrayal of a character.

✔ **Food servers:** The wise server gives you choices of drinks, appetizers, meals, and desserts. He doesn't just ask to take your order. Why? Because when he employs a bit of salesmanship, he's almost guaranteed to receive a bigger tip.

(continued)

(continued)

Doctors: Doctors get tremendous rewards when they know — and use — selling skills. Not only is your doctor better prepared to convince you to follow his professional advice, but he's also building his practice because you're so happy with his advice that you tell your friends and family how great your doctor is, thus sending him referral business.

Lawyers: Lawyers need selling skills in every aspect of their profession. Lawyers have to sell not only to get business but also to persuade judges and juries that their clients are in the right.

Politicians: How does the public develop its expectations about political candidates? How do politicians get elected? They persuade the most people that, if they're elected, they can and will do the job the voters want done.

Parents: Whether by words or example, parents constantly sell their children values and beliefs. They convince or persuade their kids on what to wear or eat, how to act, who to have as friends, how to be a friend, and thousands of other things children need to learn to grow into happy, well-adjusted adults.

Kids: Few children can go into a store and resist the things shopkeepers purposefully place on the lower shelves to tempt the young. (Considerate of those shopkeepers, isn't it?) Get ready: You're about to observe master sellers at work. Notice what kids say and how they act when they try to persuade Mom or Dad to get them what they want. It's selling at its best.

Spouses-to-be: If you get married someday, you'll put forth one of the most important sales presentations of your life in persuading your significant other of the value of spending the rest of his or her life with you. And if you're already married, the trick is to keep persuading your significant other that he made the right choice.

Friends: If your friends enjoy a movie, they'll probably want to tell you about it — and sell you on going to see it yourself. Your friends may recommend a place to eat or persuade you to go to concerts or sporting events with them. All of these are examples of selling — but they're also examples of ways your friends build relationships with you. The more memories you share, the closer you'll continue to be — and so it is with the art of selling.

You're not immune from selling situations in your daily life — even if you don't come into contact with professional salespeople — and you may not even be aware that selling has occurred. We had a saying in our household when my children were young: "You've got to sell to survive." If this list hasn't convinced you of that, nothing will. (And if it has, then I've sold you on my ideas.)

Chapter 2

The Seven-Step Selling Cycle

I like to think of selling as a cycle because, when it's done properly, the last step in the cycle leads you back to the first. Your new, happy client gives you the names of other people she feels would benefit from your product or service, and then you have your next lead or potential client to work with.

I also like the fact that selling breaks down neatly into seven steps. Everyone can remember seven things, can't they? The seven steps I cover in this chapter are an overview of what I dive deeply into in Part III. Each step is equally valuable to you. Rarely are you able to skip a step and still make the sale. Each step plays a critical role and, if done properly, leads you to the next step in a natural, flowing manner.

Step #1: Prospecting

Prospecting can also be called *finding new business*. It involves strategies for finding the right potential buyers for what you're selling. When considering your product or service, ask yourself, "Who would benefit most from this?" For example:

✔ If the end user is a corporation, you need to make contacts within corporations. Usually, a purchasing agent is assigned to make buying decisions on behalf of the company, so you need to find out whom that person is and how to get in touch with her.

✔ If your end user is a family with school-age children, you need to go where families are (for example, soccer games, grocery stores, dance classes, the park, and so on). Or acquire a list from a credible source (go to Chapter 7 for more on finding contacts) and start contacting those people at home or through the various organizations they belong to.

To make an informed decision about which people to approach, you need to find out some information about them or the companies you've chosen as possibilities. Most of your research can be done online. This legwork is sort of a prequalification step in prospecting. You do even more qualification when you meet a prospective client — but why waste time on an appointment with a company or person who doesn't have a need for your offering or the ability to pay for it?

Prequalifying helps you just like market research helps companies determine their best target markets. In fact, one of the best places to begin your research in finding the most likely candidates for your product or service is your company's marketing department. The marketing department has done research during the product development stage to determine what people want in the product or service you sell. Study their results, and you'll get a handle on where to begin.

If your company engages in advertising to promote your products, you'll likely receive *leads* — names of people who called or otherwise contacted the company for more information about the product. Treat any client-generated contact like gold! What better person to contact first than someone who called you for information!

Other valuable assets are your friends, relatives, and business acquaintances. Tell them what type of product or service you're selling. Listen to the ideas and suggestions they come up with. Who knows — one of them just may know people at one of your prospect companies who would be happy to talk with you because of their relationship. If there's something good going on, people are always willing to share their stories with others.

A word of advice here that applies to all selling situations: Never begin any selling cycle until you've taken a few moments to put yourself in the shoes of the other person. Take yourself out of the picture and look at the entire situation through the eyes of the buyer. Mentally put yourself in her shoes and think about what would motivate you to invest your valuable time learning about your product or taking a salesperson's call. If you can't come up with solid answers, you may not have enough information about your product to even be selling it in the first place. Or you may not know enough about your potential audience to sell to them. If that's the case, it's back to the books for you. Study more about both areas until you're comfortable with being in that person's shoes. In other words, don't start prospecting until you have something of value to share with your prospects — something you're confident is worth their while to investigate and, hopefully, purchase.

If you ever face challenges getting through to potential clients, you may need to take a somewhat unusual approach to get their attention or bring about a positive response. Some ideas my students have used include

- ✔ **Including a photograph of your warm, smiling, professional self or even a video of your product in action.** If your goal is to arrange to meet with these people in their homes, they'll need to make some sort of connection with you other than seeing your signature line on a letter or email.

- ✔ **Including a tasteful comic about the situation your potential clients find themselves in without your product or service.** Your potential client will recognize the relief or benefit the product provides much sooner.

- ✔ **Adding a clever quote or anecdote to the bottom of a cover letter or email.** You can find books that have quotes for nearly any occasion. Check out BrainyQuote (www.brainyquote.com) to find just the right quote online. Taking a few moments to find this kind of attention-getter can make your initial contact stand out from the rest.

- ✔ **Using letters in place of numbers for your telephone number so it's easier to remember.** If your telephone number is 344-6279 and your name is Mary, you can use the alphabet on the telephone pad to ask your potential buyers to call 344-MARY. (If your name is Optimus Prime, this approach won't work for you.)

These ideas may be a bit gimmicky if you're selling corporate jets, but they've worked for some of my students who were marketing everyday products and services. The idea is to open your creative mind to unusual ways of reaching people and capturing their attention.

To ensure that your name gets in front of the prospective client more than once, send a thank-you note the day you make your first contact with her. Handwritten thank-you notes are the best and a wise use of the time they require. Thank-you notes are always read — and if the prospect hasn't had the time to review your letter and/or brochure when she receives your thank-you note, don't you think she'll go looking for your name among other mail or emails she's received? You'll make a positive first impression that will very likely bring you closer to getting an opportunity to connect on a deeper level.

Step #2: Making Initial Contact

You've found the right people as potential buyers. Now you actually get to meet them. To persuade another person to give you her valuable time, you need to offer something of value in return. For instance: To gain entrance to someone's home, you may need to offer a free estimate or gift in exchange for her opinion on the demonstration of your product. With a business-to-business appointment, getting an appointment may be a bit easier because you often work with a purchasing agent whose job it is to meet with and gather information from people like you. Depending on your product, you may also need to meet with a financial officer or owner of the business. When you meet via phone or online using Skype or a Google+ Hangout, treat the appointment the same way you treat an in-person meeting.

Your goal is to make agreeing to spend time with you as easy as possible. I strongly recommend giving your potential client two options with regard to dates and times. Say something like, "I have an appointment opening on Tuesday at 9:30 a.m., or would Wednesday at 3 p.m. be better for you?" This makes the other person look at her calendar and consider the open blocks of time in her schedule. Whereas, if you just say, "When can we get together?" she's likely to look at how busy she is and hesitate to commit at all.

When you get a commitment, confirm all the details such as where and how the meeting will take place — and get directions if it's an in-person meeting and you haven't been there before. Sure, you may be able to get directions from an online map site or by using a GPS device, but only the people who drive there every day will think to tell you if the street in front of their home or building is under construction and you have to take an unusual route. Besides, when a potential client provides this information it gives you an opportunity thank her, and your expression of gratitude makes her feel good, which is the first step in helping her like you.

Also, get a commitment as to who will be present. If you sell products to consumers and know you need to have the agreement of both spouses, you need to confirm that they'll both be present. If you're talking with a young, single person, she may decide to have a parent or other adult present to help her make a decision. In business situations, there may be a committee designated to consider and approve all purchases.

When you visit with a potential client, be sure to appear at ease so your prospect is comfortable with you. After all, the number-one need of people is the need to be comfortable. If you're uncomfortable, chances are good that unless you're a really good actor, your discomfort shows — and it may make your prospect uncomfortable, too.

Any tension at this point in the selling cycle will take a bit of doing on both sides to overcome. If you don't get past the tension, you can end up turning a potential win-win into a lose-lose situation. You won't make the sale, and the potential client will miss out on benefiting from your talents and fantastic product.

So what can you do to avoid or break any tension? Consider the following guidelines:

- First and foremost, consider what you look like to your prospect. We all know the old saying "You never get a second chance to make a good first impression." When in doubt about what to wear to an appointment, err on the side of conservatism. Your goal is to be dressed like someone your potential client turns to for advice. So if you're selling farm equipment, skip the business suit; jeans or khaki slacks and boots may be perfectly appropriate. On the other hand, if you're selling to a corporation, you'll want to choose a more formal style of clothing.

  You want to look your best. But also remember to be comfortable. If your new shoes are too tight or they squeak, you'll be conscious of that fact and you won't be able to put all your concentration into the meeting.

  In a prospective client's mind, any shabbiness in your appearance translates into shabbiness in work habits or a lesser quality product or service.

- Think twice before you wear your favorite cologne or perfume. Subtlety is the motto here. You never know if you'll meet someone who is allergic to your added scents. If the potential client opens the window, goes into a sneezing frenzy, or just keels over, you went a bit heavy on the fragrance — and you probably lost the sale.

- A special concern for women is jewelry. If it's attractive, that's great. But if it could be considered distracting, like a diamond tiara, that's bad. You don't want to be remembered as "that woman we talked with who had those humongous earrings." You want them to remember your competence and professionalism.

- Because this is a business situation, be prepared to shake hands, make eye contact, and build rapport. Building rapport is the getting-to-know-you stage that comes with any new contact. You must immediately begin building trust. People buy from people they like and trust. They must feel your trustworthiness as early as possible in the contact you make.

See Chapter 8 for more details on getting an appointment and putting prospects at ease.

Step #3: Qualifying

When you finally sit down with your potential client, you need to find out whether she's qualified to be your client. In selling, *qualifying* your prospects means finding out not just who they are but also what they do, what they have, and what they need.

You don't have to take on every client who qualifies for your product or service. If Ms. Big Bucks could become your biggest client, you'll likely be investing a large amount of your time with her. If you can't stand the woman after your first meeting, consider how well you'll really serve her needs and whether someone else in your company may be better suited to the potential stress this client could cause you.

If you've done your homework and looked up information about the prospect, you'll know what questions to ask. You'll eventually have to know a lot of information about her, providing you get the account, so if you're truly convinced that this is a good match for you, you may as well ask questions now. The more specific your questions, the more impressed your potential client will be with your expertise. Asking pertinent questions now shows that you're interested in more than just a closed sale and that you're looking into the future as a valued business partner with your client.

Your prospects will be qualifying you, too. So be aware of what you're showing them. Most clients are looking for people who are dependable, loyal, trustworthy, intelligent, competent, and even a little fun. Do your prospects see that when they look at you? If you need to communicate a trait that's difficult to see, figure out a way, short of wearing your Scout uniform, to bring those images to mind in the answers you give to their questions and the information you offer in your discussion of their needs.

The goal of your qualification discussion is to determine how well suited your product or service is to the potential client's situation — whether she can afford it and who the real final decision makers are. Ask questions to get her talking about what she has now, how it's not fulfilling her current needs, and how much of a budget she has for making an improvement. These questions are the same whether you're selling to a business or an individual consumer. (Head to Chapter 9 for the full scoop on the qualification process.)

Step #4: Winning Over Potential Clients with Your Presentation

Your presentation of your product, service, or idea requires the most preparation. In your preparation, practice your answers to common questions with a family member or fellow salesperson. Make a list of the benefits you think are your strongest persuaders in placing your product. Then figure out a way to work those points into responses to the common questions asked by potential clients.

For example, suppose you're selling a brand-new service through which busy people can dial a number to hear all of this week's grocery sale items at their favorite store. Then they can speak into the phone the quantity they'd like of each item (whether on sale or not) and have the items delivered to their homes. Because the service is new, you don't have a track record of success to brag about. So here's where you may start:

> PROSPECT: Well, it sounds like a good idea, but you haven't proven it to be successful. I'd hate to be a guinea pig and end up having to do my shopping anyway because it didn't work out.

> SALESPERSON: Because this is a new service, we're paying special attention to the orders that come in. In fact, we have two people who listen to the recording of each call to confirm that your verbal request is what shows up on our shopping list. One of them even gives you a quick call to verify your order, ask if there's anything else you'd like to add, and arrange the best delivery time for you.

The real issue is not that the service is new but that the client doesn't feel she would have the time to shop if the service didn't end up working out. By showing that you have backup systems in place to ensure the order is handled properly, you answered the quality-control question that triggered the prospect's "guinea pig" reference.

To demonstrate personal dependability and trustworthiness, tell the prospective client an anecdote from another client situation or even from an outside activity of yours. For example, if you were an Eagle Scout as a kid, that says a lot about you, doesn't it? Even if you didn't make Eagle Scout but were active in scouting for a number of years, that fact presents a positive image, one that says you stick to things and honor your commitments. Find a way to bring up those kinds of activities.

Your clients buy more than your product — they buy you.

Amazing things can happen during the rapport-building phase of a meeting. I know of someone who was in a meeting and noticed a small golf figurine on the prospective client's desk. She asked whether the decision-maker liked to play golf — a fairly general and safe question. The guy gave her a brief answer that didn't carry the conversation too far in that direction. Then she remembered a brand-new type of golf club that her husband had talked about. She asked her prospect whether he had ever heard of these new clubs and explained briefly why she was asking. Because her husband was so crazy about them, she wanted to get him a set for his upcoming birthday. It just so happened that the prospect's son was a cofounder of the company that developed and marketed those particular clubs. Suddenly, this prospective client was very interested in hearing the salesperson's husband's thoughts on the clubs, and a deeper relationship was established.

Check out Chapter 10 for additional pointers on making winning presentations.

Step #5: Addressing Concerns

How do you handle any negative comments or concerns your buyer raises during or after your presentation? Answer in simple, unemotional terms, and have recommendations in mind. For example, if your product is available only in certain colors, and none of them quite fits the décor of your prospect's office, be prepared to point out the least offensive color as being somewhat complementary. In fact, when you get around to discussing the colors, suggest something like this: "Based on your color scheme, the Sunrise Blue would best complement your décor." That way, you've already seen and addressed the objection before the prospect brings it up.

If you sidestep obstacles during your presentation, there's a good chance they'll come back to haunt you when you do make the sale. Find a way to bring up and elaborate on any concerns about fulfilling the needs of the buyer as early in the presentation as is appropriate. Don't let unfulfilled expectations bring your potential for a long-term relationship with a buyer to a bitter end. Cover all her concerns and make sure that she understands how those concerns will be handled — and that she's comfortable with your solution.

The most common concern you'll encounter in your entire selling career is the good old standby stall: "I want to think it over." When someone says she wants to think it over, it often means she's interested in owning your product but needs more information or to consult with someone else. She wouldn't waste her time objecting if she had no interest in it at all, would she? And if she's interested, you need to strike while the iron is hot. Find out exactly what it is she wants to think over. Sometimes, she needs clarification of the finer points of your presentation. However, in the majority of cases, you'll find that it's the money that causes her to stall. Surprise, surprise! Everyone wants a bargain. Unless your product or service is severely underpriced, most of your potential clients will want to bargain or will hesitate to see whether you'll offer to include something else just to get them to buy. I cover this and other aspects of addressing client concerns in more detail in Chapters 11 and 12.

Step #6: Closing the Sale

If you've researched your potential clients properly, given yourself enough valuable preparation time, and handled all the previous steps in a professional manner, you'll likely close the sale. Closing should follow naturally and smoothly after you address your buyers' concerns. But if your buyer doesn't automatically pick up a pen to approve your paperwork or write a check, don't panic. You don't have to turn into Jo Typical Salesperson and apply pressure to get what you want. Getting your prospect's business can be as simple as saying, "How soon do we start?" At this point, if you're confident about being able to give her what she needs, you should begin taking verbal ownership of your future business relationship with assumptive statements and questions.

You may also want to use analogies, quotes from famous people, or today's news to persuade people to go ahead and get started today. Use similar-situation stories about other clients who got involved with your product or service and are happy they did. Be prepared to show the potential client how she can afford this product or service if that's her area of hesitation. Often, that's just a matter of doing the math to show her how affordable the item is compared to the benefits she'll receive.

When it comes time to close, you should have reduced any sales resistance the person had early on and increased her level of sales acceptance so that closing is just a matter of agreeing on the details of startup or delivery dates and/or financing arrangements. I cover many methods of getting that final agreement in Chapter 12.

Step #7: Getting Referrals

After you close the sale, take a moment to ask for referrals. This can be as simple as asking, "Because you're so happy with this decision today, think about your extended family and business associates who may also be interested in learning about this product. Who comes to mind?"

In a corporate situation, ask about other departments within the company that may need your same service. Then ask about other office locations the company has. Finally, ask about associates of the purchasing agent who work at noncompeting companies.

When you're given the name or contact information of a new potential client, always ask for an introduction to the new party — by phone, email, or in person. If the client seems uncomfortable with doing that, at least get a quick email or letter of introduction that you may use when you contact the person.

If, for some reason, you and the prospective client find that this isn't the best time to go forward with the sale, instead of just walking out the door and saying goodbye, make the contact a part of your network of people who can help you find *other* people who may benefit from your product or service. For example, another department in your prospect's company may have people who could benefit from your product or service. Or the prospect may know of other companies needing your product. Don't ever walk away from an opportunity to network.

Immediately upon leaving the premises or ending the call, drop a thank-you note in the mail or send a quick appreciative email to the person. This guarantees that your discussion stays fresh in her mind for at least a few days. During that time, the right lead for you may come her way, and if you've left a good impression with your thank-you note, she'll be more likely to give you the referral.

Go to Chapter 13 for additional information on getting referrals.

Chapter 3

What to Sell

The main factor that separates the top five percent of people in sales from those who struggle to accomplish their goals is elementary (you thought I was going to say, "my dear Watson," didn't you?). Highly successful salespeople actually *enjoy* the crazy business of sales. To champion salespeople, selling isn't a job. Instead, champion salespeople have discovered how to turn their job (selling) into a fun hobby.

When champion salespeople seek out new clients, go to appointments, have a chance to visit, and ask for sales, they are doing what they love to do. It just so happens that champions get paid very well for their hobbies. If you're struggling with your ability to sell *and* with finding the desire to make it to the top, be glad that you and I are having this bookside chat because I've just given you the key to excelling in sales: *Turn your career into a hobby.* Before you know it, your new hobby will be a way of life. You will live and breathe selling — all to your advantage.

The more involved you get with selling, the more selling you observe going on around you in all areas of your life. When you truly study selling, you see that selling pervades every communication you have with others; and, on a purely business level, you notice and compare the selling efforts of others to your own. The fun part is that people never know what you're up to. You get to make all the mental notes you want, and they get to be your teachers. The best opportunity for discovery often (if not usually) occurs in an informal, nonselling atmosphere. In times and situations that you may not previously have seen as sales situations, a realization will creep right up on you and whisper, "Hey, there's selling going on here. You should be taking notes."

In this chapter, I show you the way people usually approach their hobbies and help you find a way to approach selling in the same way. I show you how you can challenge yourself throughout your lifetime to discover new things and forge new trails. And I give you an idea of what to expect along the way. Attitude and passion are a huge part of success — in sales and in life — and in this chapter I cover both so you can put them to work for you.

Taking a Long, Hard Look at Your Job Satisfaction

When you don't enjoy what you do to earn money, you make a draining trade-off — interminably long hours for incalculably short vacations. My question to you is this: As short as life is, are those 2 fun-filled weeks every year worth the 50 weeks of drudgery you have to go through to earn them? I certainly hope they are. After all, you're on this Earth for such a short time that you may as well do something you enjoy.

If you're in sales, you can find a multitude of ways to enjoy what you're already doing. If you discover and practice the communication skills that are a part of selling in your everyday encounters, your life is guaranteed to be more interesting. And anything that you're interested in has to include at least a little fun or it won't hold your interest, would it?

Do you ever have to drag yourself to work? Do you ever feel guilty about taking time away from your job when you have fun on vacation? If you answer "yes" to those questions, you need to take a long, hard look at what you do for a living and how much satisfaction it's bringing you. You may even want to seek professional career advice. Don't do a job just because it provides for you and your family. Consider what kind of life you're providing if every day you leave the house unhappy to go slogging through the trenches, and you can't even enjoy the little bit of vacation time you take because you're worried about what will lie in wait for you upon your return. Too many people work twice as hard the weeks before and after a vacation. If you work double time for those two weeks, you really haven't taken a vacation at all, have you? The company has received two extra weeks of work from you without compensation.

Wouldn't it be much more fun to take each day and enjoy it to its fullest, looking forward to getting up every morning, bright-eyed and bushy-tailed, vibrant with anticipation for what the day will bring? Wouldn't it be better to enjoy your workdays as much as you enjoy your free time? What would your life be like if you could enjoy your job as much as you enjoy your hobbies? What kind of life would you be providing for those around you if the central element of your life were no longer drudgery but rather the joy that comes from self-fulfillment? If you're willing to spend a little time figuring out how to turn your job into a hobby (with the help of the rest of this chapter), you can turn this dream into a reality.

Love the one you're with . . .

A merging of passion and profession has occurred in my life with selling. For me, selling began as a career opportunity that would fulfill a need — the need to make money. When I failed miserably at first, I knew I needed help, and I started a journey of study. I knew that some people made huge incomes in sales, so I assumed that they must have known something I'd not yet discovered.

It was at that point that I chose to turn selling into my hobby. When I started to educate myself — by watching everyday people and looking for little nuances of selling that worked for them, and by reading up on the subject — I also started making a lot of money. Believe me when I say that, at first, money was my motivation for my selling hobby. But since then I've managed to transform my job-turned-hobby into something much more: It has become a way of life.

Today, I live and breathe selling. I've built my business in such a way that I enjoy what I do for a living. I don't "work" anymore, if *work* means "doing some particular thing when you'd rather be doing something else." Selling now pervades every communication I have with others.

If you're in a job you don't like in order to earn a living, stop a moment and analyze what's going on. Why don't you like what you're doing? Chances are pretty good that it's because you're not growing, achieving, or having fun. The reasons behind those feelings usually have something to do with how competent you are in your field. If you're not really any good at what you do, it's no wonder your life's no fun.

If this description fits your life, you have two ways out: You can either change what you do to something that is more fun, or you can get better at what you already do in order to make it more fun. That's the great thing about living today: You have choices. No one is going to hold a gun to your head and tell you that you have to have this career and none other. If you aren't happy with what you've got, thousands of other choices are available to you. You have no excuse for staying in a job you don't thoroughly enjoy, but it's up to you to do something about it.

Choosing What to Sell

One of the questions I'm asked most often by people who are new to the selling profession is this: "Tom, what's a really great product to sell?" My answer isn't what they expect. They want me to tell them to work in a specific industry or to sell a particular product. But that's not how it works.

In order to do the job of selling well, you must believe in your product and the benefits it provides to your clients. So, my answer is, "The best product for you to sell is one that you truly believe in and can speak about with great enthusiasm and, if at all possible, from personal experience."

When you believe in your product and its benefits, you do the work necessary to become an expert on it. You're excited to talk about it. You gain a clear understanding of what type of person or company makes an ideal client for you. And your selling job is fun.

More often than not, people buy from you because of your conviction and enthusiasm for your product rather than because of your knowledge of the product.

As an example, say you apply for several sales jobs listed online without really knowing much about the products. You get hired and start the training process to gain product knowledge. Maybe you think the product is pretty neat. Maybe you're not sure about it, but have heard others in the company talking about Joe Champion and how he made $400,000 last year and won the all-expenses-paid trip to Fiji. And now, you want to be Joe, so you get excited. But you're not excited about the product. You're excited about what selling the product can do for you.

What happened? You just put dollar signs in your eyes. You've just made selling this product all about you. And your motivation will show in some way when you're with potential clients. Maybe you'll push a little hard to get them to buy. Maybe you'll avoid answering some of their questions and not make many sales.

When you love your product, it's a totally different story. Think about how you speak with friends when you find a new restaurant you enjoy. You can't wait to tell them about it, describe it in great detail, and get them to want to go there, too. That's the level of enthusiasm you must have about your product. So, rather than seeking a product that can earn you a lot of money, seek out a product you believe in and the money will come.

Attitude makes a difference

Studies prove that having a great attitude is one of the major traits that separate so-so salespeople from their highly successful colleagues. And I believe this is true in life in general, not just in sales. Think about the happiest, most successful people you know. How do you usually find them? Are they depressed, negative, or even apathetic? I doubt it. They're probably upbeat, smiling, and positive about life no matter what's going on in their lives. And, they're interested in what's going on in yours. They don't weigh you down with the drab details of their trials and tribulations.

That's the attitude you need to have with all of your clients all the time. Even when you have worked with someone for a long time, keep in mind that it's because he likes your product and enjoys being served by you. None of your clients are interested in becoming your shoulder to lean on when things are less than great at your company or within your industry. Be the shining light of positivity in their lives, and you'll do well in yours.

Do what my colleague, the great Zig Ziglar, recommended and turn your car into a classroom. While you're driving, you can listen to the radio, or you can inspire yourself to greater success by listening to selling skills audios. Don't limit this to your car. Listen to e-books or audio recordings on sales practices, positive messages, and self-development material on your smart phone or MP3 device while you exercise, while you shop, while you do just about anything.

Give yourself permission to explore some creative ways of starting conversations with others who may have a need for your product or service. Observe how the next salesperson you encounter makes you feel. What did he say or do that brought about that feeling? Challenge yourself to pay attention, and you'll soon find yourself eagerly anticipating the next selling situation.

You may already believe in something that you could sell. Why not take the hobby you love so much and figure out how to market that hobby or yourself? If you're involved in craftwork or handiwork, like woodworking or knitting, you may be able to sell the things you make. I'm not saying this change will make you a millionaire, but money isn't the only measure of success. If you can support yourself comfortably on the earnings from your hobby, I would deem you as having a successful life. Think about it! You already have the built-in enthusiasm, excitement, and knowledge of your hobby. Now all you need to do is show others why they need to feel the same way. If you do a little research, you'll find that many very successful businesspeople started out by selling their hobbies. Determine what you love to do, and then figure out a way to get paid for it. What could be better?

Success can fit many definitions — including yours

I always enjoy asking my seminar audiences for definitions of the term *success*. I've probably asked well over 40,000 people to define *success* for me over the years. I haven't kept strict records of their answers, but I have to guess that I have rarely gotten repeat answers. That's because success is like a fingerprint — it's individual. Of course, many of the answers I've received reflect a desire for monetary riches, love, and security, but few people have come up with a definition of success that can be understood and agreed upon by all who hear it.

Because of the variety of answers, I developed this one that I teach my students. It seems to cover most of the answers I've heard.

> **Success is the continuous journey toward the achievement of predetermined, worthwhile goals.**

I like the phrase *continuous journey* because I don't think anyone really wants to arrive at success and be done. In fact, I don't think it's possible to reach a place called *success* and be happy there forever. Look at Olympic athletes: At very young ages, they achieve greatness, worldwide acclaim, and medals that many people say show they're successful. If that achievement were success and if after achieving success they just stopped, what would those athletes do with the rest of their lives?

The other phrase that I like in my definition of *success* is *predetermined, worthwhile goals*. *Predetermined* shows that a choice was made, a course was set. It was something that required thorough consideration, and perhaps inspiration, to commit to. *Worthwhile* is key because I truly believe in the good of all humankind and that the majority of people in the world want to do something of worth with their lives.

Consider using this definition for yourself and lay a course for an exciting journey toward success!

Passion supplies meaning

If you decide to sell something you love as a hobby, you're already passionate about it and that's great. Consider this example: If your hobby is an outdoor sport, such as mountain biking, nothing is more exciting than cresting mountain peaks at sunrise or soaring downhill so fast that you have a permanent grin on your face. It's not just a physical experience either: It's charged with emotional involvement. When you schedule a biking event, it becomes a highlight that gives you a great feeling whenever you think about it. You plan every detail to make the outing the best one yet. You live and breathe for the next opportunity to get out there with your mountain-biking cohorts. When you think about your biking events, you feel an emotional jolt. Mountain biking also involves a great deal of physical preparation and can be quite challenging. But if the emotional involvement is strong enough, you can hurdle those barriers with no sweat (so to speak). When you get right down to it, avid mountain bikers have become sold on their pastime because they want to experience the passion that others have shared with them.

But people often lack that passion with their choice of what to sell. Too many people who are disillusioned with their products become detached from what goes on in their work environment. They become disinterested observers. They don't join in the company's extracurricular activities or interact much with others.

Those who are emotionally involved with their work, however, bring enthusiasm to their jobs. And for those people, life is much more interesting and more fun.

Many of the salespeople I talked with over the years love meeting new people. They are curious and interested in how other people live their lives. They seek out new ideas and opinions on topics that they previously barely knew existed. Some enjoy the challenge of the selling cycle — meeting a perfect stranger and, before too long, turning that person into a lifelong client. I think nearly everyone in sales gets off on the high of satisfying a need that someone had. It's a service attitude for most. For some, especially in the beginning, it's the knowledge that only they set the limit on how much income they earn. For those sales positions that require travel, many people enjoy meeting other travelers, seeing new sites, visiting different climates. Finding out about cultures different from their own inspires many salespeople who are involved in international business. For some, the flexibility that's often available in certain sales positions allows them to schedule valuable family time or to participate in events that occur when the rest of the world works. In some industries, entertaining clients involves attending sporting events that some salespeople wouldn't otherwise choose to attend.

If you're having trouble finding even one little thing to like about the product you're selling now, I suggest that you seriously consider making a change: Either change yourself, or change your job. No one should have to suffer through a job he hates. And if you're suffering through, you aren't doing yourself or your employer any good by continuing on with it. (See the earlier section "Taking a Long, Hard Look at Your Job Satisfaction" for more information.)

Becoming a Lifelong Student of Selling

Starting a career in selling is pretty simple. You don't need any special tools or equipment. No large financial investment is required. And you don't have to travel far to participate.

So what do you need to do to start selling successfully? Pay attention to the way your children or parents communicate with you about family matters. Watch how retail clerks treat you, and notice how you feel about the store in response. Get into the habit of really *reading* billboards and newspaper ads. Which ones speak directly to you and why? Listen carefully to radio spots; those that hold your attention the longest deserve some analysis. In general, become a student of selling situations presented to you daily by everyone from sales and marketing experts to your friends and family.

In the following sections, I explain the importance of setting aside time to learn about selling, and I provide tips for working your way through the learning process.

Making time to learn about selling

Although people allow their children the privilege of ample time to learn, they often don't allow themselves the same privilege. The large majority of people discontinue their conscious learning experiences in life when they complete their formal education. Hundreds of thousands of mature adults have not learned in the past 20 years half as much as they learned in their 4 years of high school or college courses.

Adults make excuses for themselves, saying that they don't have the time to take educational courses. Or they think that they can learn faster on their own. Or they assume that they don't really need to know much more than they already know. (Tune in to *Jeopardy!* or another quiz-type of program sometime to find out exactly how much you don't know if you fall into that last category.)

Most adults fail to continue the learning process not because of a lack of desire, but because of a perceived lack of time. They expect youngsters to spend most of their time on education, with a strong dose of fun thrown in for good measure. But somewhere along the way, as people grow into adults, that focus shifts to the responsibilities they have. Their desire for achievement overwhelms them, and creating time for education just doesn't happen.

Do you recall the old story about the two men cutting wood? One worked hard and steadily all day. The other worked hard, too, but every now and then would stop. At the end of the day, the second man had cut more wood, much to the surprise of the first. When asked how he did it, he said, "Every time I took a break, I sharpened my saw." I challenge you to set aside a specific amount of time every week, or at the very least, every month, to sharpen your saw. Register for a seminar that's coming to your area. There are many free webinars available online. At the very least, browse the list of TED talks you can watch (go to www.ted.com/talks/browse for topics). They're fairly short and concise (18 minutes or less) and provide a wealth of information. Invest a couple hours in the bookstore or library to find out about the latest books published on the field of selling or on your industry in particular. Put your hands on one and read — even if it's just while you're in the bathroom! After taking in that new information, you won't be the same person you were before. You'll see the world just a little bit differently, and your hobby of selling will progress even further.

From now on, challenge yourself to think of training seminars and educational events as professional necessities. Take these learning tools out of the realm of things to do "when you have the time" and put them into the category of things that you *must* do to reach the levels of success you set for yourself. Shift your perspective only that much, and you will *make* the time to continue your education — you will become a lifelong learner.

If you're truly serious about your selling career, consider attending the high-intensity sales seminars my company offers. You will leave having mastered much of the material — ready for your very next sales call. Visit my website, www.tomhopkins.com, for details.

Working through brain cramps

When you begin to develop a new skill, you can absorb only so much before you experience what I call a *brain cramp*. This happens when you reach a point of information overload. You've taken in the information, but haven't yet processed how to make it work in your life. The best approach to learning something new is to learn, practice, learn some more, and then practice some more. You can internalize only so much information at once. If you take on a whole new subject, such as selling, all at once, it may overwhelm you. You can become so uncomfortable that you may decide to give it up. Rather than giving up, break the learning down into smaller steps. Get a good understanding of one step before taking on the next.

If you're new to sales, concentrate on prospecting and qualifying strategies first (I cover those topics in Chapters 7 and 9, respectively). That way you spend more of your time with people who may actually need your product or service. Too many new salespeople think that all they need to know is how to close sales. That is so far off the mark. Why bother trying to close someone who isn't qualified to own your product? It's a waste of your time and his.

If you're a bit shy or uncomfortable with first-meeting greetings, work on just that step of selling for a while (see Chapter 8 for guidance). Write yourself a script and stick to it. Then change one word or phrase and continue to use it — refining it as you go until you find the one that breaks the ice faster with new people.

Another important area of selling is communication. This includes asking good questions and really listening to the answers. If this is your area of weakness, see Chapter 9.

Many novices who choose to consciously develop sales skills want instant success. I think it has something to do with being an adult and the expectation that adults must be quick studies. It's an assumption many people make: "I'm an intelligent adult. I *must* be able to figure out something as simple as this rather quickly." Well, figuring it out isn't too difficult, but the application can be tricky. Don't look at others who are more successful than you are and try to duplicate their sales techniques overnight. They are successful because they practiced, drilled, and rehearsed their material over a period of time. They already experimented with the nuances of body language, voice intonation, and inflection that you're just introducing yourself to. Keep in mind that old saying, "Don't assume anything about another person until you've walked a mile in his shoes."

Accepting productive mistakes

Giving yourself permission to be a lifelong student can change your life dramatically. But students don't always do things right the first time. So when you give yourself permission to be a student, you also give yourself the right to make mistakes. It takes some of the pressure off when you do. You don't have to be right all the time just because you're an adult.

If you have the attitude and mindset of a student, you won't beat yourself up over your failures and mistakes. Instead, you'll look at your mistakes as learning experiences. As a student, you must admit that you are fallible. Until you make that admission, you won't move far off the mark you're currently standing on.

After you do admit that you can make mistakes, though, seek out others who can teach you, people who can help you grow into the person you want to become. When you open yourself up to the possibility that you don't know everything and don't have all the answers, you start a quest to discover what you don't know — and that's an important step in the learning process.

One of my favorite reminders about learning is this: You can recognize true professionals by how much they learn *after* they "know it all." If you ever assume you know all there is to know about something, or even if you accept that you know enough, you have just doomed yourself to mediocrity.

Moving out of your comfort zone

To get to the level of comfort and success you want in your selling career, you need to step outside of your comfort zone. Your *comfort zone* is where you are today, and unless you change who and what you are today, you will never change what you get out of life. You can't let the desire to be comfortable rule your life. You see, when you open your mind to learning something new, you're not the same old comfortable person you were even a minute before. With that realization, you make yourself *uncomfortable* with the extent of your own ignorance.

But everyone wants to be comfortable more than anything else. So, even after you start your quest for growth, you set goals, do some research, and invest your time learning until you again reach a level of comfort with the knowledge you have and use in your everyday life. The trick is to find a way to make yourself *keep* growing — to make yourself just uncomfortable enough about today that you'll better yourself for tomorrow.

This striving for knowledge can become wonderfully habit-forming. It's such a kick to learn and benefit from new concepts and ideas that the highest achievers in life have become addicted to it. They wouldn't think of facing a single day without the anticipation of learning something new.

Develop a picture of the new you who will take the place of that old comfortable you. I teach my students that, at times, developing the "fake it 'til you make it" approach is extremely valuable. I don't mean this in a negative way at all. I mean for you to think about the person who already has all the traits you desire; visualize yourself as the person who uses selling skills effectively to get the raise or promotion he wants or as the person who experiences great satisfaction as a result of persuading others. When you act like that person, you try to say and do what he would say and do. Eventually, you begin having small successes with the material and, before you know it, you *are* that person. You wear the suit of success. And the more you wear it, the more comfortable it gets.

Professional athletes use this method of visualization all the time. Basketball players develop a clear picture in their mind's eye of just how the basketball will leave their hands for a three-point shot. They picture their fingers releasing the ball and see nothing of the crowd, only the net. When they first begin visualizing this, their bodies may not be up to speed with the picture, but if they play the picture often enough, chances are good that their bodies get the hint and soon perform accordingly. And you can do the same with your selling skills if you're willing to move out of your comfort zone long enough to learn something new.

Preparing for the Learning Curve: Changing from Caterpillar to Butterfly

No one masters something new the first time he tries it — whether it's a new hobby or a career in selling. Of course, some people have natural talents or skills (or even a certain level of interest) that apply to the new experience, but mastery cannot occur on initial impact. Learning anything takes time and practice. This is what people refer to as a *learning curve* — the time it naturally takes for someone to progress from being a complete beginner (or a caterpillar) to an expert (a butterfly). With any learning curve, you go through four major phases, or levels, of competency. I cover each of them in the following sections.

Unconscious incompetence

The first level of competency is known as *unconscious incompetence*. In this most elementary phase, you find people who don't even know that they don't know what they're doing. These people are the hardest ones to help because they haven't yet recognized or won't admit they need help. In daily life, these are the people who drift into your lane on the freeway and never realize you were there. They unknowingly leave grocery carts perilously close to new cars. They tend to live rather mediocre lives because either they haven't realized there's more to be learned — more to be aware of — or they have simply resigned themselves to be whatever they are at the present moment.

Everyone is at the unconscious incompetence level of learning whenever they first try something new. Watch a baby learning to walk. He doesn't know he doesn't know how to walk. He just tries it. When he learns, by falling, that it's not as easy as it looks, he reaches for helping hands. The instant he reaches for help, he moves to the next level of competency.

In business, someone who's unconsciously incompetent may include someone who's been in sales for a little while. He knows the product, how to fill out the paperwork, and thinks that's all there is to the story. He thinks that Joe Champion is so good because of his looks or his tight connections with the boss. He doesn't even know there are better strategies to close sales, more effective methods of asking questions, and so on.

A second type of individual falls into this category as well. That includes you and me. "What?" you say, "I never do things like that." You may not *now,* but chances are pretty good that you did before you became aware.

Conscious incompetence

The second level is *conscious incompetence.* People abandon unconscious incompetence when they suddenly realize that they don't know what they're doing. In the wonderful world of sales, you're very likely at the conscious incompetence level right now simply because you're reading this book. You've admitted that you don't have all the answers and that you want to find out more. And how do I know such an intimate thing about you? Because you wouldn't be reading this book if you hadn't admitted that you still have something to learn about selling.

But heed one word of caution here: Now that you realize you need to discover more, take action right away! Too many potentially great careers stall at this level because people don't know where to turn for help or won't expend the effort to find the right kind of help. Your lack of competency can be overwhelming if you don't take charge. Don't be like the deer you see in your headlights at night, frozen to a spot on the road. You must *move* in order to rise to the third level of competency.

Begin by reading this book, of course. Then move on to *Sales Closing For Dummies* and *Sales Prospecting For Dummies,* both written by yours truly. (The folks at Wiley are trying to be as helpful as possible in providing resources for you.)

If you learn better in person, start reading the ads in the business section of your local newspaper or business journal to find out what seminars are coming to your area (including mine) and make a commitment to attend. If you prefer to listen to something while you exercise or drive, borrow audiobooks or MP3s from a friend or the library, or invest in some yourself. Then listen to each of them a minimum of six times to achieve maximum retention of the material. The next step takes you to the next level of competence — trying the strategies in the real world.

Once upon a time, a future champion salesperson froze in his school production of *Sleeping Beauty*

For an example of acutely conscious incompetence in action, think about the first time you had to give a presentation in front of a group. It probably wasn't much fun, was it? If it was anything like *my* first time, you came out of it with strong misgivings about making public speaking your hobby.

My first public performance was in the second grade, where it was my honor to be chosen to be Prince Charming in our class presentation of *Sleeping Beauty*. This was pretty cool. I got to wear a neat costume and carry a sword. I was even going to get to kiss the Princess. At that point in the learning curve, I was definitely at the unconscious incompetent level in terms of my understanding of performing.

When it was time for me to go on stage, I walked out and saw the smiling faces of dozens of parents . . . and I froze. After I stood there for a couple of consciously incompetent minutes, my merciful teacher came out and led me off the stage. Needless to say, I eliminated public speaking from my list of potential careers. The irony is that my success in sales demanded that I give at least acknowledgment speeches at awards presentations, so I later had to face my dragon in order to continue on my journey toward success.

In fact, the first time I was contacted to give a formal talk, I responded with a reflexive but polite, "No, thank you." No trophy was involved, so I had little desire to get anywhere near a podium. But my dear friend, my mentor in sales, the great sales trainer of the 1950s and 1960s,

J. Douglas Edwards, urged me to use the opportunity to overcome my fear of public speaking. He stressed that the ability to speak in public is extremely valuable if you want to be a leader in any field. His words etched themselves upon my mind, and I've been able to apply them to many situations in which I once was uncomfortable:

Do what you fear most, and you will conquer fear.

You see, I was afraid of the unknown. The fear became so big in my mind that I couldn't see around it, over it, or past it to any sort of positive ending. I couldn't predict the outcome of giving that talk, so I convinced myself that there were too many ways it could go wrong for the talk to be worth the risk. All I could think of was that second-grade boy standing frozen with fear onstage. I had determined that I'd never put myself in that position again.

Doug encouraged me, though, and I reluctantly consented to give the talk. I prepared for hours. I made meticulous notes on index cards, and I rehearsed my speech many times over. When the day of the presentation arrived, I was so nervous that I was afraid the sweat from my hands would smear my notes. My heart raced as I walked up to the podium.

I covered my well-prepared 45 minutes of presentation material in 15 minutes, leaving me with half an hour to go and no idea what to do! So I went through it all again — and my time *still* wasn't up! Thinking fast, I said, "I can tell by the intelligence of this audience that you have some great questions, so let's hear them." Luckily, they did have great questions and I was able to answer them.

Overall, my presentation wasn't great or even good. It was awful. But I did it, and my world didn't end. The huge fear that stood between me and the platform had just gotten a little bit smaller. I realized then — just as I did when I figured out that selling was a learned skill — that effective public speaking is a skill that I could learn. I evaluated my performance and identified what I could change for the better. In a way, that was the beginning of where I am today as a trainer.

Public speaking isn't just public speaking. It is salesmanship in the form of a speech. And if there was one thing I did know how to do well, even then, it was selling. My greatest fear and weakness has become my hobby and the greatest love of my life.

Conscious competence

When you reach the third level, *conscious competence,* you find new challenges and new victories. By this point, your desire to improve has become strong enough to overcome the discomfort of learning something new. You're testing the waters now. You know how to do the thing you're learning, but you have to think about it, be conscious of it, in order to succeed.

You're practicing the new material you've learned. You're honing the skills with your friends and associates *before* testing new strategies on qualified clients and potentially losing them due to awkwardness with the material. You're trying new things and making adjustments — and that's good.

Just don't place too high a level of expectation on yourself, and you'll do better faster. Tensing up when you try new things takes your enjoyment from the experience. The tension also clouds your judgment when you must analyze how well you did and how you can improve the next time.

Unconscious competence

At the fourth and final level of competence, *unconscious competence,* you apply all your previous knowledge without making a conscious effort to do so.

You are smack in the middle of an example of unconscious competence right now — you're reading this book. You probably aren't reading it as someone who is just learning to read. Instead of uttering each syllable individually as you point and sound it out, hoping for eventual comprehension, you're able to cruise along and seek the content you're looking for, not even thinking about what you're doing.

As an unconscious competent salesperson, the strategies are now a natural part of your presentation. In fact, if you were to record your presentation, you'd recognize each nuance and recall when and why you added it — because it sounded good at the time. You kept it because it works!

A tremendous advantage of being a lifelong student is that you no longer allow yourself the luxury of seeing yourself as a victim of circumstance. You take responsibility for your successes *and* your failures, and you're more likely to be honest with yourself when it comes to evaluating those successes and failures.

Knowing How to Sell What Your Customers Want to Own

As in any area of life, in the world of selling, if you have the wrong attitude, you can end up being your own worst enemy. Many people in selling situations have a challenge with their own likes and dislikes — they tend to sell only what they like and mostly to the people they like. You do need to like and believe in what you're selling. But if you're in a career sales position, you probably have to sell other items in the product line that may not be your favorites.

You must always keep what's right for the customer in the forefront of your mind. If you sell only what you like, you severely limit your income and you leave yourself, at the end of the day, with plenty of things on hand that you don't like. Then what will you do?

Your job is to enthusiastically sell whatever benefits your customers, whoever they may be. During your selling career, you'll have to work with some people whom you won't particularly like. (I discuss how to deal with several personality types in Chapter 7.) If you refuse to work with some people, both you and the customers lose. You lose opportunities to make sales, and the customers lose opportunities to have their needs satisfied. The people you turn down will get their needs filled by someone else. The moral of the story: Keep your mind and your opportunities open.

Be sure not to prejudge people when you're selling to them. Whether you realize it or not, you make some sort of judgment about people the moment you lay eyes on them. You judge them based on their physical conditions, their clothing, their hairstyle, their posture. In selling situations, though, acting on preconceptions is a dangerous habit that you need to control. If you're committed to becoming a professional, force yourself to look at every potential client with clear vision. Eliminate those preconceived notions before they start costing you money!

Treat your prospects with the respect you'd expect to receive were you in their shoes. This may sound suspiciously similar to the Golden Rule — Do unto others as you would have them do unto you — as well it should. Keep in mind the following tips about the kind of attitude you need to have in the world of selling, and your self-control will pay off in the long run:

- ✔ If you want others to agree with you, you must first be agreeable.
- ✔ Don't let people's outward appearances affect the way you react to them.
- ✔ Always act as though each person you contact is the most important person in your life.

If what you're offering is vitally important to you, your product, service, or idea can be a significant link for you to billions of other people who need what you have to offer.

Someone else's selling nightmare can be your dream come true

One Saturday early in my sales career, a couple pulled up outside the real estate office I was working in. They drove a beat-up truck, and their clothes suggested that they had been doing heavy labor. Another agent in my office took one look at them and said, "Tom, you can have this one." He walked away, leaving me to talk with the unkempt couple.

As it turned out, they were looking for a fixer-upper property to invest in. They had made a business out of buying run-down properties and applying their do-it-yourself abilities to turn those properties into desirable homes. They then sold the homes for a tidy profit.

I helped the couple find their next fixer-upper, and a few months later they came back to me for help in investing some of their profits into a luxurious home for themselves. Over the years, I sold the same couple many fixer-uppers — and, as icing on what turned out to be a very satisfying cake, I resold those homes when the couple finished remodeling them. Had I prejudged these folks by their appearance, I may have been the one to walk away from what turned out to be a lucrative opportunity.

Part II
Doing Your Homework Before You Sell a Thing

The Selling Triangle

For more how to prepare yourself for a successful career in selling: www.dummies.com/extras/selling.

In this part . . .

✔ Think about who your clients are and improve your chances for success, including understanding their culture, background and personalities.

✔ Know how to get vital statistics and other information on your product, and what information is most relevant to your customers.

✔ Embrace technology and discover the ways gadgets, software, and more.

Chapter 4

Understanding Your Potential Clients

Sometimes the hardest part of starting something new is breaking through old teachings or beliefs that you once felt were acceptable. I'm sure you remember the old adages "Ignorance is bliss" or "What you don't know can't hurt you." Although living by these sayings may have worked in people's personal lives in simpler times, such maxims were *never* sage advice for people who were trying to sell or persuade others. In fact, the loss of sales and the personal career damage caused by ignorance can be so disastrous that some people give up on selling altogether.

When you look at the best of the best, the cream of the crop, in the selling world, you don't see all the time those people put in behind the scenes. But that time spent behind the scenes is what selling is all about. When a pro makes selling look *natural,* you can bet that she spent hours and hours of planning and preparation before those few minutes of face-to-face selling began.

In the world of selling, preparation is key, and this chapter is a great introduction to issues you may not have considered before. I let you know some specific ways you can prepare, so you can serve your clients better — everything from researching your prospective customers before you even attempt to meet them to knowing how to listen to them when you finally do meet. I also give you some great pointers on selling to people from countries and cultures other than your own.

Understanding Why Research Is Important

Why do you need to research your prospective clients and their businesses? So that, at the moment of truth, when you're giving a presentation or getting ready to close the sale, your lack of knowledge won't trip you up. You do all your research simply to build to that final moment when your buyer gives you the okay to deliver your product and to start building a long-term relationship with her or her company.

For example, if you sell air-treatment systems to homes and businesses, and you find out that a particular business must manufacture its products according to exacting standards, that's important information to have. Why? Because it means that the business must have a high level of concern for cleanliness and precision. And your air cleaner can help them get there.

If you discover that the company is growing, but it hasn't expanded its work site, you can probably count on the fact that its employees are working in close proximity to one another. And the closer the proximity, the greater the likelihood that germs can spread rapidly from one employee to the next. No employer can afford to have people taking a lot of sick time. There's another benefit of your air-treatment system.

If the business's financial reports show solid growth and explosive future plans, you know that it's poised for change and probably wide open to new ideas. Show the company that your air-treatment system is state of the art and expandable, and you'll be more likely to get their interest.

The more you know about a potential client, the more competent you appear and the stronger you will be when you present your case.

The same principle that you use when you sell to business applies when you sell to individuals or families: The more you know about their background, the better. You'll warm people up faster when you talk about their interests, jobs, and kids than you will if you know nothing other than their address and phone number. For example, if you're still selling air-treatment systems, and you know that one of their children has allergies or asthma, that's another bullet in your arsenal of benefits when you present your product.

Adapting your message to what your clients tell you about themselves and their needs

If you doubt the validity of the premise that knowledge is power, take a look at how much information websites gather about the people who visit them. For example, Amazon.com doesn't just sell products. It offers you an opportunity to establish a Wish List of products you may be interested in buying (or receiving as gifts) someday. What does Amazon do with that Wish List? It can use the products you add to that list, along with your purchases and what you look at on its site, to find out where your interests lay. If Amazon.com begins offering a new book that someone with your interests would like, it customizes the website so that new book is the first thing you see when you log in to the Amazon.com site. Amazon is customizing its offers to your particular interests and needs. And you're the one telling Amazon what you're likely to buy.

You can take advantage of these strategies for your business, too. If your company is gathering detailed information on client interests and making it accessible to the entire sales force, you're off to a great start. If your company isn't gathering it for you, you may want to use a system that allows you to keep very detailed information on your clients' interests and needs so you can lead them to purchasing more products and services from you and from others with whom you may share referred leads (with their permission, of course).

You may be wondering how you'd find out about that child's asthma. You can do that in one of several ways, including a brief survey-type phone call asking if anyone in the home has or has ever had allergies or other illnesses that are affected by the quality of the air in the home and adding that information to your notes for each client.

In addition, companies that sell data lists, known as *list brokers,* often have enough information about potential clients that you can find out what types of pets they have, cleaning products they purchase, and whether they make a lot of long-distance phone calls. How do they get this information? Think about it. Have you ever filled out a survey about the products you use in order to receive free grocery coupons? Do you send in for rebates on products? If you do any of this sort of thing, those companies don't just send your coupons or rebates and toss your reply card. They store that valuable purchasing information about you in their databases for future reference.

 It may take a fair amount of legwork to find a good list broker. Getting a referral from someone in a noncompeting business would be great. But if you don't know anyone who has used a list broker, start by asking for suggestions from a local quick-print company. Their clients may have had great success with particular list companies.

Starting at Ground Zero to Know Your Clients Inside and Out

To be successful at selling, you must be constantly on the prowl for information. What type of information? Everything and anything about your product, your company, your competition, and (most importantly) your prospect. And with the Internet just a mouse click away, you really have no excuse for not being well informed. An abundance of information is available, quite literally, at your fingertips. All you need is the commitment to locate and internalize it. Never forget: Knowledge is power.

The most important thing to remember when you're selling is the benefit of being able to walk in someone else's shoes. You can't be of any help to a prospective client with what you're offering her until you truly understand what she needs and where she's coming from.

So where do you begin in your quest to walk in your prospects' shoes? Not at the shoe store. Instead, you need to do some basic research into your prospective clients, their businesses, and their goals. Start by following these tips:

✔ **Visit the business's website and social media pages.** Pay particular attention to the business's online product catalog (if there is one), and look for press releases posted on the site so you're up-to-date on the most recent news related to the business. Plus, always look for "About Us" and "Executive Summary" links on the website. The information you find there often gives you valuable insight into the management team and their backgrounds. And who knows? You may find out that you know someone who works there or that you know someone who knows someone there.

Take advantage of services such as Google alerts. Google allows you to request information posted about specific topics or companies . . . and to have those alerts sent to you via email.

✔ **Get copies of the company's product brochures and/or catalogs.** Talk with one of its customer service representatives about what the company offers. If you're familiar with the products that your prospective client sells, you're better able to sell her _your_ product.

✔ **Look up past news articles on the business or its industry.** If you're familiar with what's been happening in the industry in the past few months, you can work that information into your conversations with the people who work in it. The prospect will get the sense that you've done your homework about her — so you've probably done your homework about your own products, too. And that's exactly the impression you want to make.

✓ **Check out the business's financial report, if it's available.** Get the names of the company president and other key people — and find out how to pronounce and spell their names. For the pronunciation, simply call the company and ask the receptionist for that information.

If your prospective clients are individuals or families (the consumer sale), you need to gather information in a less formal manner. If you're learning about someone by referral, ask as many questions about her as you can without seeming overly zealous or intrusive. You can certainly ask for her contact information, including where she lives, how the referrer knows her (through their kids' school, church, another social venue, and so on), and what brought these folks to mind. It could very well be that the last time these people spoke, the subject of getting a new car or having the house painted came up.

Leave no paperwork or link on a prospect unturned when you do your research. Your legwork will pay handsome dividends in the long run. Knowledge is power when it's properly applied. And you should always apply that philosophy to research that helps you sell.

Although doing your research and gathering information about your prospective clients is essential, knowing when you have enough information is often difficult. In the end, it's up to you, of course. When you think you know enough to get the job done and make the sale, you've probably researched enough. If a question comes up during your presentation that you don't know the answer to, and if what you don't know may hurt your chances of closing the sale, then you don't know enough. Experience will tell you how much you need to prepare, but you're better off erring on the side of preparing too much than not preparing enough.

Working with Buyers' Different Personality Types

When you work with companies, a key concern is discovering who the true decision-maker really is. It may be the office manager, a purchasing agent, or a department head. You can usually find out simply by asking the receptionist who is responsible for the area of business to which your products or services apply. After she tells you, ask a confirming question, such as, "So, Ms. Carter has the responsibility of authorizing purchase orders, is that right?" If Ms. Carter *does* handle the area, but she has to get approval on purchase orders from someone like the comptroller, you need to know that going in (and your question will verify that for you).

When you have the name and position of the person responsible for purchasing in your area, you need to know a little about that person's style. My research has uncovered ten basic personality types of buyers (I cover each of these in the following sections). If you recognize the personality type of the person you want to sell to, you can respond appropriately. With the exception of a couple of the personality types, you find these folks in both business sales and consumer sales. Your job is to become familiar enough with the types to quickly determine how to work with each.

Your delivery style must be flexible enough to relate to all the different personality types. Never settle for having one presentation style. Having only one style severely limits the number of people you can serve. I'm not advising you to develop multiple personalities — just remember that if you don't like the personality of the decision maker, you can learn to like the opportunity she offers you to do business with her.

Note: These personality types are exaggerated for the purpose of example, and they're not limited to the genders I've identified them with. They demonstrate characteristics of buyers, but the people you encounter in the real world won't fit into boxes quite as neatly as these examples do.

Buyer #1: Believing Bart

Believing Bart is already sold on your company or brand. He knows just what to expect from your products, and he likes their reliability. He's easy to work with and, after you convince him of your personal competence, will remain loyal to you and your product. If he's *not* convinced that you're competent, Bart won't hesitate to call your company and request another representative.

How do you appeal to this personality type? Don't short-sell the product or service just because he's already sold on its quality. You need to exhibit great product knowledge to garner his trust and belief in your ability to meet his needs. Providing dependable service and follow-up will help you close the sale and gain Bart's repeat business (and referrals from him).

Buyer #2: Freebie Freddie

Freebie Freddie is a real wheeler-dealer, the guy who won't settle until he thinks he has the upper hand and you've agreed to give him something extra. Today's market is full of these types of buyers. If you give Freddie any extras in order to consummate the sale, he'll probably brag to and upset others who may not have received the same benefit.

So how do you handle this type? Let Freddie know that he's important and special — that he drives a hard bargain and that you admire his business savvy. If you think Freddie's business is worth giving something extra to, consult with your manager or the business owner about the best way to handle it. You may not have to give away much to entice this guy to buy. The enticement can be as simple as providing a little extra TLC (that's right — tender loving care), such as sending him thank-you notes or making a few extra calls after the sale to let him know how important he is.

Buyer #3: Purchasing Polly

Purchasing Polly is a distant, matter-of-fact type who carries a high level of responsibility. (You find her in business-to-business sales situations.) As with many other purchasing agents, she may have little personal contact throughout the day besides the contact she gets from the salespeople who parade through her office. She can't risk liking you too much because she may have to replace you with the competition at any time.

When you're dealing with Purchasing Polly, give a no-fluff presentation. Don't try to become too familiar. Stick to the facts and figures. She'll be grading you every step of the way. By being low-key, you'll be different from the other all-too-typical salespeople she encounters — and she'll remember you for that. Let her know that you understand how important and challenging her position can be. Send her thank-you notes. Present all figures to Polly in the most professional manner possible. And do everything in writing — she needs the certainty of documentation in case she needs to present it or defend her purchase to upper management.

Buyer #4: Evasive Ed

Evasive Ed is your most challenging buyer. He refuses to return your phone calls, he postpones appointments or reschedules at the last minute, he likes to shop around and keep you waiting in the meantime, and he tests your patience at every turn.

If you find yourself up against an Evasive Ed, enlist the aid of his secretary or support staff. (If you have an Evasive Ed in a consumer sales situation, enlist the aid of his spouse or someone else who knows him well.) A second person may be able to tell you how to get and keep Ed's business. If she tells you "that's just the way he is," you need to work on creating urgency in your presentations so he'll see the benefit of making a decision quickly and, just as important, what he'll lose if he doesn't make the decision. A good example of this is a special reduced investment or closeout on a product where you can only offer it for a short period of time or on a first-come, first-served basis.

Buyer #5: Griping Greg

Griping Greg always has something to complain about or something negative to say. He wouldn't be your first choice for a companion if you ever got stranded on a deserted island.

If you're dealing with a Griping Greg, you have to decide whether the income his business generates for you is worth all the energy he'll steal from you. If his business is not one of your bread-and-butter accounts, you may want to consider finding other clients who don't take so much out of you. *Remember:* No client is worth risking your mental and physical health for.

The most important thing you can do for the Griping Gregs of the world is listen and be empathetic. (Maybe he can't afford a therapist, and you're the next best thing.) To limit your exposure to Greg's negativity, call him just a few minutes before his normal lunch hour or just before the end of the day, so he won't want to talk long. If he calls you at other times and begins to cost you valuable selling time, find polite ways to get off the line.

When you first get on the line, you may want to say something like this:

> Greg! Glad you called. I'm just heading out for an appointment. What can I do for you in the next five minutes?

Stay pleasant and helpful; after all, that's why Greg gives you his business. If Greg gets to be too much to handle, the easiest and least costly thing to do may be to refer him to someone else in your organization. The person receiving this new client may not be as strongly affected by Greg's personality and may be able to get along with him just fine.

Buyer #6: Analytical Anna

Analytical Anna knows exactly what she wants — and she wants it written in blood or at least carved in stone. She nitpicks everything and needs to feel as if she has complete control. This may stem from a bad past experience with another salesperson who wasn't as professional as you are. She may have felt ripped off before and blame not only the salesperson but herself for not having everything in writing.

Disorder in any form shatters Anna's day, so don't be a source of disorder for Anna — if you want to get and keep her business. When you're dealing with Analytical Anna, be *very* organized. She appreciates — nay, she craves — organization. Handle every detail in writing. Be punctual. Double-check everything and let her see that you do. When she knows she can depend on you, she will do just that. Confirm appointments, and always reconfirm details of your meetings with her in writing. Send a recap to Anna of every meeting you have with her. Also, contact her ahead of every meeting to let her know what information you need for your next appointment. In other words, treat her as she treats others. Everyone wants to be around people who are just like themselves.

Buyer #7: Domineering Donna

Donna is a strong-willed ball of fire who will most often be found in a business situation. She most likely has designs on a more powerful position in the company. She often hides her needs because she expects you to have done your homework — and if you have, she figures, then you already know her needs.

In talking to Donna, perhaps the most important thing you can do is to compliment her on her importance and remind her of the value of her abilities to her company. She likely bowls others over with her ambition for power — and most people try to avoid working with people who dominate like this. But you don't have that option. Besides, Donna can become a positive force for you if you have challenges with billing or want to sell your product to another department or branch of her company. If Donna believes in you and your product, she'll be your best supporter. She chose to work for you and she'll want others to prove she was right by using your product, too.

Buyer #8: Controlling Carl

For Controlling Carl, it's his way or the highway. He's a self-proclaimed expert, even though his expertise may be limited to his own company. He's also poor at delegating authority. Carl wants everyone and everything to be reported to him. He may also be rude and interrupt your presentation while he takes calls or gives directions to his subordinates.

When dealing with a Controlling Carl, be extremely polite, prepared, and concise. By all means, don't make any assumptions. Let him know that you value his time. If the interruptions become too distracting, offer to reschedule your meeting off the premises — for, say, a lunch appointment — so that you can have Carl's undivided attention. Or you can simply enlist the aid of Carl's secretary or assistant in keeping interruptions to a minimum during your appointment. Unless Carl has a rule carved in granite that he takes all calls and sees all visitors, you're likely to get the assistance you want just by making a polite request.

You may encounter Carl in a consumer setting as well. He's the guy who asks you a question and then takes a call on his cell phone before you can engage him in conversation. It's important that you be agreeable with him and say things like, "This will only take a minute," or "Let me take you directly to that product." This strategy lets him know that you're cognizant of how valuable his time is but keeps you in control of the sale.

Buyer #9: Cynical Cindy

Cynical Cindy is the first to say, "But we've *always* done it this way." She fights change, is suspicious, and questions your every move. She's very likely part of the old guard where she works — a long-term employee. In consumer sales, Cynical Cindy may be an unwilling spouse or even a child. She has no interest in whatever the other party wants and will do her best to make your job more difficult.

Welcome Cindy's objections — even compliment her for being smart enough to bring them up. Impress Cindy by dropping the names of people and companies she trusts; in order for Cindy to bring down her wall of doubt, she needs to know who else uses your product or service. For you, though, Cindy's hesitancy can become the best thing about her. Why? Because if *you* have such a difficult time overcoming her objections, you'd better believe that your competition will get discouraged trying to win her over. It'll be hard for your competition to persuade her to change her loyalties once she sees the value of becoming *your* client. And loyalty like that is what you're after.

Buyer #10: Drifting Dan

Drifting Dan is typical of many potential clients. He has a lot on his mind. The purchase you're discussing is just one of many duties or tasks Dan needs to handle. If your presentation isn't designed to keep him both mentally and physically involved, you lose him. It will take you longer to close the sale and complete the agreement.

Be prepared to deliver your presentation in small bites, and include several brief summaries of what you've already covered in order to bring his attention back to the matter at hand.

When you notice Dan's attention has drifted, simply pause in your presentation as if you have lost your train of thought. Dan will catch the silence and rejoin you mentally to determine what just happened. Say, "Let's see, we just covered how our product will bring you a speedy return on investment. Do you have any questions about that, Dan?" This gives him an opportunity to catch up on what he missed without embarrassing him.

Being Aware of Unique Cultural Needs

If you're planning to do business with people from countries different than your own, you need to invest as much time understanding their culture as you do understanding their needs in terms of your products and services. The same rule holds true even if you do business within cultural groups different from your own in the country in which you live. Even if you're not actively doing business in another country, but you're building a website that may be viewed by people from many different countries or cultures, you need to be aware of words and phrases that just don't translate or may be offensive when a translation is made.

In the following sections, I let you know about different cultural traditions you need to be aware of when dealing with clients. But first, here are a few general pointers from Sherri Ferris, president and CEO of Protocol Professionals, Inc. (www.protocolprofessionals.com):

- ✔ **Be patient when building trust and establishing relationships.** People from countries other than the United States generally need more time to build trust. Observing a greater degree of formality when becoming acquainted is important.

- ✔ **Speak more slowly than you normally do, but don't raise your voice because you think the other person can't understand you.** Volume doesn't increase comprehension.

- ✔ **Avoid slang, buzzwords, idioms, jargon, and lingo.** These can all be easily misunderstood by those who may not speak your language as natives do.

- ✔ **If you're using an interpreter, make sure the interpreter meets ahead of time with the people for whom she is interpreting.** This allows the interpreter to learn the language patterns, special terminology, and numbers used by the people she's translating for, such as product identifiers or other codes specific to a company or industry. All of these details can change the whole dimension of what's being said.

- ✔ **Pay attention to nonverbal interaction cues.** In some Asian cultures, the word *yes* or an affirmative nod often means, "Yes, I hear you," not, "Yes, I agree."

Cultural etiquette 101: Finding the resources you need

If you need or want to find out about another culture, some wonderful resources are available to steer you in the right direction and tell you everything you need to know. Spend some time browsing credible resources to see what's out there. Or check out the following books, all of which are very helpful:

✔ *International Business Travel Etiquette: Seal the Deal with Proper Protocol* by Rebecca Black (CreateSpace Publishing)

✔ *The Etiquette Advantage in Business* by Peggy Post (HarperCollins Publishers)

✔ *Multicultural Manners: New Rules of Etiquette for a Changing Society* by Norine Dresser (Wiley)

✔ *Cross-Cultural Selling For Dummies* by Michael Soon Lee and Ralph R. Roberts (Wiley)

Some very informative websites are also great sources for tips, articles, newsletters, magazines, and even personal consultants who specialize in cultural etiquette. Here are just a few I recommend:

✔ **BusinessCulture.com** (www.businessculture.com) offers access to Worldwide Business Reports on over 100 countries, PreDeparture Reports, and Executive Business Reports. It provides a list of countries for which it does research (over 80 at last count, ranging from Argentina to Yemen), along with some expert advice about cross-cultural issues. You can also conduct a search from this site for international news posted on the ABC News and BBC News websites. The BusinessCulture.com world travel information includes weather reports from around the world, contact information for international airports and hotels, a currency converter, and advice on how to stay healthy abroad.

✔ **eDiplomat.com** (www.ediplomat.com) offers an overview of cultural etiquette by country. Entries include overviews of the people, how to meet and greet, body language cues, corporate culture, tips for dining, dress, and the proper presentation of gifts.

✔ **Protocol Advisors** (www.protocoladvisors.com) "provides customized training in etiquette and international protocol to Fortune 500 companies." This includes helping companies in cutting-edge fields to familiarize their executives, sales staff, and those who may be transferring to another country with what to expect. It's also a great source for students who may be taking courses abroad. Find out about the idiosyncrasies of the culture, as well as the do's and don'ts, so that your experience abroad is a positive one.

✔ **Protocol Professionals, Inc.** (www.protocolprofessionals.com) is "an international relations consulting firm specializing in protocol and etiquette training." This organization has worked with very high-profile groups, including the Diplomatic Corps and U.S. Ambassadors. If your involvement in another country is going to be with higher-ups, this is a great resource site.

If you're planning to sell to clients from cultures other than your own, check out any of these resources before you make your initial contact.

Culture is as much an influence on people as their personal experiences, so knowing about your clients' customs and traditions only makes sense. That way, neither you nor your client will be made to feel uncomfortable. Knowledge is power!

Arranging meetings

Getting together with people on neutral, or at least acceptable, territory can be the most difficult aspect of selling. Knowing your client's customs and routines is critical. Be sure to not make any mistakes before you get your foot in the door.

When you're planning to sell to a client from a culture other than your own, determine the best way to approach her for a meeting. In some countries, for example, mail delivery can be unreliable, so convey important messages, such as requests for meetings, by fax, telephone, or email. Find out whether the country you'll be selling in requires any similar considerations.

After you determine the best method to use to reach your client, decide which environment is most conducive to doing business with her. Although many business people prefer formal, corporate, conference room settings, others prefer more relaxed locations (such as restaurants or clubs) for business discussions. In the Chinese culture, for example, the *feng shui* of the location (an ancient Chinese system of aesthetics regarding favorable positioning in relation to *qi,* or life force) can play an important part in how the business goes. Paying attention to details such as those may be the key to your success with Chinese clients.

When you have an appointment, confirm all the details and do your homework on what to wear, what to bring with you, and how to give your presentation. Always be punctual, but don't expect the other person to be. In many cultures, relationships are much more important than time clocks. Value the time your client gives you, but don't count the minutes.

Dressing appropriately

Because your appearance is the first cue others get about how you feel about yourself and your business, take extra care in dressing for business meetings and events. When in doubt, dressing conservatively and more formally than you would if you were meeting with a client from your area is always wise.

In many countries, it is considered inappropriate for women to wear slacks or shorts. Find out about this before you even begin to pack; otherwise, your potential business may be over before you even get close enough to shake the client's hand.

Getting names right

A person's name is the most important thing to her. You can lose everything else in life and still have a name. When a client hears you use her name correctly, she knows that you put forth the effort to get it right — and that goes a long way toward earning her respect and trust. If you forget a client's name — or mispronounce it — you'll have to work that much harder to remedy the situation and earn the client's respect in the future (if she'll even give you a second chance).

When introduced to Mrs. Roberta Jones, call her Mrs. Jones unless and until she tells you otherwise. When meeting a couple you know to be married, use Mr. and Mrs. There will be cases where the woman didn't take the man's name; you can't be expected to know that. If they don't bring it up, you've done nothing wrong. However, don't assume that a man and a woman shopping together are a married couple. When your type of sale requires you to know first and last names of clients, it's wise to ask directly, but not bluntly, for each person's name. Never address someone by her first name unless she specifically asks you to do so. And never abbreviate a name unless instructed to do so. Robert is Robert, not Rob, Robbie, Bob, Bobby, or any other version. Margaret is Margaret, not Maggie, Marge, or Peggy.

If your potential client has an unusual name, it's fine to ask her to pronounce it more than once and to spell it for you. Repeat the name to ensure you have it right. This shows that you care enough to get her business right as well — something that works toward building clients' trust in you.

In some cultures, a person's *surname* (or last name) is given before her *proper name* (or first name). Take the time to find out which cultures place the surname first, or you may find yourself addressing Ms. Ling as Ms. Amy.

For example, Hispanic names often include both the father and mother's family names. The father's name comes first and should be used as the term of address. So, if you're dealing with someone by the name of Luisa Mendoza Trujillo, *Luisa* is her first name, *Mendoza* is her father's family name, and *Trujillo* is her mother's family name. And you should address her as Señora or Señorita Mendoza.

In Germany, the preference is to be addressed by your job title as opposed to the German equivalent of Mr. or Ms. So addressing someone as Vice President Schmidt is considered appropriate. In Italy, including someone's profession when introducing or referring to her is considered more appropriate (for example, "our engineer, Ms. Puccini").

Meeting and greeting new people

In every country, including the United States, people shake hands when meeting and departing, but in some countries, particularly Middle Eastern ones, embraces are also included. Determine in advance whether your potential client is more likely to welcome an embrace or a handshake. Inquiring about the person's health is a positive gesture in Middle Eastern culture. Also, when the relationship becomes closer, don't be surprised if you are given a kiss on the cheek — even from one man to another.

Don't extend your hand to shake a Middle Eastern woman's hand unless she extends hers first.

Taking time to read up on the details of how people meet and greet one another in the country you'll be visiting can make a huge difference in how the balance of your contact time goes with each potential client.

Presenting your business card

Having some business cards made with your contact information in the language of the recipient is a good idea. If your card is two-sided, with your language on one side and another language on the other, always present your card with the client's language facing up. Doing this makes your client comfortable with understanding the information. Allow the client a moment to read the card before talking or moving on to the next aspect of your presentation.

If you're the one in charge of having this printing done, seek out the advice of a professional, such as the protocol folks mentioned in the earlier sidebar "Cultural etiquette 101: Finding the resources you need," to ensure that it's done properly.

Be sure to find out what rules apply in the culture or country you'll be visiting; some countries have specific etiquette surrounding the use of business cards. For example, if you're going to Japan, take plenty of business cards and give one to every person you're introduced to. Also, academic degrees are important in Japanese culture, so if you have a Master's degree, be certain to show that on your card. Only pull out one card at a time; holding a stack of business cards in your hand is considered bad manners in Japan as is writing on a business card.

In any culture, taking a moment to read the card of each person who gives you one before accepting another card is wise. Do not set the cards aside quickly — that would be like dismissing the person to move on to someone else. Putting the cards in a business card case shows respect for the person who gave it to you; shoving it in your pocket or notebook does not. Treat business cards the same way you treat the people giving them to you. If you feel the need to write a reminder note on someone's card, do it in private — after their card is in your possession.

Knowing regional manners

Even if you're doing all your business within your native country, you may need to pay attention to differences among various regions. Although you all speak the same language, you may do it with different accents or in a dialect different from the client's. For example, people in nearly every region of the United States have accents or certain ways of saying particular words. These accents can be charming or irritating, depending on your existing assumptions.

If you're from the Southern United States and do business with folks in the Northeast, be prepared to talk a bit faster than normal in order to keep their attention. Also, you may want to train yourself to listen more effectively because people in that part of the country tend to talk faster than the people you're used to being around.

The opposite is true if you're a Northeasterner doing business with Southerners — or even a city person doing business with people who live in small towns. Some people from the South and in small towns handle business in a more relaxed manner than do folks in the Northeast.

Unless your name is Meryl Streep, you probably can't do much to change your accent, but you can be aware of the speed with which you speak and you can pay attention to the speech patterns of your clients. As much as possible, try to adapt to your clients' way of conversing — that way they'll feel more comfortable and focus more on what you're saying than how you're saying it.

Warning: If you're from Seattle, be sure that you don't pick up a Tennessee twang while doing business with someone from Memphis. Although it can be easy to do, the Memphian may think you're making fun of her.

Respecting personal space

All people, regardless of the country they live in, have a need for *personal space* (the distance between you and another person when you're talking to one another). Personal space is just that — personal. But in each culture, the amount of personal space people need is different from what you may be used to. For example, the British want more personal space than people from the United States. (Next time you see a photograph of the Queen of England, pay attention to the people standing next to her. The people most likely won't be standing hip to hip.) Russians and people in the Middle East, on the other hand, need less personal space than most Americans do.

If you want to be sure that people feel comfortable around you (a necessity in the world of selling), don't invade another person's space. If you're working with people from cultures where less personal space is required than you're used to, be sure not to back away when they step into your larger personal space. That can be construed as a sign that you are fearful or hesitant about the other person. Neither are good things to have happen with potential business clients.

Making presentations

In some cultures, getting down to the bottom line as soon as possible is critical. In others, you need to spend more time telling your clients about the history of your company and helping them feel comfortable with you and your product. In yet other cultures, underscoring the personal and emotional benefits of your proposal is important. In some cultures, people prefer to touch and feel samples of your product, whereas in others they may prefer to just read analyses, complete with graphs and testimonials.

When you give a presentation in another country, always be organized. Have professional-looking paperwork to explain all the details of your proposal, and bring a copy for everyone in the room. Leaving anyone out or asking for additional copies to be made is a major mistake.

In some countries, the negotiation is the best part of the game. Negotiation may include shouting orders, banging fists on tables, or simply silence. In other countries, you present, and they either accept or decline and then move on with little or no chance for you to reiterate important points or give a benefit summary. So, your first shot needs to be your best shot.

You simply *cannot* prepare too much for a presentation to someone from a culture other than your own. Expect to be asked for any and every little detail about your company, product, service, and location, as well as about yourself. That way, no matter what comes up, you'll be ready.

Giving gifts

The decision makers at most companies understand the value of appropriate gift giving and usually establish certain parameters for gift giving by their staff. If your company doesn't have specific guidelines for you to follow, ask what they prefer. Or, better yet, suggest some appropriate parameters based on the potential value of each client to the company. If you're the sales representative who is the main source of contact with the client, you want to ensure that the client thinks well of you when she receives the gift. So, don't be afraid to jump in there with some solid suggestions.

The stronger your relationship with your client, the more personalized your gift should be. You wouldn't send a long-standing client whose business represents 20 percent of your sales volume a vinyl datebook. If you've done business with the client for a while, you should know what that person likes and select a gift that will provide her highest level of enjoyment.

Some cultures find the giving and receiving of gifts a personal matter, not a business matter. For example, in France, business gifts aren't given. If you're invited to a French business associate's home, however, be certain to bring flowers, chocolates, or a bottle of high-quality spirits, such as vodka or scotch. Don't bring wine, however. The French are considered by many in the world, including themselves, as wine experts. The host has already chosen the proper wine for the meal.

In some cultures, gifts that would be considered very appropriate where you're from may be completely offensive to people in the country you're visiting. For example:

- In Japan or Latin America, a gift of a letter opener may imply that you are severing the relationship because the letter opener looks like a knife.

- Someone from India would not appreciate a gift made of leather because the cow is considered sacred in that country.

- In Japan, white is used in funeral services, so you want to make sure that you don't wrap gifts in white or send white flowers.

> ✔ In Germany, red roses are given only in personal relationships, never in business ones.
>
> ✔ In many Asian cultures, singling someone out with a gift or a compliment may be considered offensive rather than polite.

Just be sure to read up on the country in which you'll be selling so that you avoid offending your clients, and everyone's attention is focused on what you're selling instead of on an unfortunate faux pas.

Be sure that the recipient doesn't construe the gift as being inappropriate. Giving a Rolex watch to a client who only purchased $500 worth of product from you is probably not a wise move — financially or for the business relationship (and this goes for gift giving in your own country as well). If the client is uncomfortable at all with the gift, she may wonder whether you're offering a bribe for future business — and that's exactly the opposite of the reaction you're going for.

Before you give a gift to a client, determine whether the recipient's company has a policy on receiving gifts. Many companies don't allow their employees to accept gifts; if you offer one, your client may be in the uncomfortable position of having to decline or return your gift. If the company doesn't allow its personnel to receive gifts, ask the person with whom you have the best relationship in the company what you can do. Maybe you can send a box of candy or a basket of fruit for the department to share but not a pen-and-pencil set for the individual.

Some countries require duties or other fees to be paid on shipments from outside that country. Be sure to find out whether this applies in the country you're visiting, and pay any duty in advance so the gift you're sending is truly free. You can get this information from the nearest consulate for that country. Or you can simply order the gift from a major supplier within that country.

Dining out with ease

Asians, on average, dedicate more hours to work-related activities than do people from the United States, which means that they include after-hours dinners as a normal part of their workday. So, if you're working with an Asian client, you may be expected to wine and dine with her as part of the meeting. If you're the one being wined and dined in her country, be prepared to reciprocate before you leave.

In some cultures, slurping, burping, and even drinking from another person's glass during dinner is perfectly acceptable; in others, it's absolutely not.

When you're visiting another country, you don't necessarily have to join in on behaviors you have trouble with, but you should at least be aware of them so you don't act inappropriately shocked if your guest does so. And at the very least, know what's considered rude, and avoid those behaviors during your meals.

Be sure to understand your potential client's needs with regard to specific foods or preparation of such foods. When dining with a client, make certain you're not taking her to a restaurant whose menu will not provide appropriate foods for her. Also, consider customs the client may have, whether cultural or religious, with regard to taking a meal. You may need to allow a few moments for prayer or indulge the client in eating very slowly and consuming many courses.

Etiquette, in any country, is all about behaving in such a way that everyone feels comfortable. As that old saying goes, "When in Rome, do as the Romans do." And when you're entertaining foreign clients in your own country, do everything you can to make them feel at home.

Responding to Your Clients' Fears

In all its forms, fear is the greatest enemy you will ever encounter in persuading your clients. The toughest part of your job is helping other people admit to and overcome their fears so you can earn the opportunity to do business with them. Fear is what builds those walls of resistance that salespeople so often run into. You need to know how to climb over or break through those walls if you're going to travel the road to sales success.

In the following sections, I identify eight common fears you need to help your prospects overcome. When you recognize these fears as barriers to your ability to serve your prospects with excellent service, you're ready to discover how to dismantle those walls, one brick at a time, thus gaining your prospect's confidence and trust.

Your goal is to get your prospects to like you, trust you, and want to listen to you. They do that when you serve them with warmth and empathy.

Fear of salespeople

At first, every prospect is afraid of you. Why? You're a salesperson, and you want something from them — a commitment, their time, or their money. Plus, what you want usually involves some kind of a change on the prospect's part, and most people are afraid of change, at least to some degree. Even if you're selling to someone you already know — a friend, an acquaintance, or even a relative — when you meet that person in the role of a sales professional, certain fears inevitably arise. The only exception may be selling to your parents or grandparents, simply because they probably believe in you and trust you no matter *what* role you play with them. To them you come across as you should to everyone — with a natural, nonsales personality.

As a salesperson, when you meet with someone who, like most people, tries very hard to hang on to her hard-earned cash (or at least not to part with it too easily), you can safely assume a certain amount of fear is involved. Most people separate themselves from their money only for products and services they believe they need. Your job is to help them recognize the need, and build the value of your product's ability to serve that need to a point where their fear now becomes a fear of what happens if they *don't* allow you to help them.

Most people, when you first encounter them, show their fear in their body language. They may cross their arms or lean back away from you. In retail settings, they may actually take a small step backward when you approach them on the sales floor. A wise tactic to help overcome this is to warmly invite them to stand or sit beside you while you show them all the good stuff your product does or has. This way, you're looking at it together. You encourage them to put their hands on the product, push buttons, turn dials, make things light up, heat up, or move. When they get involved with the product, their fear of you lessens. After all, you're the one who introduced the prospects to the product, and look what great fun they're having now!

Fear of failure

The fear of failure is one you're likely to encounter in your clients because virtually everyone has this fear to some degree. Why? Because everyone has made mistakes, and everyone has regrets. Whether your failure was in choosing the wrong hair color or purchasing a vehicle that wasn't right for you, you know the frustration of making a mistake. Somewhere in your psyche, you have a fear, not necessarily because of your bad decision, but because you remember that mistake as being associated with a salesperson (the hairstylist who told you that you'd look great with green hair or the car salesman who convinced you that your five kids didn't have to ride with you all the time when she sold you a two-seater convertible).

No one wants to handle a transaction in which the customer may be dissatisfied with the result. Believe me, the grief you get from a dissatisfied customer isn't worth the fee you earn on the sale. Although dissatisfied customers aren't (and shouldn't be) the norm, you must go into every presentation with a sharp interest in the who, what, when, where, and why of your client's needs. When you've satisfied yourself that owning your product or service is in your client's best interest, then it's your obligation as the expert to convince her that this decision is truly good for her. Take the time to talk your prospect through every aspect of her decision very carefully, giving her the time she needs to make a choice she'll be comfortable with.

Fear of owing money

Prospects are tremendously afraid of owing too much money — to you, to your company, to a finance company. Your fee for service is almost always a point of contention with prospective customers — and not just because they're being stubborn, but because they're legitimately afraid of paying too much money.

Most people won't attempt to negotiate with a company about its fees, but as a salesperson your clients don't see you as an institution. You're not cold, forbidding concrete walls and walkways. Instead, you're a warm, flesh-and-blood fellow human — and because of this, your clients often try to negotiate with you. Depending on your clients' negotiation skills, they may do any or all of the following:

- ✔ **Put off making a decision, forcing you to draw them out.** I cover what to do in this situation in Chapter 11.

- ✔ **Tell you point-blank that they're concerned about the cost.** In this situation, you need to sell them on the value of the product or service you provide.

- ✔ **Voice their concerns in a roundabout way.** For example, a client may say something like, "Another company I talked with will charge a lot less."

If your client has reservations about the cost of your product or service, I recommend saying something like this:

> You know, I've learned something over the years. People look for three things when they spend money. They look for the finest quality, the best service, and, of course, the lowest price. I've also found that no company can offer all three. They can't offer the finest quality and the best service

for the lowest amount. So, for your long-term happiness, which of the three would you be most willing to give up? Fine quality? Excellent service? Or the lowest price?

Most people say that quality and service are of the utmost concern, which overcomes their concern about the fee. Your next move is to reiterate everything you will do for them. Again, sell the value of the product you and your company provide.

If you run into a client who is truly concerned only with getting the lowest investment and you can't provide it, you may have to bow out of the picture. Do it gracefully and stay in touch. Chances are good that she'll get what she pays for and eventually will see the wisdom in investing more for the quality product or service you can provide.

Fear of being lied to

One common fear in buyers is the fear of being lied to. As a general rule, clients who are afraid of being lied to doubt everything you're saying about how much they'll benefit from your product, service, or idea.

When you face a client with this fear, a strong past track record comes into play. Having a long list of happy clients should help you calm this fear. If you're new and you don't yet have an established track record, tell your prospect you made a point of choosing your company because it has a great track record. If you're doing something entirely new with a new company, new product or service, or new concept, you have to build on the personal integrity and credentials of those involved in the project. For some products, there is a salesperson (you), a technical advisor who reviews technical details of either manufacture or installation of a product, the actual installer, and the after-market customer service folks.

There is *never* any reason to lie to a customer. When you're honest with your customers, they will respect you and give you the benefit of the doubt even if they don't necessarily care for what you have to say. Honesty and integrity in every selling situation makes you a winner each and every time.

Fear of embarrassment

Many people fear being embarrassed with anyone who can possibly know about the decision if it's a bad one. Have you ever made a poor decision that was big enough that most of your friends and family members knew about it (and then kept reminding you about it)? They may have only been teasing you. However, it may have demeaned and embarrassed you. Bad decisions make you feel like a child again — insecure and powerless. Because many potential clients have this fear of being embarrassed by a bad decision, they put off making any decision at all.

If you're selling to more than one decision maker (such as a married couple or business partners), odds are that neither person will want to risk being embarrassed in front of the other. Chances are they've disagreed about something in the past and they don't want to have that uncomfortable situation arise again.

Knowing that this fear can block your sale, your primary goal when working with clients who are afraid of being embarrassed should be to help them feel secure with you. Let them know that they're not relinquishing total power to you — you're merely acting on their behalf, providing a product or service for which they have expressed a need.

Fear of the unknown

Fear of the unknown is a common fear in buyers. A lack of understanding of your product or service, or of its value to the prospect's company, is a reasonable cause for delaying any transaction. National name recognition will dispel some of this fear. But if you work for a local company, I recommend that you join forces with the rest of your company's sales staff to earn a great local reputation as a competent business with great products. Over the years, a great reputation saves you a bundle of time in the selling business.

Former teachers (at least the good ones) often make the best salespeople. Why? Because selling is all about educating people about the benefits of doing business with you. When you educate them past their fear of the unknown, they feel confident about their decision to do business with you.

Always spend a little extra time on what your product actually does and the benefits it brings when you're working with a customer who is unaware of your offering — and afraid of the unknown.

Fear of repeating past mistakes

Having a bad past experience generates fear in the hearts of some potential clients. If they've used a product or service like yours before, find out what kind of experience it was for them. If they hesitate to tell you, you may assume that their past experience was bad and that you have to overcome a lot more fear than if they've never used a product or service like yours before.

Try offering the product or service on a sample or trial basis. Give the prospect the names of your satisfied customers who will give unbiased testimony as to the value of your offering. (Check with those customers first to make sure they don't mind if you have prospects contact them.)

Fear generated by others

A prospect's fear also may come from third-party information. Someone she admires or respects may have told her something negative about your company, about your type of product, or even about another representative of your company. Either way, that third party stands between you and your prospect like a brick wall until you convince or persuade her that you can help her more than that third party can because *you* are the expert on your product or service. You'll have to work hard to earn the prospect's trust. Enlist the aid of some of your past happy clients as references, if necessary.

Choosing Your Words Wisely

Before you even get to know your clients, you need to think about the effective power of language. Every word you utter creates a picture in the mind's eye of the listener. Do you use that power to your greatest advantage?

Every word paints a symbol or picture in your mind. When you hear a word, you picture a symbol of what that word represents. Each symbol often has emotions attached to it as well. Words — such as *spring, summer, autumn,* and *winter* — can generate positive or negative emotions in you. If you love gardening, the warm spring air brings to mind beautiful blossoms, the opportunity to get your fingers in the dirt, preparing your soil for a summer crop. If you are a hay fever sufferer, the picture painted by the word *spring* is totally different.

The same rule applies to the words you use in your contacts with customers. You don't know in advance which words about you, your product, and your company will generate positive feelings in your clients. So you need to become extra sensitive to the way you use words if you want to have a successful sales career. In the following sections, I share the best selling-related words and phrases to use, I explain the importance of using the jargon your prospects use, and I provide tips on fine-tuning your vocabulary to create positive mental pictures.

Knowing the best sales words and phrases to use

Many words common to sales and selling situations can generate fearful or negative images in your clients' minds. The experience of millions of sales professionals confirms that replacing such words with more positive, pacifying words and phrases (like the ones in Table 4-1) is crucial. I discuss these words and phrases in more detail in the following sections.

Table 4-1	Words and Phrases to Eliminate from Your Sales Vocabulary
Instead of . . .	*Use . . .*
Sell you	Get you involved or help you acquire
Sold them	Got them involved or helped them acquire
Contract	Paperwork, agreement, or form
Cost or price	Investment or amount
Down payment	Initial investment or initial amount
Monthly payment	Monthly investment or monthly amount
Buy	Own
Deal	Opportunity or transaction
Objection	Area of concern or concern
Problem	Challenge
Pitch	Presentation or demonstration
Commission	Fee for service
Appointment	Visit, as in "I'll pop by and visit"
Sign	Approve, authorize, endorse, or okay

Concentrating on what appears to be such minor details may seem like overkill, but some of those details pack a hefty punch. You may consider the following words minor and feel that all my fussing over them is misplaced. But if you really think about it, you'll likely see what I've been hinting at all along: Language is a salesperson's *only* tool — period. The salesperson who uses language well, for the genuine benefit of other people, is a salesperson who sells, and sells, and sells. The words you use aren't minor details at all.

They're the very center of your profession. So, when you write down and practice your own product presentation, go through it and make sure your words stress comfort, convenience, and ownership from your prospects' perspective. After all, satisfying your prospects' needs is what the business of selling is all about — and the words you speak to them are the only way that you, and not your competition, can earn the opportunity to satisfy those needs.

Replacing "sell" and "sold"

The first terms I recommend that you remove from your vocabulary are *sell* and *sold.* Many salespeople tell prospects how many units of their product they have *sold.* Or they brag about having *sold* the same product to another customer. What are the mental images these words create? No one likes the idea of being *sold* anything. The word reminds people of high-pressure sales tactics and usually turns them off. It makes the transaction sound one-sided, as if the customer really had little say in the matter.

So what can you use in place of these common words? Replace *sell* or *sold* with *helped them acquire* or *got them involved* — phrases that create softer images of a helpful salesperson and a receptive customer becoming involved together in the same process.

Replacing "contract"

A commonly used word in sales is *contract.* What images does that term bring to mind, especially when you picture yourself as a consumer? For most people, *contract* evokes negative images — something Mom and Dad have warned you about all your life. Contracts bring with them fine print, legalities, and being locked into something. Where do you go to get out of a contract? To court — not a pleasant image for most people. So I recommend that you stop using the word *contract,* unless your particular line of business requires it. Instead, use *paperwork, agreement,* or *form.* Do those words bring to mind threatening images? Maybe, but they're a lot less threatening than the images the word *contract* evokes. And that's exactly what you're going for.

Replacing "cost" and "price"

What about *cost* and *price?* When I hear those words, I see my hard-earned cash leaving my pocket. That's why I train people to substitute the words *investment* or *amount* for *cost* or *price.* When most people hear the word *investment,* they envision the positive image of getting a return on their money. For products for which the word *investment* just doesn't fit, use the word *amount* — it's been proven to be less threatening to most consumers than *cost* or *price.*

Replacing "down payment" and "monthly payment"

Most people envision *down payments* as large deposits that lock them into many smaller *monthly payments* for, if not an eternity, at least a few years. They see themselves receiving bills and writing checks every month — not a pleasant image for most people. So replace those phrases with these: *initial investment* and *initial amount* or *monthly investment* and *monthly amount.* In the selling business, we call these terms *money terms,* and anyone who wants to persuade someone to part with money needs to use these terms well.

Replacing "buy"

What about the word *buy?* When people hear the word *buy,* they see money leaving their pockets. Use the term *own* instead. *Own* conjures images of what they'll get for their money, where they'll put the product in their home, showing it with pride to friends or relatives, and many other positive thoughts.

Replacing "deal"

One term overused by salespeople is *deal.* This word brings to mind something people have always wanted but never found. Images of used-car salesmen are only too closely associated with the word *deal.* Top salespeople never give their clients *deals.* Sales pros offer *opportunities* or get them involved in a *transaction* that is good for them.

Replacing "objection," "problem," and "pitch"

Customers don't raise *objections* about your products or services. Instead, they express *areas of concern.* I never have *problems* with my sales. Every now and then I may, however, face some *challenges* with my transactions. I never *pitch* my product or service to my customer. Instead, I *present* or *demonstrate* my product or service — the way any self-respecting professional would.

Replacing "commission"

As an authority or expert on your product or service, you don't earn *commissions,* either. You do, however, receive *fees for service.* If a client ever asks you about your *commission* on a sale, elevate your conversation to a more appropriate level with language such as this:

> Mrs. Johnson, I'm fortunate that my company has included a fee for service in every transaction. In that way, it compensates me for the high level of service I give to each and every client, and that's what you really want, isn't it?

Replacing "appointment"

One word that can potentially raise concerns in the mind of a consumer is *appointment*. Now, in the business-to-business world, this may not be as strong. However, consumers will view the appointment as interfering with their regular schedule even if the schedule shows that time as free time. Rather than equating meeting with you to an appointment with a doctor or dentist, use the softer term *visit:*

> I'd love to have the opportunity to visit with you, would Wednesday evening or Thursday afternoon be better?

Better yet, offer to "pop by and visit." What mental image does that create? That you're going to pop in and pop out. That you'll only be there a short time. In the business world, a "pop by" can conjure the image of a brief handshake and exchange of information in the lobby with no sit-down, conference room involvement at all.

Replacing "sign"

The last but definitely not the least important term I recommend that you replace is *sign*. If you replace nothing else in your selling vocabulary after reading this book, never again ask a customer to *sign* an agreement, form, or paperwork. What happens emotionally when people are asked to *sign* something? In most cases, a warning goes off in their heads. They become hesitant and cautious. They want to review whatever it is they're signing, scanning the page for the infamous fine print. Anytime now, they may even head for the door. It's been drilled into almost everyone from early childhood never to *sign* anything without careful consideration. And why would you want to create that emotion in anyone you were trying to *get happily involved* with your product or service?

Instead of asking your clients to *sign*, ask them to *approve, authorize, endorse,* or *okay* your *paperwork, agreement,* or *form*. Any of those word pictures carries the positive associations that you want to inspire in your clients.

I know a man who helps people acquire recreational vehicles. An RV isn't a minor investment for anyone. So when the moment of truth comes, he simply turns his paperwork around and says these words: "Bill and Sue, let me make you famous for a moment and ask for your autograph." While he's saying these words, he's handing them a pen and smiling. Nice picture, isn't it?

Using only the jargon your clients know

Today more than ever, your selling vocabulary matters because of the phenomenon of *trade talk,* or jargon. *Jargon* is defined as words and phrases particular to a given field of work. If you sell medical supplies to doctors, you need to know the jargon medical professionals use and use it yourself, liberally. But if you sell medical supplies to the general public, limit your use of technical terms to the bare minimum until you can determine your client's level of knowledge about the product. You don't want to alienate or confound your customers by using acronyms or words they're not familiar with. ***Remember:*** Your goal is to make your customers feel important — and it's tough to feel important when you don't feel very smart.

The human mind can assimilate information rapidly only when it comprehends what is being said. If you're talking to Jo Consumer about bits and bytes and she doesn't understand those terms, her mind stops at those terms and tries in vain to find an image that fits them. Many people won't stop to ask you for explanations because they're afraid of showing their lack of knowledge and being embarrassed in the process. Others may get the gist of what you're talking about but struggle to keep up. While they're trying to keep up, they miss the next few valuable points you relay to them. In other words, you've lost them. If your subject sounds more complicated than your buyer can comprehend, you risk squelching her desire to ever own or use your product or service *and* you risk losing the sale. More often than not, you lose such buyers to a salesperson who uses lay terms and simple definitions.

Good things come to salespeople who take the time to find out how to speak their client's language.

Developing your vocabulary to create positive mental pictures

Words are readily available to anyone who wants to use them. Webster didn't reserve certain words and their meanings for the rich. Everyone has access to the same dictionary, and everyone has the same opportunity to choose the words that make her speech outstanding and memorable. Every time you need to convey a concept to someone, you have a choice of any one of thousands of words to establish your meaning. You have no excuse *not* to choose your words carefully. Because you know that your words reflect the person you are, investigate the word choices you make and the reasons you make them.

Developing your selling vocabulary isn't about mastering the words you were tested on in school. It's about taking the time to make a list of powerful but easy-to-understand words and phrases that are specific to your product or service. Then test those words on a friend or relative — someone who is *not* a qualified prospect. If your test person doesn't have a clear understanding of the terms, prepare brief definitions of those terms in lay language (language your test person — and anyone else — can understand). The first time you use the terms with new or prospective clients, be prepared to give them the definition in lay terms if it's something vital to the transaction or if the term will recur frequently in your discussion with these customers.

You need to strike a balance between speaking the language of your clients and educating them about the terms they need to know if they're going to use your product or service. The key is to not make any assumptions about the terminology your clients are familiar with — and to be ready to explain any terms they don't know.

Anyone who wants to persuade others (and if you're in the selling business, that's you) should recognize and choose appropriate language. Take a look at the two following examples. Be aware of the differences in language between the two situations. Even though you can't *see* these two salespeople, pay attention to the mental picture you get of each of them and their selling styles.

Here's the situation: The manager of Continual Hair Care (CHC) has been courting an account with a major chain of salons (owned by someone named Ms. Dunn) for two months. Ms. Dunn's salons now carry the products of one of CHC's competitors, but Ms. Dunn has agreed to hear a presentation by a CHC representative. The CHC manager needs to choose the salesperson who can consummate all the manager's hard work — making a sale and landing the account. The manager calls a meeting with each salesperson she is considering: Dawn and Sue. The one who succeeds in representing the company can receive a sizable increase in earnings. Which one would you choose?

Dawn goes first:

> MANAGER: Now that you understand what will be expected of you, how would you give this presentation?
>
> DAWN: I would just love the chance to tell Ms. Dunn how much better our products are than what she's using. I would go to Ms. Dunn's salon tomorrow morning. I know I can convince her to dump what she uses now and replace her stock with ours.
>
> MANAGER: What's your next step?

DAWN: Well, after I got all the information, I would tell Ms. Dunn what we can do for her, and I would try to get her on my side before the presentation to her staff so ahe can help me sell her stylists on the products.

MANAGER: I'm interested to hear how you would do this, Dawn.

DAWN: Well, I guess I'd tell her how much money she would save and how much more she'll make by selling our products.

Now, here's the same situation — a hopeful salesperson talking to CHC's manager — except now the salesperson is Sue:

MANAGER: Now that you understand what will be expected of you, how will you handle this presentation?

SUE: I believe the first step would be to contact Ms. Dunn and request a meeting at her convenience. Then, with your approval, I would examine your files on the salon, so I'm prepared for the presentation.

MANAGER: What's your next step?

SUE: I will ask Ms. Dunn to show me her salons. I will familiarize myself with Ms. Dunn's needs, her stylists' needs, and those of the salons' clientele. Then I will offer Ms. Dunn the opportunity to use Continual Hair Care products and ask her permission to present the products to her stylists.

MANAGER: I'm interested to hear how you would do this, Sue.

SUE: Although considering her financial benefits is important, I will encourage Ms. Dunn to examine the improved condition of hair that has been treated with Continual Hair Care products. Making hair more beautiful will give Ms. Dunn happier customers as well as increased profits. Would it be possible to take a few company models with me on the presentation?

These two conversations create two pictures in the mind of the manager. Who will represent her company with the most success? The answer is Sue. Why? Because Sue radiated calm enthusiasm and a thoughtful manner. But the turning point in Sue's interview is her choice of the phrase *I will* instead of the indefinite terms like *I guess* or even *I would* that Dawn uses. Sue speaks as if she's already been chosen, whereas Dawn uses iffier, less-confident language. This difference is subtle but very effective. And it isn't long before the manager agrees to send models out with Sue for her presentation.

Sue is an *above average* salesperson with a powerful command of language. She creates positive word pictures with every word she utters. Here are some words you may hear an *average* salesperson deliver. Think about the pictures they create in your mind.

> SALESPERSON: All the kids in your neighborhood will love playing in your new pool.

> PROSPECT: I'm probably going to have trouble getting my kids out of it.

> SALESPERSON: When should we start digging? Would this Saturday or next Monday be better?

What's wrong with this dialogue between the salesperson and the prospect? What image comes to your mind from the salesperson's statement that "all the kids in your neighborhood will love playing in your new pool"? Loads of kids jumping, splashing, running, and yelling at the tops of their lungs comes to my mind. It's not too peaceful a scene.

Think about the word pictures you paint. Just a few careless words can destroy hours of hard work. In this case, the salesperson would do better to say, "Most of our customers tell us they enjoy spending quality time with their families in their new pools." This image is much more pleasant — and it leaves the picture more open to interpretation. So if the client would *enjoy* a bunch of kids playing in the pool, that's what she can see, but if she would prefer a more laid back atmosphere, she can see that as well.

The salesperson's next words — "When should we start digging? Would this Saturday or next Monday be better?" — carry their own negative images. With the word *digging,* the prospect may envision a huge tractor roaring through her yard digging up plants and mound after mound of dirt, making a general mess of the prospect's home — and on a weekend to boot.

The salesperson would do better to say this:

> Some people prefer to be present when we begin the first phase of their new swimming pool. Others prefer to just tell us when and then have us tell them when the pool is ready to swim in. We can begin Phase 1 Saturday or next Monday. Which would you prefer?

I can't emphasize enough how important your choice of words is to your selling career. Your words can make or break the sale without you even knowing it. In many cases, if you ask a customer why she *didn't* buy from you, she may not be able to put her finger on any one deciding moment. She "just didn't feel right" about going ahead.

Words create images, which in turn evoke emotions, so start paying careful attention not only to your prospects, but also to the effects your words have on them.

Knowing How to Listen to Your Clients

The human body has two ears and one mouth. To be good at persuading or selling, you must find out how to use those natural devices in proportion: Listen twice as much as you talk, and you'll succeed in persuading others nearly every time. When you do most of the talking:

- ✔ You aren't finding out about either your customer or your customer's needs.

- ✔ You aren't hearing buying clues or concerns.

- ✔ You may be raising concerns the prospect may not have had in the first place.

- ✔ You're shifting your buyer's attention away from your presentation.

- ✔ You're giving your buyer more opportunity to disagree with you, to distrust one of your statements, or both.

- ✔ You're taking center stage away from the customer.

- ✔ You aren't able to think ahead.

- ✔ You aren't able to guide the conversation.

- ✔ You aren't able to convince the other person of the best decision for him.

Most people don't think they talk too much, but if you had listened to as many sales presentations as I have, you would have developed a keen ear for how much talking is done compared to how much is needed — and the answer, all too often, is too much.

To develop your ear, try these two simple exercises:

- ✔ **Listen to a salesperson selling others or trying to sell you.** Pay attention to what her words are doing. While you're listening, ask yourself these questions:

    - • Do her words paint positive or negative mental pictures?

    - • Do her words say anything that may raise a new objection to her product or service?

    - • Are all her words necessary?

    - • Does she ask questions and then carefully listen to the prospect's answers?

    - • Does she move forward with questions, or does she get off course by talking about features and benefits the customer has not expressed a need for?

✔ **Record yourself when you're talking with a customer.** You may be shocked at how much chatter you can cut out. To detect what you need to cut, ask yourself these questions:

- What is the quality of the questions I ask?

- Am I asking information-gathering questions to help myself move forward with my sale, or am I just asking questions to fill a sound void? (Questions don't mean much unless the answers are helping you get the information you need to help you serve your customer better and keep the sale moving forward.)

Watch and listen to others and to yourself more carefully than you're used to listening in everyday conversation. Acquaint yourself with what good listening really *sounds* like. It should sound like the voice of others, not your own voice. As you discover more and more about selling well, the phrase "putting your foot in your mouth" will gain new meaning for you. After all, you can't put your foot in your mouth if it's closed. So close it, and listen more.

Chapter 5

Selling What Your Product Does Instead of What It Is

In This Chapter

▶ Noting the product details that your clients need you to know

▶ Getting the vital statistics on your product with a variety of techniques

*O*ne of the best advantages of a career in selling is that good selling skills are portable. By that I mean that after you master basic selling skills, you have the education you need to sell any product that you believe in once you master your product knowledge.

Product knowledge is one whole side of the selling triangle I discuss in Chapter 1, which tells you that it's one-third of what you need to know to be successful.

In this chapter, I offer specific suggestions for ways you can develop your product knowledge and be prepared for nearly any question that comes your way when you're with potential clients. Investing time in product research upfront pays off when you're ready to put your selling strategies to work.

You can't know too much about your product or service. Customers love to feel that you have the inside track on the latest and greatest products and services; they want to believe that you're the most competent person in your industry. Face it: No one wants to be represented by a dud!

The Stuff You Need to Know about Your Product

What must you absolutely, positively, truly *know* about your product in order to sell it? Always begin with the obvious:

- ✔ **What the product is called.** Know the specific product name and models, as well as the product/part number. Clients may refer to frequently ordered products by number. This is what's called *insider jargon.*

- ✔ **How the product is represented in the marketplace.** People are more likely to ask questions related to the benefits or features of a product than by using its name and model number. Become familiar with what it does because you're bound to run into potential clients who refer to it as, "that type of vacuum that picks the lint off of fleas. At least I think that's what it said in the ad I saw." Potential clients may not recall the brand or name of your product, but they always remember what grabbed their attention in your advertising.

- ✔ **Whether the product is the latest model or release.** Many of the potential clients you encounter want the latest version of your product. Others hope to find a discount on a discontinued model. Either way, you need to be prepared.

- ✔ **How the product improves on a previous model or version.** Be able to list the new features or options and what they can do for your customers. This is especially beneficial when you talk with existing clients who might be interested in upgrading or taking advantage of a technical advancement.

- ✔ **How fast, powerful, or accurate the product is.** Be able to offer up a comparison of your product to its competition so you can tell your customers how your product stacks up. It's better if the comparison was done by an independent group. If it's just your word against that of the competition, you may not have much of a leg to stand on with doubters. If there's no independent study available, at least have your satisfied clients who are already using it give you a testimonial stating that it's better than what they had before.

If you must create a comparison yourself, base it on something the competition provides so you can show your clients that you're very exacting in the information you provide — that your comparison is truly apples to apples.

✔ **How to operate the product during demonstrations.** Nothing is worse than trying to demonstrate a product to a prospective customer, only to find out that you're not sure how to make it do what he asked. Be able to operate the product as well as you operate the car you drive every day — by reflex.

✔ **What colors the product comes in.** Being able to tell your customers right away whether you have a specific color available comes in handy when they want to know whether or not it meets their needs. Some companies discontinue colors and release new ones to meet and match current fashion and decorating trends.

✔ **What your current inventory is for setting delivery dates.** Your client may have seen a review of your product in a magazine, even though it's not due out for two more months. You need to know what he's talking about, be prepared to inform him of delivery delays or future release dates, and see whether he needs the benefits of the product sooner. If the product is currently in production, but on back order, brag about its popularity and know the projected delivery dates. This is where you want to focus on the new model being worth the wait.

✔ **How much of an investment is required.** Be sure to phrase the price of the product in terms of an *investment* or *amount* as opposed to a *cost* (as I note in Chapter 4). Also, be prepared to reduce that amount to a monthly amount if your product is something that requires financing. Many purchasing agents consider how much something will add to monthly overhead. Other clients want to know how quickly they will receive a return on their investment (ROI). Be prepared to do that math with them as well. It can be as simple as calculating the cost of your product and dividing it by the annual, monthly, or weekly savings you project after your product is up and running. The answer you get tells the client when you project he will earn his money back on the initial investment.

✔ **What terms and financing are available.** If your company offers financing, consider it another product and know how the payment plan works as well as you know the product itself. Don't risk losing a sale when you've gotten all the way through to the financing stage of things.

✔ **Know whether distributors or competitors offer the same product for less.** Know who these distributors or competitors are and what price they're selling the product for. Don't be caught shortsighted by a client who is willing to do more research than you are.

Even companies with the most basic product training should cover these topics with new salespeople before asking them to meet with buyers. Unfortunately, however, some companies provide only the bare minimum of information, and you have to develop the rest on your own. With all this preparation, you should be pretty well off.

Be prepared to encounter a potential client who asks an odd question — something out of the ordinary that you can't answer with your current knowledge. When that happens, never make up an answer! Tell the person that you'd be happy to find out the answer to that question for him and then do it — quickly — before he considers the competition's product over yours. In cases such as this, you may have to do a lot of additional information gathering in the course of researching the answers to your buyers' questions. And that's okay because you build your product knowledge as well.

Keep in mind that if a potential client ever comes to you with valid information about your product or service that is a surprise to you, your credibility with that client is on shaky ground. After all, you're supposed to be the expert clients come to for information or advice. If they know more than you do, why do they need *you?* Make a commitment to stay on top of your game!

How to Get the Product Information You Need

How can you be sure you're armed with the product knowledge you need before you head out to make a sale? Take advantage of as many different resources as you can, starting with your company website and social media sites.

If your company offers training sessions on products, attend. If they hand out brochures and pamphlets, know them backward and forward. Talk with your existing customers about the product so you know what questions or comments they have, discuss the product with your fellow salespeople to get suggestions, and, if at all possible, tour the facilities where your product is made.

Also, be sure to know your competition's product so you can tell your customers how your product measures up. I cover each of these resources in the following sections.

Product information doesn't just come from the technical booklet that comes with the product. It's everywhere the product has been. In seeking out as much information as possible, you will earn and keep your expert status, and more people will want to take your advice.

Attending training sessions and reading product literature

Your company or the manufacturer of the products you represent may hold regularly scheduled training sessions about the product. If so, then by all means go to these training sessions. They're your best opportunity for getting the scoop about your product from reliable sources. And *always* attend these sessions with a list of questions and a notepad for writing down the answers. If the speaker doesn't answer your questions during the presentation, find a way to ask your questions of him before this knowledgeable person gets away.

Average salespeople resist training after their initial orientation period with a new product. That's why they remain average. Keeping your eyes and ears open to new and better information or ways of selling your product is critical to achieving success in your selling career.

Between training sessions, watch for email or Web updates of product information from the company as well. Visit your own company's website every morning and look for a product revision date, if those are posted on the site.

If something has changed in the past 24 hours, you need to read it and be familiar with it as soon as possible. After all, your best new prospect may have read that information already, and you want to be able to show that your knowledge is current.

Many online news sites, including CNN (www.cnn.com) and MSNBC (www.msnbc.com), let you tell them what industry or company you need the latest news for. When you visit your customized home page on the site, links to that information show up automatically.

Your company probably inundates you with technical information on your product or service, even if it doesn't offer specific product-training sessions. Set aside a specific amount of time in your schedule to sit and read — but don't just read through it the way a customer would. Study it. Read it every day for at least three weeks.

By the end of that time, you'll have the information memorized and know exactly what your customers are referring to when they ask questions. Nothing is worse than having to look to a higher source when your buyer asks a question that you should know the answer to.

If what you sell is a tangible product, get your hands on a product sample right away. Be like a kid with a new toy: Play with it, experiment, read through suggested demonstrations, and try it out as if *you* are the customer. Make notes on things you find challenging. Chances are good that at least one of your prospects will have the same issues that you come up with. Resolve those concerns now, and you'll be well prepared for your future presentations.

Try sending the questions you come up with to your customer support department online. See how long it takes them to provide an answer and how detailed the answer is. What you receive from them is what a customer would likely receive when using that service after a sale. If the return time is unacceptable for the type of question you asked, see if you can do anything within the company to help speed things up. Or if you know the response time is slow, you may recommend, during your presentation, that your clients contact you directly with questions. This strategy shows that you provide added services *and* that you're knowledgeable about the product.

Make sure that responding to customer support questions and concerns doesn't take up so much of your time that it interferes with your selling time. After all, you're paid primarily to find and serve new customers for your business, in addition to satisfying those you've already gained.

Talking with current clients

Get as much feedback as you can from the people who already use and benefit from what you sell. Ask what their experiences have been with your product. Do it in person as often as possible. However, if you have a large client base, consider using a short survey of maybe two or three questions.

Your surveys can be printed pieces mailed to your clients or, for even better response, emails or Internet surveys clients can quickly complete with a few clicks. If you prefer the personal touch and feel the time is valuable, handle those surveys in a personal phone call. The advantage to talking to people personally is that you can get each client talking and, hopefully, discover something new that will help you serve all your clients better.

Your current customers are an extremely valuable resource — *if* you keep in contact with them. Pay close attention to how they describe their use of the product and what they like about it. Your company tells you what your product is; clients speak of what it does. The benefits of your product are more valuable to clients than any list of features the developers come up with. Several strategies for keeping in touch with existing clients are covered in Chapter 14.

Learning from your colleagues' experiences

Veteran and top salespeople have all kinds of information about products that they may never document. Talk with them as much as you can in order to put their knowledge to work for you. Get them talking about their happiest clients and their most challenging sales. Also, ask about the ones that got away and how they would handle those situations differently when a second chance comes along.

Keep your meetings with other salespeople focused on product knowledge and information; otherwise, your time will not be well spent. When two or more salespeople get together, it's easy to get off the subject at hand and descend into old sales stories or other unrelated matters. If you want product knowledge, focus the conversation there. Now is not the time for gossip.

Ask your sales manager for permission to do a ride-along with the top salesperson in your territory. You almost always get a thumbs-up because the request shows your manager that you're sincere in wanting to become the best salesperson you can be.

Watch how the top salesperson handles everything — himself, the client, brochures, proposals, visual aids, and the product itself. Listen to the word pictures he uses in describing it. Notice the mood he sets. *Remember:* The *how* of handling products and information is as important as the what and why.

Being a student of selling

When you're in a learning mode, you need to set the stage for learning. That may mean gathering pen and paper, brochures, and a demo piece of equipment and locking yourself in the company conference room to study. It may mean setting appointments and interviewing with a training director, company owner, or top salesperson. It may involve watching hours of product training videos or attending classes on the products. It may involve interviewing current clients.

It doesn't matter what the type of education is, you must begin every session with a clear respect for what's to come. Treat the sessions like gold. Show up on time, if not early. Be prepared to take plenty of notes. Bring a couple of pens in different colors to highlight the most important information. And be courteous to those sharing their knowledge with you. What they are imparting will make you money.

Treat them and their messages with the utmost respect. The better you treat the people helping you, the more they'll relax. You'll be making them like you and trust you, which will lead them to offer you even more valuable information. Hmm, sounds a lot like selling, doesn't it?

Have the veterans provide you with their research website addresses. If these salespeople are as good as you think, they have tremendous databases where they get their latest and best information about your product — and that of the competition.

Going directly to the source: Seeing things firsthand

Whatever type of product you sell, try to create an opportunity to tour the facility where your product is designed and built. Better yet, try to visit with the originator of the idea. Find out what he was thinking when it all came together.

Such an occasion may include attending a company meeting where the founder is present. If there's an opportunity for a question-and-answer period, be prepared to ask questions and take great notes. If the idea for your product came from someone else on the company team, seek out that person. At the very least, make a connection with someone in the headquarters of the company who can provide you with background information.

With most products, the original idea comes from a need that wasn't being met. Some are stumbled upon while seeking the answer for a completely different need. Knowing your product's story comes in handy when selling to clients. If it's a particularly interesting story (and not too long) consider weaving it into your presentations.

Keeping an eye on the competition: Know what you're up against

Many companies designate a person or department to gather information on the competition and to prepare analyses of that information for the sales staff. If your company has this situation under control, sing their praises and encourage them to keep up the good work, because doing such research can be a voraciously time-consuming feat.

If your company *doesn't* provide this service, you need to take it on yourself. At least once a week, make a point of doing online searches that include a list of relevant keywords such as your competitor's company name, your product name, and so on.

Search for the competition's latest news releases as well as products — good things to know, especially if the competition is in trouble with the government or involved in a lawsuit based on one of its products, for example.

Don't rely on just one source for information. If you're in business on your own, you may want to enlist a family member to find juicy tidbits of information on competitors' products for you. Because you're the one who's out there every day slogging in the trenches, facing off against the competition, you need to keep your eyes and ears open for any information available, too.

If you call on customers who've had past experiences with your competitors, ask them if they would mind sharing their thoughts on the product and service with you. Ask what they liked about the product — particular features and benefits.

How were their contacts with customer service handled? What would they like to see improved upon? Asking in a sincere, caring manner sends the message that you want to do better, be better, and help them have a better experience than ever before.

When customers tell their tales, take good notes and keep them handy for future reference. If a new customer has just switched from the competition to your product, find out exactly what the deciding factor was and work it into any presentations you make in the future where circumstances are similar. Also, if a certain feature brought a client to your product, be certain that feature remains in the product when the client considers making an upgrade.

Chapter 6

Technology as a Sales Tool

∙∙∙

In This Chapter

▶ Overcoming techno-phobias

▶ Making your selling career easier with gadgets, software, and more

∙∙∙

Gone are the days of 3-x-5 index cards with handwritten notes about clients. Also gone are the giant Rolodex wheels of name and address information. If you haven't yet organized using today's technology, now's the time! Any time you spend putting effort into low-tech tools is time you could be spending with clients. The whole idea of using technology is that it saves you time and frees you up to do more selling. Part of doing your homework as a sales professional is getting up to speed with the technology that can make your life — and your selling — more effective.

In this chapter, I start by lessening some of your fears and helping you get motivated to get up to speed. Then I share some great resources that can help you sell better — everything from tools to use when making presentations to mapping services to help you get where you're going. I don't even come close to describing all the technological resources available today, but I do highlight a few of the best, letting you know which ones to check out first. View this as a jumping-off point to the wide range of innovations at your disposal.

 As the mind thinketh, so it shall appear online. What I cover in this chapter is just the tip of the iceberg in terms of what current and developing technology can do for you in your sales career. I suggest allowing yourself at least 30 minutes a week to investigate new sites, talk with fellow sales associates to find out what they've discovered, and explore up-and-coming technology. Keep an eye out for those truly wonderful developments that will help you save time in tracking all the details of your career and allow you more time to do what you're paid to do — acquire new clients.

Conquering Any Misgivings You Have about Technology

Advertising has changed in recent times. Advertisers assume when you see something that interests you that you'll pop onto the Web to find out more. The term "Google it" has replaced Mom's advice to "look it up" when you have questions about something. As a culture, we're more mobile than ever before, and to do business with us, companies need to be accessible on our terms. If that's what you expect from the people you do business with, you need to be prepared to have your information be just as accessible to your clients.

In the following sections, I help you overcome your fears about technology and get motivated to use it to your advantage. So if you get a chill down your spine when you hear talk about apps and texting, read on.

Setting aside your fears

If you've been in the sales profession for decades, the developments in technology may have left you reeling. In the past several years, I've talked with many veteran salespeople — people who consider themselves professionals — who are afraid that technology will take over their jobs, like the Industrial Revolution took much of the manual labor away from workers. These salespeople fear that if consumers can place orders from any device, they won't have any need for a salesperson. They fear that consumers will get the jump on them by knowing more about the competition's products and services and latest announcements than they do. In other words, they fear becoming obsolete.

I firmly believe that technology couldn't possibly bring about the demise of the sales profession any more than automation eliminated the need for living, breathing people in the industrialized world. Sales aren't made to machines; sales are made to people. And even though more information is accessible than ever before, technology hasn't yet mastered people skills — and as a salesperson, you still have the upper hand on the capacity to develop those skills to better serve your buyers.

Being able to persuade potential future clients to like you, trust you, and want to listen to you when making buying decisions is still critical. Real people with real challenges will always want to talk with other real people — that's where the fun is. Technology can't empathize with clients. It can't understand their needs and calm their fears the way a living, breathing sales professional can. An electronic device can't build a caring, mutually respectful, long-term relationship either.

When it comes to using any of today's technology solutions, having some fear at first is completely natural. It's fear of the unknown. We all have it. What most humans want more than anything else is to be comfortable. Figuring out how to use something new requires change. And change of any sort leaves most people feeling at least a little bit uncomfortable.

Motivating yourself to change

Many people hesitate to discover something new, even if they're assured it will make their jobs easier or make them more effective — and even if the new knowledge or behavior is guaranteed to extend their lives (like exercise) or help them earn more money (like sales training). They know that in order to get from here to there, they'll have to invest extra time and effort — and who has an abundance of either of those?

So where will you find the time in your already busy schedule to master new technology for your career? What do you give up in order to change? If you're like most people, when you're motivated by your belief of how much better you'll be *after* the change is complete, you'll quickly plan the time and be energized to put forth the effort.

 Flexibility and adaptability are the keys to success in today's ever-changing business world. As you've seen over the last 15 to 20 years, computer literacy is no longer just a business skill, it's a life skill — just like adding, subtracting, or knowing how to drive a car. Using the Internet, smartphones, tablets, and certain common computer software programs all fall under this umbrella as well. The more you know, the more indispensable you will be to your company — or the more valuable you will appear to a new company if you decide to change jobs.

Using Technology to Make Your Life Less Complicated (Not More)

If you're new to some of the technological tools available for use in your selling career, you may think of all those gadgets as time-consuming things you have to spend hours figuring out. And to some degree, you're right. Anytime you use a new product or service, you have to spend a little time upfront learning how to use it — but the reward is definitely worth it when it's the right tool for the job you have in mind.

In this section, I highlight some key tools you can use in your selling career to make your life simpler. If you do your homework and get up to speed on these tools, you can put them to use — and be more profitable in the process. How can these tools make you more profitable? Because, when used properly, they can free you up to focus on your clients' needs more completely (instead of worrying about some of the other details). And that's always a win-win situation.

The techno-salesperson you talk with about any new tool should do a good job of understanding your specific needs before recommending any device. If she doesn't invest that time, she may not have your best interests at heart. Find someone who does.

Trying out some fun gadgets

If you can think of a task that needs to be handled, there is very likely a bit of technology invented to handle it. The trick to not owning so much technology that you can't carry it all around with you is to concentrate on your own priorities. Which tasks take so much of your time that it would be worth having them mechanized or, at the very least, simplified? Not only can today's gadgets organize and simplify your business and personal life, they can also help you communicate. In this section, I review some of the more common tools sales professionals are using to get organized, plan their time, and communicate — or at the very least, get from Point A to Point B with clients, both physically and verbally.

Smartphones

If you're in any type of selling other than retail sales, it's wise to have a smartphone or similar device at the very least so you can be accessible to both your office and your clients when you're not sitting at a desk.

Owning a *smartphone* is like having a computer in your pocket. You can receive email and connect to the Internet. All of these services are available for a fee, of course, and those fees vary widely depending upon the types and amount of service you need to make your life easier. For example: Your smartphone may include — or allow you to download — an app (formally and formerly known as application) that adds GPS (global positioning system) tracking to your smartphone so you never get lost again on the way to a sales call. There's software that allows you to take a photo of a new contact's business card and have it automatically upload her information into contact management software that's also resident in your phone (I discuss this software later in this chapter). It's truly a matter of holding the world in the palm of your hand!

For some salespeople, smartphones have replaced the need to carry laptop computers, digital cameras, and MP3 players. Just note that with their smaller screens, if you show PowerPoint presentations or video demos to potential clients, you may still benefit from something with a larger screen.

If you're in doubt about what you need, talk to someone else who has more experience with your company — preferably a top producer — and find out what she uses on a regular basis to increase effectiveness.

Tablet computers and laptops

The iPad and its competitors have made a huge splash in the world of technology. These lightweight and highly portable tablet computers are being touted as ideal tools in the educational arena where students can upload textbooks, connect to the Internet, and use online software to learn. Many business people are quickly finding their potential quite beneficial and fun, too. Their screens are much larger than that of a smart phone, yet they are sleek and fun to use. They fall right in between the technologies of laptop computers and smartphones.

Laptops have been around since 1975. They were designed specifically to allow people to take their desktops with them. Ever since then it seems manufacturer's goals have been to increase their power while decreasing their size and weight. Laptops were a staple of salespeople for many years, and still are for some industries. One of their advantages over tablets is that you can store your whole world on the laptop and take it with you. You can function as long as your battery lasts. You are not tied to working only where you can get Internet access.

The overall benefit in using these various gadgets is that when used properly, they enable you to serve the needs of your clients more effectively, communicate with your company efficiently, and make more sales.

Helping your clients find you

You probably have a lot of information on your business card — your company name, your company address, your direct phone number (or at the very least your extension number), your fax number, your mobile phone number, your company's website address and social media sites, and your business email address. So, if I'm your client, what's the best way for me to reach you when I have a challenge? If the challenge is causing me grief or a slowdown in my own business, you can bet I'll use every number and address I have to track you down.

Instead of allowing your clients to become frantic trying to locate you, consider using a cloud-based *unified messaging service,* in which you can have all your messages (voice mail, faxes, email, and so on) delivered to one place. You can collect all your messages from anywhere around the world using a phone or the Internet. Some smartphones have apps that allow you to get this service.

There are also services where voice messages left for you can be converted to text and sent directly to you to read, You can choose whether to receive the text in an email or as a text message versus having to dial in to a service. So, with the proper tools, you never miss a customer contact.

Making travel plans

A live person at a travel agency can be a great help when you're planning multiple business trips. But if check your email at 9:00 p.m. and find out that your boss needs you to be in a city 300 miles away for a client meeting within the next day or two, you're going to want to check the best flight arrangements for your arrival time and to get a reasonable fare — and the sooner, the better.

Most airlines have their own sites where you can check availability and purchase tickets, so if you have frequent-flyer miles with a particular airline, the airline's website is a great place to start. (See Table 6-1 for a listing of the contact information for major U.S. airlines.) But if you're flexible and can travel on any airline, you won't want to invest all your time doing individual comparisons at the airlines' websites. Instead, visit www.cheapseats.com, www.expedia.com, www.priceline.com, www.travelocity.com, or any of the other travel aggregators online. Most offer comparisons of times and fares for nearly all commercial airlines. You can find what's best for you and then book the flight right then and there if you want.

If you'll be traveling by car anytime during a sales trip, you can find maps online at several different websites. Two of the best are Google Maps (maps.google.com) and MapQuest (www.mapquest.com). Both sites give you estimated travel times, all the turns you need to take, and the total mileage of your trip — they can even estimate your fuel costs. You can print out the information or download it into your computer or smartphone. The directions are provided in step-by-step text form, along with maps of the area. You can also find the nearest hotels and restaurants along your route.

 As mentioned in the earlier section "Smartphones," some of today's smartphones include GPS that allows you to enter the address you're seeking and get voice-guided and text display of the route to take to get there. Keep in mind that using GPS for a long trip can use a lot of data.

Table 6-1	Airline Websites and Contact Information	
Airline	*Website*	*Contact Information*
Allegiant	www.Allegiantair.com	All reservations: 702-505-8888
American Airlines	www.aa.com	All reservations: 800-433-7300
Delta Airlines	www.delta.com	Domestic reservations: 800-221-1212; international reservations: 800-241-4141
Frontier Airlines	www.frontierairlines.com	All reservations: 800-452-2022
Southwest Airlines	www.southwest.com	All reservations: 800-435-9792
United Air Lines	www.ual.com	Domestic reservations: 800-241-6522; international reservations: 800-538-2929
US Airways	www.usairways.com	Domestic reservations: 800-428-4322; international reservations: 800-622-1015

Using slides in your presentations

Giving presentations is a key element in selling. Microsoft PowerPoint and Keynote are two of the most popular. They make it easy for you to tell your prospective clients about yourself, your product, and your service. These software programs allow you to create simple or intricate slide-show presentations. When you're ready to give a presentation, you can use the slides you've created in a number of different ways: You can print the slides and give them as handouts to your potential clients, or you can display the slides on a wall or screen with a projector. You can even show them on your laptop, tablet, or smartphone.

You can also customize the slide presentation for each buyer. Plus, you can include audio files in your presentation, time music to go along with the messages, or add photos or diagrams to better make your points.

Some of my students take photos with their digital cameras or phones and add them to their slide presentations. This is ideal in industries such as real estate or when working with clients long distance.

PowerPoint is often bundled together with other Microsoft software programs (like Word and Excel), so you may already have it on your computer. If you don't, you can try it for free directly from Microsoft; `http://office.microsoft.com/en-us/powerpoint/`. For more information on PowerPoint, you can check out *PowerPoint For Dummies,* published by Wiley; different books are available, depending on the version of PowerPoint you have, most of them written by Doug Lowe.

Keynote is an Apple product that allows you to create and deliver beautiful presentations. It has some fun tools to add life and engaging features to your presentations. It's available through Apple here at `www.apple.com/mac/keynote/`.

Keeping track of client contact information with contact management software

If your business is a simple one and requires only basic contact information on each client, you can get by with nearly any simple address book, such as the one found in Microsoft Outlook. But if you need to track each contact with your clients and have those contacts coordinate with your daily, weekly, or monthly calendar, using something called *contact management software* (CMS) or *customer relationship management* (CRM) software makes more sense. CMS and CRM allow you to create databases of information — as much information as you'd like to include — about your future clients and long-term clients. It's where you input information such as:

✔ Names (make sure to get the spelling correct)

✔ Company names

✔ Addresses

✔ Various phone numbers

✔ Email addresses

✔ Assistants' or secretaries' names

✔ Best times of day to reach the clients

✔ Dates, locations, and times of appointments

✔ Notes on each conversation with the clients

✔ Descriptions of correspondence sent

✔ Products or services ordered

✔ Delivery dates

✔ Challenges that arise and how you overcame them

✔ Future growth plans for the company or division

✔ Birth dates, anniversary dates, and other important dates

✔ How long the contact has been with the company

✔ Hobbies (to establish common ground)

✔ Where the client took her last vacation

✔ Just about anything you can possibly learn about the people

The best thing about CMS and CRM is that the information is quickly and easily accessible or alterable as your relationship with your client evolves. Some contact management programs also include word processing software, which you can use to generate letters or emails or to process orders for a client. The contact information can be automatically placed in the document so you don't have to worry about misspelling anything as long as it's entered correctly into the database.

Many of these programs even prevent you from scheduling a meeting that conflicts with another event you already recorded. That feature alone can help you save face with clients instead of having to call them to reschedule.

Some contact management software is even available online so you don't have to be concerned about your laptop crashing and losing all your valuable information. Others are customized to the specific needs of salespeople — with forms for travel itineraries, charting activity and productivity, meeting notes, expense reports, and so on. Take some time to find one you think you'll be comfortable using.

Your company may want the whole sales teams to use a certain software program. Many of these programs provide reporting information or sales analysis information for management so sales managers can see how efficient their staff is being and where clients may be dropping off. So, your decision may be made for you by someone higher up. If that's the case, you simply need to take advantage of whatever training is available — even if that's just a training manual to read through — to gain the most benefit from it.

If your company doesn't offer or suggest a software program to use, you'll need to spend some time researching your options and choose the one that's right for you. Although I don't recommend one program over another (because what will work best for you is your call), I can share some basic information about some of the programs my students use successfully:

✔ **ACT! by Sage** is an economical investment. It has various levels of programs. If you buy from an online store, you can also download it directly onto your computer instead of having to wait for the CD to be shipped to you. This software is also available in a cloud-based version. It's great for salespeople who work out of an office as opposed to actually going off site to visit with clients. ACT! allows you to import contact information from Outlook or almost any other format you may already be using. For more information on how to use ACT!, you can check out *ACT! by Sage For Dummies* by Karen S. Fredricks, published by Wiley; different books are available, depending on the version of ACT! you have. To read about the many features of this software visit www.act.com.

✔ **Infusionsoft** (www.infusionsoft.com) is more of a small business CRM program. It includes standard CRM functions as well as the ability to create and manage marketing campaigns from within the system. There's also a store feature for handling actual sales transactions.

✔ **NetSuite** (www.netsuite.com) is rated as easy to use and a good tool for tracking leads as well as managing email marketing. It's billed as an all-in-one solution that includes accounting, Enterprise Resource Planning (ERP), e-commerce, and CRM. It's a cloud-based business management software. The real-time reporting feature is very popular with its users.

✔ **Salesforce.com** online Customer Relationship Management service allows you to keep your database online rather than on your own computer. That way, you're not bogging your system down with a huge amount of data, and the information is available to you online from any computer. No more lugging your laptop home every night. The investment varies depending on the number of people in a company or group who subscribe to the service. Visit www.salesforce.com for more information; you can also pick up *Salesforce.com For Dummies* by Tom Wong and Liz Kao (Wiley).

✔ **SalesLogix.net** helps mid-market companies manage their customer relationships. Similar to salesforce.com, this service is subscriber-based and offers access to the contact management database as well as many other linked services, including travel information, motivational and training tips, and so on. Visit www.saleslogix.com for more information.

✔ **Siebel Systems** (www.siebel.com) offers software geared to larger businesses and is a high-end investment. It involves a complete server-based administrative system and includes tools for sales needs, service needs, and administrative needs. You can keep track of your clients, be sent notices from corporate, and file your expense reports all on one system.

Part III
The Anatomy of a Sale

Five Types of Buyers

Buyer	Summary
Believing Bart	He is already sold on your company or brand. But if he's *not* convinced that you're competent, Bart won't hesitate to call your company and request another representative.
Freebie Freddie	The guy who won't settle until he thinks he has the upper hand and you've agreed to give him something extra. If you give Freddie any extras, he'll probably brag to and upset others who may not have received the same benefit.
Purchasing Polly	A distant, matter-of-fact type who carries a high level of responsibility. She can't risk liking you too much because she may have to replace you with the competition at any time.
Evasive Ed	Your most challenging buyer. He refuses to return your phone calls, he postpones appointments, he likes to shop around and keep you waiting in the meantime, and he tests your patience at every turn.
Griping Greg	Griping Greg always has something to complain about or something negative to say. If you're dealing with a Griping Greg, you have to decide whether the income his business generates for you is worth all the energy he'll steal from you.

For more on closing sales, visit www.dummies.com/extras/selling.

In this part . . .

✔ Seek leads for potential business and understand how to approach people and business with positive results.

✔ Connect with your clients and win over the difficult decision makers over by building solid rapport and standing out from the pack.

✔ Apply sales pointers such as building on answers you get, making potential clients feel valued, and relieving any tension that may arise.

✔ Win clients through effective presentations by putting the focus on the product benefits using the right language, staying in control, and mastering visual arts—among other pointers.

✔ Eliminate client concerns by knowing how to address them strategically.

✔ Use effective closing statements and overcoming hesitancy or fear from your client.

✔ Spread your good name by understanding how to request glowing referrals from clients who are satisfied and happy to recommend you.

Chapter 7

Connecting with the People Who Need What You Have

The first step in the selling cycle is what most people call *prospecting.* *Prospecting,* essentially, is the process of searching for people to whom to sell your products or services. I compare it to prospecting for gold where you would require the use of a burro, a pick, and a shovel, except that the prospecting you do as a salesperson uses the Internet, phones, email, and word of mouth instead.

If you already know the people you'll be selling to, you probably don't need this chapter right now (although the tips and suggestions you'll find here may help you find even *more* qualified buyers, which is always a good thing). On the other hand, if you have a great opportunity, service, product, or idea, but you don't know where to find other people who would be interested in getting involved with it, this chapter is exactly the place to start.

If you don't know whom to contact to help you get from Point A to Point B, you doom your product, service, or idea right from the start. You soon lose your enthusiasm or invest too much of your own time and money with little or no payoff at all. You run out of gas before you even get on that road to success. That's why this chapter is vital. You can master everything else in this book, but if you never get the opportunity to get in front of the right people, all the selling techniques you've honed add up to naught. You won't even make enough profit to feed your burro.

Knowing Where to Start Looking for Potential Clients

When you're finally prepared enough with knowledge about your product, service, or concept (see Chapter 5), and when you feel comfortable with your selling skills, you need to begin finding buyers. Because you won't have a lot of qualifying, presenting, closing, or follow-up to do when you're new, your primary focus should be on prospecting. In fact, in the beginning, your daily plan should be to invest about 75 percent of your time prospecting. The other 25 percent of your time should go toward developing your product knowledge and presentation skills.

The key to success in a people-oriented business like selling lies in how many people you can see in the time you dedicate to your business life. Initially, you'll probably find yourself working very hard just to find a few candidates for your offering. But with every experience, you'll refine your strategies and techniques, and eventually start working smarter.

The simplest place to start prospecting is with the people you already know, such as the groups I cover in the following sections. Talking with these people first helps you find easy leads and give you an opportunity to practice your prospecting presentation with people who are less likely to give you a dose of rejection than are complete strangers.

Many successful sales veterans will tell you how important prospecting continues to be even after they have built a large customer base. They, however, can prospect among their existing clients (also known as getting referral business; I cover this topic in greater detail in Chapter 13). Successful sales professionals — those with a strong desire not only to reach the top but to stay there — make prospecting a part of their everyday selling strategy. They understand that achieving success doesn't mean they can stop looking for new business opportunities. Successful sales professionals explore every avenue in search of new clients, no matter how long they've been in the business.

Starting with a few prospecting basics

The best place to start prospecting is with people who have already paid money for products and services similar to yours. If you're selling exercise equipment, begin with people who jog, belong to health clubs, or join local recreational sports teams. Why? Because you *know* they're already health conscious. The convenience of being able to exercise at home may be just what they're looking for. If you're selling graphic design, start with the people responsible for handling advertising for local companies. If you've already worked for people in a certain type of business, such as gift shops, you may want to concentrate on other gift shops in the area. The items in your portfolio will then be very appropriate outlets for your work.

Where you'll find your prospects depends on what you represent. If you sell products or services for a company, you probably discovered the likeliest places to find your products or services in use during your product-knowledge training (if you didn't, ask now). Those places are, obviously, the best places to begin prospecting. After you have made a few sales, you'll have time to get more creative with staking out other claims.

If you're on your own (as opposed to representing a company), use your local Chamber of Commerce as a resource. Go online to see what others in your industry are doing to attract leads for business. (If you conduct business in your local community, it's wise to become a Chamber of Commerce member and attend its events. Most are hosted specifically for members to get to know one another. This can be an excellent source of leads for your business.)

Conduct online searches for businesses of the type that would use your product or service. For example, you may search for all manufacturers of computer software if your product applies to that field. All you need to do to narrow down your list of potential prospects to the right ones to begin contacting is ask the right questions. If you have some money to invest in lists, you may want to contact a *list broker,* which is a service with all sorts of lists available that can review your particular demographic needs with you to provide you the best list of potential customers to contact.

If you choose to seek out a list broker, start by asking fellow salespeople, clients, or other business people what their experience has been with purchasing lists. Getting a referral to a reputable company is best. If you don't know anyone who has purchased a list, contact some of your local printers to see if they can make a recommendation or referral. Don't ask just one person and go with that broker unless the person you asked had unbelievable success with a list of demographics similar to yours. You want to get several recommendations for the same company before trying to work with it.

Some list companies offer to provide you with a small sampling of their lists so you can test the response to your offer before making a purchase. Always ask for that. (Your clients ask you for freebies. Why not ask when you're the client?)

In the case of needing consumer contact information versus business contacts, note that a reputable list broker will find you a list that has had telephone numbers checked against the national Do Not Contact list. You don't want to pay for a list of folks who do not want to be contacted by telephone if that's the type of campaign you're planning.

A lot of companies are out there with lists that haven't been updated or may not have been collected in the most appropriate manner. If you plan to reach out to your clients via email, you want a list with a double opt-in process and names that have either been verified or added within the last six months.

Searching for prospects among your friends and family

When you're new in the world of selling, honing your selling skills may draw you out of your comfort zone. So prospecting among those people with whom you're most comfortable — your friends and relatives — can take away a little of the stress of selling. I refer to a salesperson's friends and family as his *warm* or *natural market*. Friends and relatives are less likely to reject you (which means you're less likely to fail), and rejection and failure are the two biggest fears among those who are trying anything new. Your friends and family like you, trust you, and want to see you succeed. That means they're almost always willing to help. Besides, if you truly believe in the goodness of what you're doing and these people are candidates for your product or service, why would you want to deprive them of the chance to benefit from what you're selling? If you truly care about them, they'll respond in kind — and possibly become some of your best clients.

Be selective when you prospect among your family and friends, though. If you're selling exercise equipment, don't get discouraged if 90-year-old Aunt Minnie doesn't buy two of everything.

Start by contacting your friends and family and telling them that you're in a new business or you're starting a new career and that you want to share the news with them. Unless you've started a new job every six months for the past several years, they'll be happy for you and will naturally want to know more. This interested audience gives you the perfect opportunity to test your presentation skills.

A key phrase to use in getting your friends' permission to share with them your new product, service, or idea is this: *Because I value your judgment, I was hoping you'd give me your opinion.* This statement is bound to make a person feel important and be willing to help you — if he wasn't already.

After you contact all your family members and close friends, move on to acquaintances. Consider talking with your child's baseball coach, other parents, your accountant, and the checkout person you always see at the grocery store. When approached properly, most people are more than willing to give you advice or opinions. Ask the right questions, and they can advise you right into a great connection with a big client.

Always be aware of other people's time constraints. Don't try to contact them while they're working unless the questions you ask need only a quick reply or if they're responsible for making purchases for their companies.

Even if your friends and relatives aren't good candidates for your offering, contact them anyway. The first rule in prospecting is never to assume that someone can't help you build your business. They may not be prospects, but they may know others who are. Don't ever be afraid to ask for a referral. If someone can't help you or has strong opinions about your chosen career or offering, don't let it deter you. Just thank him for his time, and move on. That little strategy alone will do a lot for your career.

Using the help of professionals

Getting advice from others who have already been where you're going and are willing to share their knowledge is always a wise move — no matter how long you've been in the selling business. The Service Corps of Retired Executives (SCORE) has an excellent reputation for matching people who are new in a field (or those who may be struggling a bit) with retired or semiretired professionals from similar fields. SCORE is a U.S. government program with contact offices in most major metropolitan areas. You can visit the SCORE website at www.score.org to find out more about its services and to locate help near you.

The experience the helpful people of SCORE can provide is exceptional, but you must be open to discovery. Although some of its experiences may not apply to your current marketplace, the information available through SCORE can be like a life jacket thrown to you in the middle of the ocean.

If SCORE doesn't have an office in your area, keep an eye out for a mentor who can offer similar assistance. A *mentor* is someone who has more experience than you, an interest in what you're doing, and a willingness to take you under his wing to guide your actions. Mentors want to help others overcome obstacles they faced in order to help others learn from their experiences. You can find a mentor through Sales and Marketing Executives International, a professional support organization that has offices in most major cities. Check them out at www.smei.org. And you can always contact your local Small Business Administration office for advice by phone or online at www.sba.gov.

If you're new to sales, the company you work for may partner you up with one of its veteran salespeople for a brief training period. This type of company-sponsored mentoring program is working wonders around the world. It gives recognition to the vets for their knowledge and expertise and at the same time helps to train the new people in tried-and-true methods of conducting business. If you have the opportunity to take advantage of a program like this, be sure to do so. And if your company doesn't have an organized mentoring program, talk with your manager to see if you can be paired with someone anyway. Your interest in learning, and becoming the best salesperson you can be will most certainly be looked upon favorably.

Taking your search online

Unless you represent a product or service with a very small and particular demographic, the opportunities you have for making contact with prospective clients are practically unlimited. You simply need to test a variety of methods to narrow down those that bring you the best people.

If what you sell is good for businesses, begin with your local online Yellow Pages (www.yellowpages.com). Businesses invest their money in listings because they're serious about being in business. Their listings also should tell you that they're serious about *staying* in business. Online listing service providers like the Yellow Pages have made it easy for you to narrow your searches by category, location, and services offered by those companies listed. If your product or service can bring a business even more business or make that business more efficient, you owe it to them to contact them.

And if you want to broaden your field of potential clients, check out a toll-free directory. You'll find one online at www.inter800.com. Businesses are listed by company, number, and type of industry, regardless of long-distance carrier. ATT Anywho directory (www.anywho.com) allows you to do reverse lookups, when you have the phone number but don't know where the company is located. You can get company email addresses here as well.

If you're not online, your local library will likely have an Internet connection that you can use, or it may even have an actual toll-free directory in its reference section. Your local library is a wealth of free information. Use it!

If you're new to the Internet, refer to *The Internet For Dummies,* 12th Edition, by John R. Levine and Margaret Levine Young (published by Wiley) to get a clearer idea of how you can use this phenomenal tool to your greatest advantage.

Seek out resources via social media as well. Begin by asking your fellow sales associates which ones they find most helpful. I recommend the sales groups on LinkedIn for my type of business as I participate in some of them myself. Search through your industry news publications. Some of those sources may reference groups for users of your type of product.

When you find a group that suits your product offering, follow simple etiquette rules for engaging others. Introduce yourself to the others who use it. Don't go straight into a sales presentation. Rather, ask questions of the other members about their uses of your product or how they feel about it. After you begin to see what needs are being expressed, you can offer advice in the form of solutions. Using this type of strategy requires a soft-sell approach but can get you great exposure to a large database of people who are already interested in your type of product.

Because there is no editor on the Internet, not everything you see there is 100 percent correct and accurate. Information posted by large, respectable corporations probably provide source listings, but you should verify information without source listings through a reputable source before relying on it yourself — or passing it on to your clients.

Hiring someone else to do the dirty work for you

If you work for yourself, are really pressed for time, and are able to cough up the money, you can hire an advertising agency and a public relations firm to handle much of your market awareness and generate leads for you. Agency assistance varies; an agency can take on everything for your business, or it can help you with occasional, one-shot promotional ideas.

The fees agencies charge for their assistance differ across the country, so be sure to do your homework when researching agencies. As with any search, begin with people you know. Find out if anyone can refer you to a reputable agency. If you must search on your own, consider contacting another company that sells a noncompeting product to your same demographic group. If you ask its marketing person about any outside sources it uses, he will probably be happy to make a recommendation. If you cannot get a referral, once again, you need to search online.

Warning: Never hire an agency just because you like its website or see that it has a strong client list posted there. The biggest challenge with the Internet is that you can post pretty much whatever you want and let the buyer beware. When you are the buyer, do your homework. Any agency should be willing to show you its portfolio *and* provide you with contact information for its clients so you can speak with them yourself about the projects that were done. You want to know exactly what

the campaigns were, how long they took to put them in place, what they charged, and the statistics on what was generated for the client. If an agency is unwilling or unable to provide that much detail, move on to another that can. In marketing, it's not about the beauty of a campaign. It's about the results.

Always check out the people who give testimonials and references for a business. You never know when an agency's best testimonial will turn out to be from Grandpa Smith, who may have a personal (and maybe even a financial) interest in the agency's success. If an agency hesitates to give you references, don't waste your time considering doing business with it.

Even if you do hire an agency or agent to find prospective customers for you, never, never stop prospecting for yourself. If you ignore this valuable step in the selling cycle, you may walk by your best potential client without even a glance.

Tip: A local college or university may have a need for its advertising and public relations students to do internships or case studies. In these cases, there is typically no fee to the client. You're not getting experienced people working for you, but they should be knowledgeable in the field. Start by contacting the head of the marketing department. If he doesn't have any interns available, he should be able to refer you to an instructor in the department who does.

Taking advantage of lists generated by your company

When you work for someone else's company, the company usually handles the details of advertising and marketing to generate leads for you and the other salespeople. But to become a great salesperson, you should always be prospecting on your own, too. That way, if the company lead program hits a lull, you're prepared. A slow period isn't the time to begin developing your prospecting skills. If you're prospecting all along and encounter a minor setback, you'll barely break stride in your business activity level.

You may be in a position to help answer questions emailed to your company by customers or prospective clients. If that's the case, don't just reply; make the inquirer curious for more information. Do your best to capture more than the person's return email address. Get the person's name, address, and phone number if at all possible. Add him to your contact list and follow up with him to ensure he's satisfied with your reply. Offer to provide him with additional service as well. This strategy is just one more way to add to your list of prospective clients.

Finding the Right People: Proven Prospecting Strategies

In this section, I cover ten of the most effective methods I've used to find people who are the best candidates for what you have to offer. When you apply yourself to finding these people, and if you continue to do so on a regular basis, you'll be off and running on a successful selling career.

Mining the people you already know

You don't conduct your normal daily activities in isolation, do you? That means that you already know a horde of people who may be potential prospects for your product, service, or idea.

Think beyond your closest circle of friends and relatives. (Besides, you probably tapped them out during your first two weeks of selling, anyway.) If you're like most people, you shop every week (at grocery stores, hardware stores, discount stores, at shopping malls, and so on). And unless you live in the middle of nowhere, you have neighbors. You may go to a house of worship or community functions on a regular basis. You may have a spouse or significant other who works or who is involved in other activities through hobbies. And chances are good that several people in this wider circle of acquaintances may be able to benefit from your product or service in some way — or they may know others who do. In prospecting with the people you come into contact with on a daily basis, your job is simply to communicate. Letting others know the benefits of what you do opens many doors of opportunity for you. All you need to do is start a conversation.

Make a list of all the people you know, and start there. Here's a list to get you started:

✔ Your parents

✔ Your grandparents

✔ Your siblings

✔ Your aunts, uncles, and cousins

✔ Your coworkers

✔ Members of your sports team

✔ Fellow congregants at your house of worship

✔ Parents of your children's friends

✔ Your neighbors

✔ Your hairstylist or barber

✔ Your friends

✔ Members of business or civic groups you belong to

✔ Your mechanic

✔ Grocery store cashiers

✔ Your drycleaner

✔ Your pest-control person

✔ Your pet's veterinarian

✔ Your doctor

✔ Your dentist

✔ Your lawyer

✔ Your accountant

✔ Your kids' teachers

✔ Your teachers

✔ Your kids' coaches

✔ People you used to date

✔ Tellers at your bank

✔ Fraternity or sorority friends

✔ Your kids' babysitters

✔ Friends of your spouse or significant other

Tapping your business contacts

Whether or not you're new to selling, you've probably been involved in some sort of business. Even if you're just out of school, you've probably held part-time jobs. Business contacts can be easier to talk with than some social contacts because business contacts prospect all the time, too. You can probably cut to the chase more quickly with business contacts than you can with your personal contacts.

Visit the websites of the companies where your business contacts work. Look for the names of other companies they have affiliations with so you know before contacting them whether they may have another good contact for you. If the affiliates posted on their websites aren't good candidates for your product or service, or if they could be considered part of your competition, don't waste their time or yours in asking for them.

When you're prospecting, think not only of the people you know in your business life, but also get involved in clubs or organizations for business professionals and prospect there. Excellent opportunities have been found in sales and marketing clubs and at functions held by Chambers of Commerce.

Prospecting . . . an imaginative way

One student of mine always wore his company logo on a lapel pin — upside down. He made a specific point of putting it on upside down when he left the house. Hardly a day went by that some well-meaning do-gooder didn't tell him it was upside down, thus opening the door to a pleasant conversation about his business. As soon as he left that person's presence, he would turn the pin upside down again and move on to the next do-gooder.

Pay attention to emails you get from your business associates. You may have received an email as part of a group of recipients — and one of those people may be a prospective client for you. Getting a new lead may be as simple as having the person who sent you the message give you those other people's contact information so you can reach out to them. Or see if you can get permission to contact each person who received the email along with you.

When you receive a group email from a business contact, you may be able to see the email addresses of all the recipients. If you want to try prospecting with them, contact the person who sent the email and see whether the people you want to contact would mind if you contacted them (as opposed to just sending emails without checking first). That way, you can contact the person and say, "John Smith asked me to contact you," which is much more professional and courteous to all parties involved.

When you're sending emails to more than one person, put your recipients' email addresses in the *blind carbon copy* (BCC) field instead of the *To* or *CC* field. That way, you're not sharing your personal or business lists with others.

I can't recommend highly enough Toastmasters (a public-speaking organization) for anyone in sales. When you're involved in Toastmasters, you win through what you give to the group *plus* you gain access to lots of potential clients. Go to www.toastmasters.org to find a chapter in your area.

Many industries also have their own associations through which you can discover valuable new strategies for approaching people in your specific industry. Staking your claim in these groups can be highly beneficial. Ask your business contacts if they have a back issue of an industry publication available. Studying it will give you a good feel for the type of potential business you may find within that organization. You can do an online search for specific industry associations, such as the American Heart Association, the American Association of Retired Persons (AARP), or the American Bar Association.

When you find a prospective company, do further research with reputable resources. A great one is Dun & Bradstreet. Visit www.dnb.com and request a Business Background Report. Information on more than ten million U.S. businesses is available at the Dun & Bradstreet website. You're charged a fee for the reports, but you know the information you're getting is from a reliable source — which makes the fee worthwhile. Other websites that offer business listings and specific company information include Hoover's Online (www.hooversonline.com) and infoUSA.com (www.infousa.com).

For free information on businesses, try the Internet Public Library at www.ipl.org. It's an easy-to-use research site, but the information available is not as detailed as what you find at Dun & Bradstreet.

Talking to salespeople you currently buy from

Talking to salespeople you buy from is one of the most overlooked strategies of prospecting. Other companies send you highly knowledgeable, professional salespeople who already know loads of other people. They wouldn't be coming to you if you were in a similar business, right? So, because you're in a noncompeting business, why not talk with them about any leads they may have? Or at the very least, ask them to keep you in mind the next time they call on their customers. Any extra sets of eyes out there looking for prospects on your behalf are of tremendous value, especially when your only investment most likely will be returning the favor sometime down the road.

I've used the idea of a swap club to generate many leads for my business. I would get between four and six top people in other fields to join me once a month or every other week for breakfast at a local restaurant. Each of us would bring at least five to ten new leads for others in the group. There may be times when one of the people just doesn't have that many, but be sure to emphasize that sharing leads is the goal of the meeting — not devouring the fresh sticky buns. Each person pays for his own breakfast and provides the leads as his "fee" to stay in the group. If you set it up that way in the beginning, no one will have to tell someone else to leave for nonperformance. He'll know he's out if he fails to hold up his end of the arrangement.

Parlaying your adventures as a consumer

Imagine that you're at a restaurant and your server does an especially excellent job. If you're looking for someone to join with you in business (such as network marketing), not work *for* you, and if this person already has great people skills and is competent at performing his duties, he may be a good candidate for being in business for himself. You probably run into these kinds of people every day, everywhere you go — so take advantage of the situation and talk with them about the opportunities (or products or services) you have to offer.

Be careful how to approach people while they're working. Professional etiquette dictates that you don't interfere with other professionals while they're conducting business.

So what do you say to such people when you have the opportunity to talk? Here are some words that have proven to work in this particular situation:

> I can't help but notice that you have a nice way with people. I'm curious, are you achieving all your goals working here? The reason I ask is that the firm I represent is in an expansion mode, and we're looking for quality people to take advantage of the opportunity. Do you have an interest in knowing more?

If the person asks, "What's this about?" say

> Ethically, because you're working now, I'm not at liberty to discuss it. However, if you'd like to jot down a number and time I can reach you when you're not working, we can visit and see if it's a win-win possibility.

You can then either arrange a time to call or, at the very least, leave him with your card and a time to contact you. It's a harmless strategy, but it still gets the person's attention.

Another way to prospect through other businesses is to send the business a letter or thank-you note for providing you excellent service. Many business-people publish or display these letters in their places of business or on their marketing literature. If they have your permission to use your name in promoting their business, they're also pretty likely to list your profession or business name. When other people read your words, they'll see how professional you are and, hopefully, remember your name when they need the type of services you offer.

If you market a consumer item, chat with people you meet when doing your own shopping to see if they're good potential candidates for your product or service as well. Your grocery checker surely needs insurance, doesn't he?

The key to successful prospecting is to acquire the mind-set that *every* person you meet is either a potential client or knows someone else who is qualified.

Benefiting from the itch cycle

Face it: Nearly every tangible product brought to market has a limited life span. At one end of the spectrum are computer software and hardware, which can have a life span as short a few months. At the other end of the spectrum are things like refrigerators and freezers, which have life spans of close to 20 years. No matter how long a product's life span is, every product has one.

The precise life span of your product doesn't matter. What matters is that you know what its life span is. When you know your product's life span, you have a goldmine of opportunity waiting for your pickax to strike. If you're new to the product, ask people already in the business about your product's life span.

When you review your past customer files (see the following section for more information), you'll see that Mr. and Mrs. Lopez's washer needs to be replaced in the near future. It's bound to happen if it's getting up in years — say, 10 or 12 years old. So don't wait for the Lopezes' washer to break down and then quietly hope they come see you again. Get in touch with the Lopezes *before* their washer breaks down, and let them know you have some great new products with greater energy efficiency, more cleaning options, and other all-around better features. Put a reminder on your calendar or tag their file for follow-up in your contact management software. Your call just may help them move a little *quicker* in replacing that old machine!

Chances are good that the Lopezes know that their washer is on its last legs and they've just been putting off making the purchase. Maybe they've been waiting for a good buy or sale to appear in the paper — that doesn't matter. What matters is that they haven't acted *yet*. And these facts matter, too: The Lopezes already know you and/or your company— and they know that you're the expert they can turn to when the time for decision making arrives.

Always make sure strategies such as this one are approved by your manager or are acceptable according to company policy before you implement them.

If your company allows it, take advantage of a strategy I call *puppy dogging*. How do you sell a little puppy? You let someone take it home for a few days to see how things go. Almost every time, the person — that is, the *prospect* — becomes so attached to the new puppy that he can't bear to part with it.

If you're a car salesperson, you let a trusted client try out the latest model of the car you think he'd like, and before 48 hours are up, he loves the new car and wants to keep it. Even if he doesn't want that particular model, he's started itching for a new car and will need to get back in touch with you to return the loaner. You've provided yourself an itchy customer to serve. Such personalized service is guaranteed to keep clients coming back for more. Some salespeople even send clients links to high-quality videos of the latest model of the car they currently drive. This helps them to fantasize about owning it, all in the comfort of their own home. Offer to bring one by for him to test-drive. All he needs to do is reply with the word "Yes," and you have permission to confirm an appointment with him.

If you don't already know the replacement cycle for your line of products, find out what it is. When do people begin getting that itch for something new? All you need to do to find out this kind of information is make a few phone calls to people who currently use your products or services. You can treat this like a survey or market study and simply ask for their help. If they know it won't take long, most people love to help you. Begin by verifying that they're still using the product your records show them owning. Then ask what they used prior to the product or service they bought from you. The only time such research will fail is if the product or service that you got them involved with is your customer's first foray into your market. If it's the second, third, or later product or service of this type that they've owned, ask how many years, overall, they've used such products or services before replacing them.

You can also look at your own records to determine the lifespan of your product or service. For example, if you sell copiers and your customer has used your copiers for 17 years, trading in only four times during your association, you know he'll need a new copier after he's owned his present model for about 4 years. Toward the end of the third year, you may want to ask the client a few questions about his current needs and get permission to send him information about the latest and greatest models. If he says he won't need another machine for two more years, thank him for his time and make a commitment to stay in touch.

With replacement products, the salesperson who gets to the customer at the right time is often the one who wins. Plan to be that person, and you'll be doing a lot of the winning. The early bird makes the sale!

Using your client list

Any business that's been around for at least three years should have a detailed client list. If you don't already know, ask the business owner or manager how many salespeople have come and gone during that time. It may be that those salespeople haven't necessarily gone away but are now in other positions in the company. Find out what happened to past clients. If they weren't reassigned to another salesperson, you may want to ask to be given the authority to contact those clients yourself. If nothing else comes of your contacts, you leave a positive impression of the type of follow-up your company provides. And, hopefully, you update your database along the way. Be sure to get email addresses and website addresses (for business contacts), too.

With the many changes that occur in business these days, managers don't automatically invest the time to complete the basic task of transferring clients to new salespeople when the former salespeople move on. If the company is growing rapidly, some customers may get left in the dust. Why not be the one to pick them up and take care of them? They've already bought your brand or service before, so they're likely to do so again.

If your company has lived up to its promises, your customers should want to continue to work with such a fine organization. If they haven't made any purchases lately, it may be simply because no one has asked. Don't leave the door open for a competitor to come in and snatch up valuable customers. Prospect your list of past customers, and you may not only solidify their future business but the business that they will refer to you as well.

Riding the wave of technological advancement

Earlier in this chapter, I cover the inevitable itch cycles of various products. Why do you suppose people itch to get something new? In some cases, it's simply because the product wears out. In others, though, it's because of something more personal, like status. They want to have the latest, greatest, shiniest, top-of-the-line products with all the bells and whistles you can provide. When people have the best and latest products, in their minds they appear to be doing well in life and in business.

Few people really want to have the old model of anything unless they're collectors and the old model is a true antique or classic. Because most businesses today sell the latest equipment, peripherals, and support products and services, knowing and using this method of prospecting is tantamount to success.

Whenever you have a new model, an updated version, or even a change in the investment for your product, you have a solid reason to reconnect with the people you've already sold to. Being the kind of people they are, it's only natural that they'll want to be kept apprised of the latest changes. The key to success with this strategy is in how you contact them. Take a look at the following examples to see how you can put this strategy to work for you (and how it can backfire if you're not careful).

Bill invested in a top-of-the-line home entertainment system a couple years ago, but now some improvement has been made in the product that wasn't available when he bought it. Don't just call up old Bill and say, "Hey, I've got something even better for you." That would be both pushy and presumptuous and would very likely have the opposite effect of what you wanted — you may turn Bill off to even hearing what you have to say, because you've just, in effect, criticized his current system.

Instead, call Bill and ask him how he's enjoying listening to his favorite music on his home entertainment system. Being sure that he's still happy with what he's got before bringing up anything else is critical. If he has a complaint you didn't know about and you start talking about new products, you can lose Bill as a customer forever.

When you've determined that he's happy, say the following:

> Bill, I know how diligent you were in your research before investing in the T-tronics system. Because I value your opinion, would you mind evaluating something else our company is coming out with?

See the difference? You've complimented Bill, acknowledged his intelligence, *and* asked for his opinion. You've made him feel important. Of course he'll be happy to look at your new product now. And if it's truly better than the one he has, he'll probably want to upgrade his system.

If you take the time to know what's going on with your current customers, you'll know exactly when and how to contact them with new products or innovations and increase the volume and number of sales you make to each one. Now that's what I call working smarter.

Reading the news

One of the greatest prospecting tools around can be delivered to your doorstep or your email inbox for under a dollar a day in most areas. It has an intimidating, ultra-technical name; it's called the *news*. I used to read my printed version with a felt-tip marker so I could circle all the opportunities I found. But today, you can cut and paste the most pertinent information you read online into a single document or right into your customer management software.

Unless you do business internationally, you'll probably want to stick to the local news, business, and announcements sections. Stay away from the latest crime statistics and headline-making stories unless that's your field of interest. For most people, the most beneficial portion of the paper is written about John and Jane Q. Public.

John and Jane are the people who get promoted in business. They have babies. They buy and sell homes. They start new businesses. Do you get my drift here? If John Q. Public has been promoted, what else usually comes along with that promotion? A raise in pay. And what do most people do with their raises? Invest in stocks and mutual funds? Some do. But most buy new cars, bigger houses, nicer clothing, and season tickets to entertainment events — and buy the products and services you sell.

Knowing how to read the news for leads only takes a little practice. When you get started, you'll be amazed at the number of leads you used to glance over. Here's just a brief list of some of the things people need and want when they go through life changes (all of which you can find in your local news):

- ✔ People having babies need more insurance, bigger homes, minivans, delivery services, and diapers.

- ✔ Families who are moving into new homes need garage door openers, security systems, ceiling fans, window coverings, homeowners' insurance, landscaping, and aspirin (lots of aspirin).

- ✔ New or expanding businesses need equipment, personnel, and supplies.

I know of one real estate agent who benefited tremendously from a single news item in the sports section. The local professional football team acquired a new player. So the real estate agent sent a note to that new sports player before his arrival, congratulating him on making the move and welcoming him to the area. He included a copy of the news article and offered his services if needed. Being new to the area and to the team, the football player didn't know anyone in town, but he did need a place to live — so he contacted the real estate agent who sent him the letter. The agent not only helped the player find a new home but put him in touch with an insurance agent, landscaper, local doctors for his family, a hairstylist, and so on, illustrating exactly how the news can pay you much, much more than the few cents a day it costs.

Take today's local news and read every headline. Copy or highlight those with stories that may hold some business prospects for you. Then do what any top salesperson who's striving for excellence would do and *contact* those people. Cut out the article (or print it if you're reading online), make a copy for your records, and then send a brief note, saying, "I saw you in the news. I'm in business in the community and hope to meet you someday in person. I thought you might enjoy having an extra copy of the article to share with friends or relatives." Be sure to include your business card. People love seeing that they were in the news. And they love having extra copies of the articles to send to friends and relatives who aren't in the area. By providing this little service in a nonthreatening way, you can gain a lot of business.

Knowing your service and support people

If you're in touch with the people in other departments of your company, you may be able to discover valuable information that may help you keep the clients you already have (and get more down the road).

For example, someone who works in accounting for your company may know that one of your clients has been late several times in making his monthly investment in your product or service. That's a valuable piece of information for anyone in sales. By reconnecting with that client, you may be able to make other arrangements for him. Perhaps his growth rate isn't as high as he anticipated, and your equipment or service just costs too much for him. Instead of letting information like that get away, help the client cut back on his equipment or make other financial arrangements. He'll never forget you and will become a loyal, long-term client, referring his friends and business associates to you when they need the product or service you provide. If you let such information go without addressing it, you may lose that person as a customer just because he's overloaded with unnecessary equipment and is too embarrassed to approach your company about it.

Get in the habit of periodically checking your company's service and repair records. Even better, see whether your company can set up a system so that when a service call comes in, the salesperson is automatically emailed a notice of it. Consider asking the folks in your customer service department how many times your clients call with questions about the product or service you've sold them. Also, find out the type of questions being asked. If your clients are calling frequently, you need to get back in touch with them. Maybe they're in a growth phase, and you can help them acquire new services. Or maybe they're having some challenges with particular equipment. If they got stuck with a lemon, you need to be the one to turn it into lemonade — before they demand a replacement, a refund, or your head, and you get squeezed out!

Always strive to provide service above and beyond what the average salesperson would give. You'll build long-term relationships, trust, and referral business in the process.

Practicing the three-foot rule

Many businesspeople subscribe to the three-foot rule when it comes to prospecting: Anyone who comes within three feet of them is worth talking to about their product, service, or business.

When you get comfortable with what you're selling and with talking to people about it, I highly recommend applying this strategy. All you need to do is say, "Hello, it's nice to meet you." Pay attention to the people you talk to. Notice something about them you can compliment. For example, if you're a woman and you're talking to another woman, you can say, "That's a great purse (or dress, or coat). Where did you find it?" After she answers, go on with another question about her response or bring up something else you have in common, such as why you're standing in line at the grocery store at 11:00 p.m.

After you establish a little bit of rapport, that's when you can bring up the subject of your idea, product, or service. Ask a question such as, "Have you ever found a product to get gum off kids' sneakers?" (if what you sell gets gum off sneakers). Or use a question such as, "Have you been to the new gift shop on Fifth and Grovers?" (if the new shop is your shop). If you market security products, you can say, "I see you carry mace on your key ring. It makes you feel a bit more secure, doesn't it?" When she answers in the affirmative, talk about the great security product that you found (and sell). Personal testimony moves more products than any other method.

I know of one man who has gotten some of his best leads from fellow elevator passengers whom he knew only as long as it took to ride six floors up or down! Many business contacts have been made while standing in checkout lines at the grocery store or order lines at the coffee shop. Be ready to talk about your product or service wherever you go — and don't pass up any opportunity to speak with a prospective client.

Get creative with how you seek out information. For example, car handlers at valet parking services can be a valuable source of information. They discover a lot about people by their cars and how they treat the valets, and they overhear conversations about business. I'm not advising you to encourage people to eavesdrop on your behalf, but never turn away a valuable source of leads, either. If you've been trying to get an appointment with Mr. Warbucks, and the valet knows he's in the restaurant and will be leaving promptly at 9 p.m., it may be convenient for you to be next in line at that time, don't you think?

So how do you handle these brief encounters with people and get leads to build your business? I have to admit that this method won't bring you great leads *every* time. Even so, why walk by a potentially beneficial opportunity without knocking? So here's what you do: Grab a few of your business cards. (Salespeople are notorious for ordering thousands of business cards at a time. In fact, you can often tell the people who are newest to sales by the huge bulge of cards in their pockets. So make sure you start with just a few.) Across the front of each card, in very neat handwriting, write, "Thank You." (Hopefully, you haven't printed every one of your vital statistics on the cards; if you did, you may have no room to print your *Thank You*.)

When you meet a new person — someone who has entered your three-foot space — be warm and friendly. Introduce yourself and ask what his business is or why he's at that place. Making such banter sort of obligates him to do the same. When he asks what your business is, you simply hand him one of your cards. Most people take whatever is handed them as long as their hands aren't already full. (Thousands of servers of legal documents requesting your presence in court can't be wrong!) When the prospect gives you the courtesy of looking at the card, he'll probably ask about that *Thank You.* (Curiosity gets the better of most people, and they blurt out their questions almost as a matter of reflex.) That's the moment you've been waiting for. At that point, you simply smile and say these words:

> I guess I'm thanking you in advance for, hopefully, the opportunity someday to serve your [whatever your business is] needs.

Be sure to use those words exactly. *I guess* makes it sound spontaneous. *Thanking you in advance* shows that you're a nice person. *Hopefully* shows humility. *Someday* places your offer way out into the limbo of the future; it's a very passive, nonthreatening word. *Serve your needs* elevates your prospect to a place of importance in your life — and *everyone* needs to feel important. When someone feels like he's important to you, he's more likely to make a move that can help you.

He'll probably do one of four things, any one of which is a move in the right direction for you:

- ✔ He'll agree to call you to discuss it further.
- ✔ He'll give you a time to call him to discuss it further.
- ✔ He'll ask you to send something.
- ✔ He won't be interested, but he'll refer you to someone who may be interested in what you have to offer.

What have you got now? A lot more than you had a moment ago, standing there in line waiting to order your coffee. You've got a prospect . . . with a bonus opportunity of getting referrals.

Chapter 8

Arranging to Meet and Putting Your Clients at Ease

. . . .

In This Chapter

▶ Knowing how to get in touch with your potential clients

▶ Using communication tools to your best advantage

▶ Figuring out how to get in touch with the difficult-to-reach decision-maker

▶ Winning people over with a good first impression

▶ Standing out in a retail setting

▶ Building rapport with your prospective clients

. . . .

*I*n virtually every situation in which you can use selling skills, if you don't connect directly with the decision maker, all your hard work developing your selling skills goes for naught. If you don't connect directly with your clients — whether face-to-face, via video chat, phone, or email — you'll never be able to discover their needs in order to figure out how you can satisfy them.

So how do you get directly involved with the people you want to persuade? To connect with people long enough to discuss business, you first must sell them on confirming to meet with you.

Of course, to begin with, you have to find the right people to contact, and you do this by prospecting, a topic I cover in Chapter 7. But you also have to be firmly convinced that what you have is right for the people you're selling to. If you're not convinced of that, you won't deliver your presentation with enough conviction to persuade them to give you the time of day, let alone consider your product or service.

In this chapter, I let you know exactly how to get an appointment (which, as a sales professional, you call a *visit* or a *meeting*) with your prospective clients. Then I take it a step further and give you some great pointers for putting them at ease when you finally do meet — no matter the venue. When they're comfortable, they'll listen to what you have to say.

Knowing the Basics of Contacting Potential Clients

Your first line of approach when you're contacting a prospective client may differ depending on how you received the person's contact information:

- **If the prospective client contacted you by telephone, returning the call is always the most courteous response.** I give you the full scoop on telephoning prospects in the next section, "Reaching Your Prospects by Telephone First."

- **If you got the person's name from a referral (in other words, another client or business associate recommended you call her), ask the person doing the referring to introduce you to the new prospect.** Or, at the very least, contact the prospect and let her know that so-and-so asked you to contact her. Then you need to decide what type of meeting would be best — and this most likely depends on the formality of the situation. If you're selling luxury yachts, dropping a note first may be wise as opposed to interrupting the prospect's life with a sales phone call.

- **If the person left her name and email address on your website, she probably prefers to be contacted first by email.** Many websites ask in their visitor registration area how the client prefers to be contacted. If your website doesn't already ask this question, ask your company to change it. It's a simple yet powerful courtesy that can open the door to further business if you use it right.

Your goal when you contact a prospective client (whether by phone, mail, or email) is to get in direct, live contact with her, so you must approach the sale of the appointment very carefully. You first have to sell the prospect on the fact that she'd be better off speaking with you than not speaking with you. And that means you must offer benefits to her in your very first contact.

Keep the following tips in mind when you're trying to get a potential client's attention:

- **Always be courteous.** Say "please" and "thank you." Refer to the person as Mr. or Ms. Last Name; don't be too quick to use the first name. And don't ever assume a woman is a Mrs. or Miss. Getting that wrong can start you off on the wrong foot with her.

- **Do anything to meet the prospect.** Even if you have to drive miles out of your way to be where she is and all you get is an introduction, those miles can turn into smiles when you close the sale later.

✔ **Hit the high notes early.** That means you must pique her interest right away. Tell her about a benefit that she would be likely to enjoy — saving money, making money, and improving lifestyles are big ones for most people.

✔ **Confirm all the details about where and when you'll meet.** Verbal confirmation is a must. Written confirmation is even better. You can include in your confirmation that you'll invest plenty of time in researching just the right information for the meeting to make it worth her while. This often prevents the person from canceling your meeting lightly.

These instructions may seem too simplified at first glance, but many a novice salesperson gets so excited about getting an appointment that she lets her etiquette slip and says, "Hell yes, I'll be there!" (And although a little swear word among friends may be acceptable, it's something you should avoid at all costs when you're dealing with clients.) Or, she gives up too easily when a customer is tough to meet with, losing the chance to gain a new client. Or, she fails to reconfirm details about when and where to meet — and not knowing for sure when the appointment is, loses a potentially big opportunity. If you do your best to be courteous, secure an appointment no matter how busy the prospect is, and confirm the details of when you will meet, you're well on your way to a great sales call.

Reaching Your Prospects by Telephone First

The important thing to keep in mind when you've come up with a list of prospective clients is that not all of those clients need your product or service. You may have to contact 20 people to find 1 who wants just what you have to offer. But every one of those other 19 calls brings you 1 call closer to the right person. So you just need to stay focused on your ultimate goal; don't let a little bit of rejection send you scurrying to the nearest hidey-hole.

So what do you do when you're ready to approach those potential new clients? What strategies work best? You go through seven steps, all of which I cover in the following sections. Use these steps no matter the type of appointment you're seeking — whether the goal is for in-person, via conference call, Internet app, or whatever:

1. **Offer a greeting.**

2. **Introduce yourself and your business.**

3. **Express your gratitude for the person's willingness to talk with you.**

4. **Tell the person the purpose of your contact.**

5. **Get an appointment to speak with the person about your product or service.**

6. **Thank the person while you're on the phone.**

7. **Write a thank-you note and send it either by regular mail or email.**

The rest, as they say, is selling.

When you're about to contact your prospective clients, keep three things at the forefront of your mind: your belief in what you're offering, the happiness of your current clients, and your desire to serve others. This advice remains the same whether you're selling yourself as an employee, your skills as a freelance writer, or a million-dollar computer system as a career sales representative for a Fortune 500 company.

Step #1: The greeting

When you call a prospective client for the first time, begin by using the most important thing for anyone to hear: her name. Using a formal approach, such as "Good morning, Ms. James" or "Good morning. I'm calling for Ms. James," is best because it conveys respect. (But be sure to check your watch before you call, and take into account time zone differences. You don't want to look like a complete flake by saying "good morning" when it's 1:00 in the afternoon wherever Ms. James is.)

I recommend the use of *Good morning, Good afternoon,* or *Good evening* because it sounds more professional than just saying, "Hello." This phrasing distinguishes you from all those other people who call your prospective client — and this time the difference definitely favors you.

Too often, people are tempted to use a person's first name over the phone. The use of the familiar Bob or Judy doesn't bother some people (especially those whose names are Bob or Judy), but it does bother others. So don't risk being too familiar with Ms. Catherine Smith, whose mother and friends always call her *Catherine,* by souring the conversation at its beginning by calling her *Cathy.* Wait for Ms. Catherine Smith to say, "Call me Cathy, why don't you?"

Common courtesy goes a long, long way in making initial contacts. If you aren't confident in your skill level in this area, attend one of the many classes offered on business etiquette. Visit the Web sites I recommend in Chapter 4. Or, if you can't find an etiquette class in your area, pick up a book on the subject. I don't know of many situations in which you can be *too* polite, except maybe wrestling matches.

Step #2: The introduction

After offering your greeting, introduce yourself and give your company name. If your company name doesn't explain what you do — as it would if the name were, say, Jensen Portrait Studios — then you must also mention briefly what type of business you're in. The key word here is *briefly*. I once asked a salesman what he sold, and I got 45 minutes on the features and benefits of owning my very own magnetic resonance imaging scanner. Yikes!

To keep your potential client on the line and awake, you may not want to say that you're in the carpet cleaning business, for example. Instead, describe your business in terms of benefits to the prospect. For example, you may say,

> We're a local business that helps companies like yours enhance their image with customers and reduce employee sick time.

Clean carpets give a good impression. Dirty carpets harbor germs. Is Ms. James ready to hang up? Probably not yet. Your description is creating all kinds of pictures in her mind because you haven't been so specific as to mention carpet cleaning. Your business could be anything from sneeze guards to high-tech air-cleaning systems. Because she probably doesn't have that clear a picture yet of what you're selling, she's probably curious to know more. After all, no one likes to end a conversation with all the blanks not yet filled in.

Paint a tantalizing picture with the words you use, but keep it simple. If you hear snoring on the other end of the line, you've gone on too long. Keep in mind that this all happens in a matter of seconds. You're trying to get Ms. James to give you anything with which you can extend the conversation.

Step #3: The grateful acknowledgment

After you introduce yourself and your business, you need to acknowledge that your prospect's time is valuable and thank her for taking your call. This lets her know you consider her to be an important person. Say something like this:

> I appreciate you for giving me a moment of your valuable time this morning. I promise to be brief.

Or you may want to try this:

> Thank you for talking with me. I'll only be a moment, and then let you get back to the important work you do.

It doesn't matter if she was just walking into the room with nothing in particular planned for the moment. Acting as if you called her when she's just out of a meeting with the president never hurts the impression you make.

You don't need to gush at your prospects with gratitude, though. Just be professional and businesslike in your manner.

Step #4: The purpose

After you express your gratitude for your prospect's time, you need to get right to the heart of the matter by letting her know why you're calling. You should always express your purpose with a question. Something like this may be appropriate:

> If I can show you how to reduce employee sick time while improving the image your company presents to its customers, would you be interested?

If she says *yes,* ask permission to ask her a few brief questions. When you have her permission, start with your qualifying questions to determine what she has now and what she'd change if she were to make a new product purchase. (We cover qualifying questions in great detail in Chapter 9.)

If she says *no,* be prepared with one more question that may pique her interest, such as:

> Do you believe an improvement in the image of your business would have the effect of increasing sales?

If she still says *no,* you may want to be more direct and ask:

> When was the last time you had the carpets in your facility steam cleaned to eliminate germs and improve the experience your clients have in your store?

If she says it's only been a week, you may just need to remain polite and ask for permission to contact her when she needs the service again. (**Hint:** Ask how long ago she had her carpets cleaned, and you'll find out when she'll need them cleaned again.) Thank her for her time. Put a note in your calendar to contact her a couple of weeks before she needs the carpets cleaned again, and move on to your next potential client call.

Many of my students have benefited from a strategy that I call the *survey approach*. To begin, you would have your manager or the business owner assign you the task of surveying your client base or a list of new potential clients (because you never lie to clients or potential clients.) During your survey approach, when you get to this phase of the contact, you say,

> The company I represent has given me an assignment to conduct a quick two-question survey of just ten people. You're the sixth person I've contacted. We would greatly value your opinion. You wouldn't mind helping me by answering two brief questions would you?

When you ask for the potential client's help and show that you value her opinion, she's likely to comply. After all, who among us doesn't have an opinion? Plus, by informing her that your company is having you do this, you're likely to gain her empathy and cooperation.

The purpose of conducting this brief survey is to get the person on the other end of the line talking. Hopefully, what she tells you gives you the information you need to state benefits that build her curiosity enough to commit to that vital face-to-face visit.

Be careful not to just go from one question to the next without really listening to your prospect's answers. She'll know by how you phrase the next question whether her last answer was heard. If she thinks you're just waiting to pounce on her with a canned list of questions rather than sincerely trying to get valuable information, she'll disconnect with you quickly.

So how can you show that you're really listening to what your prospect is saying? Paraphrase her responses before moving on to the next question. When she hears that you cared enough to listen, she'll be more inclined to continue — and you escape your instant journey into the vortex. For example:

> Client: We are already scheduled to have our carpets cleaned with another company.

> You: So you do believe in the benefits gained from keeping your carpets cleaned regularly. May I ask what you appreciate most about having clean carpets?

Step #5: The actual meeting

If, after sharing with your prospect the purpose of your call and asking the questions you prepared, Ms. James seems inclined to set a time for an in-person visit, be prepared to tell her just how long you'll need. I recommend that you keep your initial contact as short as possible. Most people balk at giving you an hour or even 30 minutes of their time. Twenty minutes or less seems to be an acceptable time commitment for most people. If you know your typical presentation runs longer, that's okay. State the situation this way:

> The length of time required to cover the details is flexible, Ms. James. Most of my clients find that 20 minutes is sufficient to get the gist of what we're offering. Anything longer than that will depend on you and the questions you have.

When Ms. James agrees to give you the 20 minutes you need, give her an option of when to meet, with an alternative advance question such as this:

> Would tomorrow at 10:20 a.m. be good for you, or is Wednesday at 2:40 p.m. better?

This question lets your prospect choose yet keeps you in control. What's she doing if she chooses either option you've given her? Committing to the appointment, which is exactly what you want. This is called the alternate choice question. We cover this and more questioning strategies in Chapter 9.

Notice that my example mentions off times, as opposed to 10 a.m. or 2 p.m., for example. Using off times differentiates you from all the other salespeople who call. It also shows that you must know the importance of punctuality if you can keep a schedule using those times. If your visit will last only 20 minutes, it also lets your prospect schedule other appointments around you in the more standard time slots. ***Remember:*** It all comes down to courtesy.

Step #6: The over-the-phone thank-you

After you secure an appointment, move on to thanking your prospect again, reiterating the time you agreed to meet and verifying the location of her office (or the place where you'll be meeting). Nothing is worse than showing up late and presenting the excuse of getting lost. If the location is difficult to get to, *now* is the time to ask for explicit directions. If this is The Big Sale you've dreamed about for years and you finally have the appointment, drive to the office the day before and get familiar with the area. Know at least one alternative route in case traffic presents a problem or a road crew is scheduled to repair potholes that day.

If an appointment is important enough, schedule at least the earlier part of that day in the prospect's part of town so you're already in the area when the time for the appointment arrives. You never, ever want to take a chance that you'll be late for a first appointment because you don't know where you're going or because of circumstances beyond your control.

Making sure you don't set yourself up for disappointment

When you set appointments for people to come to your place of business or to a meeting, give yourself a reality check and expect only 20 percent of those who committed to you to actually show up. Between the time you contact the person to set up the appointment and the time the appointment arrives, any number of conflicts may occur. They may decide to sleep in that day. An important call may come in. They may change their mind about the value of spending their time with you. They may just be running late. Or they may just plain forget.

The only way to guarantee that a person will come to an appointment with you is to go and bring her to the appointment yourself. When your appointment is at her place of business or her home, your odds improve tremendously.

Step #7: The written thank-you

If your appointment is more than two days from when you call, immediately send your potential client a thank-you note (either by regular mail or email), confirming the details of when you spoke and what was agreed to. A professional-looking piece of correspondence can solidify any doubts she may have about this commitment. Follow up with an invitation to add the meeting to their Outlook or Google calendar by sending a meeting invitation from within one of those programs.

Keep in mind that if your prospect has given you a home email address as opposed to a work one, she may not check that email account on a daily basis, which means it may not be the best method of reaching her. In most business situations, however, people communicate frequently by email, so the recipient will likely see your message right away.

Including your picture on your letterhead or on your business card and enclosing that with your thank-you note never hurts. Get a professional portrait taken if you choose to use a photo — sending something that looks like your driver's license photo is bad news. Knowing what you look like increases the prospect's comfort level when she meets you.

Putting Mail, Email, and Face-to-Face Interactions to Work for You

You can contact your prospects in four major ways: by phone (which I cover in the preceding section), mail, email, or face to face — either in person or via the web (I cover these last three methods in the following sections).

Most professional salespeople integrate all four methods into an effective prospecting strategy. For some, one method works better than others. Different situations call for different strategies, so be well versed in how to handle each. As you gain experience in prospecting, you'll figure out which methods work best for you and at which times.

Keep in mind that when you use any of these four methods, you're asking busy professionals or consumers to give up time that they may think can be spent more productively. So before you have a chance to convince your prospects otherwise, they may try to shut you out — and shutting you out is easy for them to do. They can just make a paper airplane out of your letter, delete your email with a simple click of the mouse, leave you on terminal hold, ignore your incoming phone call, or cancel your meeting.

Mail

If you choose to use mail as your primary method of prospecting, choose your mailing list carefully. Mailing is a great way to prospect, but mail sent to the wrong list of people is a tremendous waste of your time, money, and effort. Nothing is easier to get rid of than a piece of paper that arrives amidst a stack of other papers. And this is especially true if your prospecting piece of paper winds up in the mailbox of someone who wouldn't care about your product or service in a hundred years.

Instead of sending a piece of mail that talks about your product or service, consider mailing a single-page introductory letter to the people you know who are most likely to want to get involved with what you're doing, indicating that you'll be calling on a certain date and time. Include your photograph on the letterhead or on a magnet or other enclosed novelty item. Magnets are great because people tend to use them on their refrigerators, and every time your prospect goes to the fridge, she sees your smiling face. People buy faces. They aren't as likely, however, to buy from some anonymous voice on the phone. ***Remember:*** Prospecting is all about establishing rapport.

Whatever you send in the mail, be absolutely certain that it includes your website address and your email address. As much as most people love talking on phones, they're still more likely to check you out first by visiting your website to see if there's anything interesting that may make it worth their while to talk with you in person. Or, if the purpose of the mailing is to generate sales, let the recipients know if they can order online. They don't have to wait until they can catch a live sales representative on the phone — especially if they read their mail at 2:00 a.m.

Email

You can handle email prospecting in two ways:

- ✔ Purchase an opt-in email list from a list broker. *Opt-in email lists* are lists of people who have agreed to have information about certain things they're interested in sent to them via email. Messages to potential customers on an opt-in email list have an open rate ranging from 5 to 15 percent — a huge increase over traditional direct-mail response rates. And using opt-in email lists can help you avoid emailing unwanted information to people and making a negative impression (making no impression at all is better than leaving a negative one).

  Check out www.postmasterdirect.com to find out more about how you can benefit from email promotions.

- ✔ Search out the email address of a consumer or purchasing agent (through an online directory or corporate website) and mail a very specific, customized email.

In either case, you want to use your email like the introductory letter mentioned in the preceding section. Introduce yourself, your company, and the benefits your product would provide to the recipient. Then finish in one of the following ways:

- ✔ For the opt-in list, you may wrap up your letter with a call to action: "Reply to this email within 24 hours, and we'll have a specific proposal to you by Friday of this week."

- ✔ In a custom email you may tell the recipient that you'll be calling within 48 hours to ask her two quick questions (this is the survey approach from the "Step #4: The purpose" section earlier in this chapter).

Sending an email that looks like an advertisement is not as effective as sending something that looks more like a letter or typical email message. Your goal with email is to make a personal connection, pique the recipient's interest with valuable tips or information, and tell her how to learn more.

Face-to-face interactions

Face-to-face prospecting is almost always the best method, but it's also the most time intensive. Walking from office to office or home to home trying to find decision makers is physically exhausting, which can be tough. But even worse is the sad fact that you may not get many leads out of all your legwork.

What you will get, though, is a load of information from neighbors and receptionists. They can be powerhouses who help you either eliminate a family or company as prospects or advance your chances of obtaining an appointment for making your presentation with the decision-maker by providing great prequalifying information. I've often thought one of the best places to prospect would be a secretarial convention rather than the one where all the executives meet. Receptionists, secretaries, and assistants hold the keys to opening the doors you want to get through. Hence their title in sales jargon is *gatekeeper*. Too many salespeople think this term is negative in that their job is to keep you out. In reality it's to let in the right people. You just need to figure out how to demonstrate that you *are* the right person.

Treat receptionists or secretaries with the respect they deserve. Their time is valuable, too. If you try to rush past a receptionist or quickly ask to see her boss without first showing concern or interest in her, you may as well not have gone in at all. Introduce yourself, ask the receptionist's name, and then try to have a friendly dialogue with her before asking to see the boss. She will be more inclined to introduce a friend to her boss than she will a pushy salesperson, so try to get her to see you as the former rather than the latter.

When you engage in face-to-face prospecting, remember how lucky you are to be able to get some of the precious time out of the busy schedules of important people. Your prospects are offering something to you, too: an opportunity to show them how they can benefit from your product or service. In today's society, suspicion and distrust are rampant. When you professionally prospect (with the right attitude about your prospects), your contacts will come to trust you and welcome you into their homes and offices.

Getting to the Elusive Decision Maker

When you're seeking a meeting with a prospective client, what you really want is to get in with the person who has the ability to make decisions about the products and services are used, otherwise known as the *decision maker*. In consumer sales, it's most often the heads of the household (even though one spouse or partner may defer to the choices of the other). In some situations, the end user has the final word. The end user may be a child or parent of the person you believe to be the decision maker, or in business situations, the end user may be the person or group who will actually use your product or service.

In the case of a purchasing agent or business owner, that person may have so many people contacting her that she's established a hierarchy of people around her who screen calls or start the research process on her behalf. This situation may cause you to wonder exactly where your prospective client is and what she's doing. Images of her jetting to exotic locations for meetings or floating in a sensory-deprivation tank may come to mind. But it doesn't matter what she's doing, as long as you can eventually get to her. I provide pointers on how to get through to those elusive decision makers in the following sections.

When you have trouble getting through to the decision maker, you get the opportunity to be a little creative. Yes, this situation requires more work. But keep in mind that those people who are hardest to get to are tough on your competition as well. So if you stick it out, get to visit with them, and win their business, you'll be on the inside of that same protective wall. And those same support people will keep not you, but your *competition,* at bay.

Going head-to-head with the receptionist

If you're having trouble getting through to a company's decision maker, begin with the receptionist who answers the phone when you call. If at all possible, get the name of the decision maker on your first contact. Tell the receptionist that you need her help and ask, "Who would be in charge of the decision-making process if your company were to consider getting involved in a [whatever your product or service is]." The receptionist is the person who has to know what each employee's area of responsibility is in order to direct calls properly, so she should be a great help. Then, whenever you make follow-up calls, use the decision maker's name.

Be sure to ask for the correct pronunciation and spelling of any names the receptionist gives you. Never guess about names or take the chance of writing them down incorrectly; business practices like that are likely to haunt you later. It never hurts to get the receptionist's name as well.

If the receptionist is especially helpful — as receptionists tend to be — take a moment to send a thank-you note to her along with your business card. Businesspeople often tout the value of a good receptionist when they need to hire one, but only smart businesspeople reward other people's receptionists well. A little bit of recognition now can prove valuable later on. When you have built a solid relationship with the receptionist, she will always look forward to hearing from you or seeing you, and future visits will be much warmer. She will also help guard your account against infiltration attempts by your competitors.

Working with the decision maker's assistant

If the decision maker has an assistant, the receptionist probably puts you through to that person first. Expect it, and don't be put off by it. Treat this person with the same respect and courtesy you would use with the decision maker herself. The assistant can make or break your chances of ever getting an appointment, so the best thing to do is to ask for the assistant's help as well. You can accomplish a great deal of research with the assistant's help — and you may even be able to prequalify the decision maker through her assistant (see Chapter 9 for more information on qualifying).

First, tell the assistant the benefits the company stands to gain from your product or service. These benefits may include that you have a way of increasing efficiency while decreasing the costs of a service the company is already using. This provides that assistant with just enough information to either want to know more or to want to help. (And if you live up to a promise like that, the assistant can be seen as a hero by taking your proposal to the boss right away, so she'll probably be eager to listen.) Finally, tell her you need her help, and simply ask how to get an appointment to speak with Ms. Decision Maker.

Most businesses have an established procedure for setting up appointments with the head honchos. By asking what that procedure is, you show that you're not trying to beat the system; you just want to find out what it is so you can work with it. When you show respect for the system in place, you move up a notch on the respect scale.

Encountering voice message systems

With today's technology, many companies have gone away from having a receptionist answer the phone. Instead, you encounter a voice messaging system. Some of these systems are very clear and concise. You can quickly determine the name and extension number for the decision maker you're seeking. Other systems are very broad such as "For sales, press 2." And it may not be clear who is responsible for purchasing what you're selling. When you encounter this type of situation, I suggest you press the number or extension for someone in accounting or more specifically in accounts payable. The people responsible for paying the bills know who must approve each type of purchase order and may be able to give you the name and extension of the person you're trying to reach. And, if you're lucky, they may transfer you directly to the decision maker!

Leaving voice mail messages that build curiosity

When you're trying to connect with someone who uses a voice messaging system to screen calls, you really need to be strong in your selling skills. Your first sale, via voice mail, is to sell the decision maker on calling you back.

When leaving voice messages, it's extremely important that your message is brief and to the point.

Start by giving your name. Then tell the potential customer that you'll leave your number twice. Give the number. Then, leave a curiosity-building statement or question. Give your number again and the best time for her to reach you. Thank her for her time. Tell her you will follow up on a specific date and time if you don't hear from her, then do it.

A curiosity-building question might be "When was the last time you learned a new strategy for saving on your income taxes?" A statement to build curiosity might be, "You can save up to 20% on printer and copier ink without keeping a closet full of supplies." Leave a message that encourages the recipient to either call you back or take your call the next time.

Getting creative in your efforts to meet with the decision maker

Whatever unusual method you choose for getting in touch with the decision maker, always consider how the other person will receive it. Your goal is to find an inoffensive method for getting someone's attention — but your method has to be creative, too. You don't want to risk alienating anyone, but if she's important enough to contact, you need to find out what her hot buttons are and build your contact method around that. Again, this is where receptionists, secretaries, and assistants (along with even other family members) can come to your rescue.

I know of a salesperson who sent a loaf of bread and a bottle of wine in a basket to a hard-to-reach decision maker. She included a note that said, "I hate to w(h)ine, but I know I can save you a lot of dough if you'll just meet me for ten minutes." It broke through the barrier in a creative way, and she got a confirmed appointment.

Before sending alcohol to a prospective client, find out whether she drinks or abstains from alcohol. If she doesn't drink, this bit of creativity can make the wrong impression.

Another creative way to make a good impression on the decision maker is to ask her receptionist or assistant who she respects and listens to in her field. Our planet of billions of people really is a small world when it comes to making contacts. If you find out that your prospect is a member of the PTA or Rotary Club, think about whom else you may know who's a member, and try to network your way into an appointment that way.

If you're working your business correctly, you're bound to find some way that your circle of contacts connects with the prospect. The real skill in meeting people is turning those points of contact into strong links.

Making a Good First Impression at Your Meeting

Your prospective clients make many decisions about you in the first ten seconds when they meet you for the very first time. That's right. Within *ten seconds,* you can be either chopped liver or Prince or Princess Charming.

Take a stopwatch or check the second hand on your watch right now and find out what ten seconds feels like. When you're watching your clock, it seems like a long time — but when you're walking into a room or chatting online and meeting someone for the first time, it passes by in an instant. Your job is to come up with a way to help the people who meet you for the first time see that they made a good choice in agreeing to see you. Your clients must *immediately* see some benefit from investing their time with you.

Knowing how to maximize those first ten seconds (with the help of the following sections) allows you to make the impression you really want to make, so you can comfortably move forward in your selling.

Dressing for success

Before you meet with your potential client, consider the way you dress. Your goal is to ensure that your prospects like you and see that you're similar to them. So how should you dress to accomplish this? Dress like your clients dress. Or, even better, dress like the people they turn to for advice.

Use good judgment and common sense when it comes to the way you dress. If you sell farm equipment and show up at a client meeting dressed like a banker, the farmers you're selling to aren't likely to feel very comfortable around you. After all, in the past, bankers have foreclosed on farmers, so you want to dress less like a banker and more like the farmer herself. This doesn't mean you have to show up at your client's farm in a pair of dusty overalls, but more-relaxed clothing is probably in order — maybe khaki pants and a casual shirt or blouse. Of course, if you sell to a corporate purchasing agent and you show up in casual clothes, you won't make the impression you want to make. Know your clients, and you'll know what to wear.

If you're new in sales or new to a particular group of clients, pay attention to what the other successful salespeople at your company wear, and then dress like they do. If your company has a dress code, there's probably a good reason for that. Be sure to abide by it.

Paying attention to your body language

In addition to the message you communicate to your clients with what you wear, the body language you use also expresses something. Your carriage, your facial expression, the placement of your hands, the speed, volume and tone of your voice, how much you lick your lips as you talk … all of these govern first impressions just as much as what you wear.

Being aware of your body language may require some time in front of a mirror or video camera, or you may need to spend time with someone who truly cares about your success and is willing to give you an honest opinion. Dress for work and walk your normal walk. If your normal body language doesn't present an image of success and confidence, watch someone who does and emulate her. Basically, you want to do the following:

- ✔ Walk with your shoulders comfortably back. Your arms should be at your sides (no hands in pockets!).

- ✔ Make good eye contact with the people you meet. Don't stare them down or eye them as if you're assessing their clothing.

- ✔ Smile warmly — with both your mouth and your eyes.

- ✔ Keep your tone of voice confident. When you rehearse, if your voice sounds shaky, keep rehearsing until you've got it down.

- ✔ If you're truly nervous when meeting new people, take a few slow, deep breaths to calm yourself before beginning the meeting.

Walking into a yes

In a study of 10,000 people conducted by UCLA, each person was asked what their initial impressions were of someone they later said yes to. Seven percent said the person had good knowledge of the topic, product, or service. Thirty-eight percent said the person had good voice quality — he sounded confident and intelligent. And 55 percent said the person walked with an air of confidence and self-assurance even as he approached. If you doubt the power of projecting positive body language, think again.

Getting Your Potential Clients to Like and Trust You

When you meet people, your main goal is to help them relax with you. No one gets involved in a decision-making process when they're uptight. You want your prospective clients to like you and trust you because, if they don't, they won't do business with you. Always remember that your goal is this: to be a person other people like, trust, and want to listen to.

So how can you help your prospective clients like and trust you? Start in those first ten seconds after you meet, and move through five important steps to making a stellar first impression (covered in the following sections in more detail):

1. **Smile deep and wide.**

2. **Make eye contact.**

3. **Offer a greeting.**

4. **Shake hands.**

5. **Offer your name and get the prospect's name.**

If you handle these steps properly, you'll earn the opportunity to continue building rapport and lead into the next phase of selling, which is qualifying (I cover that in Chapter 9). Qualifying is where you determine whether you can help your prospective client, but if you can't get to that stage by making a good first impression, all your previous efforts will be about as useful as a box of wet crackers.

Most of the time, people are who you expect them to be. That's because your demeanor — what you say and how you say it — sends them a distinct message of what you think of them. People are, for the most part, reactive and respond according to what's given them. So if you expect them to be cordial, open, and friendly, they will be. When your body language and opening statements are pleasant, the people you meet are very likely to respond in kind.

Step #1: Smile deep and wide

When you first come into contact with a prospective client, smile. (Yes, it's that simple!) A smile radiates warmth. If you're not smiling, if your smile appears fake, or if it looks like it hurts when you do it, your prospect will want to avoid you and will put up a wall of doubt and fear in just a few seconds.

Some people forget how to smile because they don't do it much. I've had to ask some of my salespeople to go home, stand in front of a mirror, and practice smiling for a solid 30 minutes. (If you try this at home, make sure the door is closed when you practice, or someone may just throw a net over you and haul you away!)

If you're contacting people over the telephone, smiling still counts. Believe it or not, people can hear a smile (or a lack of one) in your voice. When I was a manager, I put little mirrors by the telephones of each salesperson, because I wanted them to see themselves when they were speaking with clients. If my people saw that they weren't smiling, chances were good that the person on the other end of the phone could sense it — and it would certainly have a negative effect on the relationship. I had the salespeople turn the mirrors over or slip them into drawers when clients were actually in the office, but believe me, having those mirrors made a big difference in the success of our telephone contacts.

Step #2: Make eye contact

When you meet a prospect, look in her eyes. This is a part of body language that builds trust. People tend not to trust those who can't look them in the eye. Think about it: People usually glance away when they're lying to you. So when you don't look your clients in the eye, they may doubt what you're saying. Developing the ability to look someone in the eye and lie to them takes a good bit of intentional practice, which is what con artists do.

If you're meeting clients online and using a webcam, practice looking into the camera, which, in effect, is making eye contact. Your potential client shouldn't see you watching their image on your screen if your camera is at the top of your monitor. Glancing is fine to watch their body language, but keep your eyes primarily focused on the camera.

Although looking your clients in the eyes is very important, be sure not to go to the extreme and lock onto their eyes. Getting into a staring contest is dangerous in any selling situation. Give your prospect a couple seconds of solid eye contact while smiling, and she'll most likely be the first to glance away.

Step #3: Say hi (or something like it)

The style of the greeting you offer depends on several factors, such as whether you're calling a longtime friend, a new acquaintance, a total stranger, or the Pope. Your greeting is also affected by the particular circumstance of how you're meeting your prospect. If you have any doubt at all about what kind of greeting is best, err on the side of formality.

Depending on the situation, any one of the following greetings may be appropriate:

- ✔ Hi.
- ✔ Hello.
- ✔ How do you do?
- ✔ How are you?
- ✔ Good morning (or good afternoon or good evening).
- ✔ Thank you for coming in.
- ✔ Thank you for seeing me.

If you already know your prospect's name, use it with your greeting (for example, "Good morning, Ms. Williams."). If you don't know your prospect's name, don't rush to get it (just wait for Step #5, which I cover a little later). Pressing strangers for their names is fine in many situations. But in others, it's seen as being pushy. If you're in a situation where you're obviously there to sell something, be atypical and establish a bit of rapport *before* asking for your prospect's name.

Step #4: Shake hands

Salespeople are well known for having a tremendous need to shake hands. So most people expect to shake your hand when they meet you unless it's culturally unacceptable. But, to avoid appearing awkward with those who aren't comfortable shaking hands, I recommend that you keep your right arm slightly bent and held by your side. If you see the other person reach toward you, you're ready. If she doesn't reach toward you, you haven't committed the grand faux pas of reaching out too eagerly.

Some people don't want to shake hands because they just don't like touching other people. Then there are those people who go to great lengths to avoid physical contact for health reasons — they may be unusually susceptible to germs and don't want to touch anything they don't have to touch. Other people suffer with arthritis and find hand shaking extremely painful. Instead of opening a first meeting with their list of physical ailments, they'll simply avoid shaking your hand. So don't take it personally if someone doesn't show an interest in shaking hands.

The handshake is appropriate in most instances, but only if you do it properly. Take some time to notice how others shake your hand. If you've ever shaken a hand that feels like a dead fish, you'll understand what I mean. Or, if you've experienced a bone-crushing handshake, you'll also see the importance of having the right kind of handshake.

To convey the highest level of trust, confidence, and competence, you need to grasp the whole hand of the other individual and give it a brief but solid squeeze — not too tight, but definitely not loosey-goosey either. Keep it brief. There's nothing more uncomfortable than to have someone keep holding your hand when you're ready to have it back.

If you're meeting a married couple, shaking the hands of both the husband and the wife is appropriate. If they have children with them, shaking the kids' hands is a nice gesture as well. After all, if the product you're selling involves the children, you want to earn their trust, too. If you can tell a child would be uncomfortable with having her hand shaken, simply give her a moment of eye contact. Don't do any cheek tweaking or hair tousling of the kids. Remember how you hated it when Aunt Minnie did it to you?

Step #5: Offer your name for their names

The handshake is the most natural time to exchange names. Depending on the situation, you may want to use the formal greeting of, "Good morning. My name is Jennifer Smith with Jones & Company." If the setting is more casual, you may want to give your name as Jen or Jenny — whatever you want your prospects to call you. Make sure they get your name right, though. Nothing is more difficult than correcting a potential client who calls you Lynn when your name is Jen. Besides, when you've won them over and they've begun sending you referral business, you don't want the referrals asking for the wrong person and letting someone else earn your sales.

What's in a name?

If you're being introduced to a group of people, be careful to use the same level of formality with each member. Don't call one person Ms. Johnson and call Ms. Johnson's associate by her first name, Carole, just because you can't remember Carole's last name. That's more offensive than having to ask again what Carole's name is.

Early in my career, I spent an entire afternoon with a couple, failing to get their names correctly during the initial greeting. The day concluded with them making an offer on a home. When it came time to fill out the paperwork, I asked the husband very warmly and sincerely, "And how do you spell your last name?" He responded, "J-O-N-E-S." Boy, was my face red!

If a woman says her name is Judith Carter, use Ms. Carter when you first address her. Don't jump to the familiar Judy. Why? Because that's what a typical salesperson would do, and calling your prospect Judy may cause her to raise her guard against you. Getting familiar too fast is also impolite. Let your prospect decide when you may become more familiar, and let *her* give you the appropriate first name to use. Don't shorten someone's name (from Judith to Judy, for example) unless she tells you to. Some people prefer their given names to nicknames.

When you're involved more deeply in the qualification or presentation stages of selling (see Chapters 9 and 10) and you feel some warmth building, using first names with most people becomes comfortable. If they haven't given you permission to do so, politely ask for it. With Judith, just ask, "May I call you Judith?" If that's what everyone calls her and she has built some confidence in you, she'll probably say yes. Or she may say, "Call me Judy." Although this may seem like an old-fashioned approach, it's what sells. People yearn for a time when they were treated with more respect and courtesy.

Establishing Rapport with Your Potential Clients

Your clients feel comfortable around you when you know how to establish *rapport* with them, which is what selling situations are all about — establishing common ground. People like to be around people who are similar to them. Bringing out the similarities you share with your prospects proves that at least one salesperson is not an alien being from another solar system. You're not even from the dark side of the moon — you're just like them: You have a family, you have a job, you have similar values, and when you're seeking any product other than the one you represent, you work with salespeople, too, just like your prospects. You just happen to be more of an expert on the particular product line or service you represent than your prospects are — and you're happy to use your knowledge to their advantage.

In fact, I have just the words to say to let your potential customer know that you're a normal person. If you sense that the other party is concerned that you may not be on the same page as they are, say something like this:

> Ms. Williams, when I'm not helping people get involved with my product, I'm a consumer, just like you, looking for quality products at the best price. What I hope for when I'm shopping is to find someone who can

---

Winning over Hell's Angels

After about my third year in sales, I had been working hard and had done pretty well. I was driving a brand-new Cadillac, which was the real estate car of the 1960s. It was long, sleek, and beautiful. I'd even earned enough to invest in a few nice suits.

I received a call from a woman who asked me to come by and look at the home she and her husband were thinking of selling. Driving over in my new Caddy and nice suit, I was feeling pretty good about myself. When I pulled up to the house, there in the driveway leaned six Harley-Davidson motorcycles parked in a line, the way serious bikers park their bikes.

Judging from the looks of these hogs, my Cadillac and suit weren't going to help me establish much rapport. A huge, bearded man wearing a Hell's Angels jacket answered my knock. Glancing into the home, I could see five other guys just like him sitting in the living room. If there were ever a time when a salesperson did not have instant rapport, this was it.

Nervous, I walked on into the home and decided to stick with what I normally did for starters. I said, "Before I can give you any figures on what your home is worth, I need you to show it to me." We started in the living room and went into the kitchen. Because the garage was just off the kitchen, it was the next stop. As we went into the garage, there on the floor was a motorcycle all in pieces, one they were obviously customizing. I asked them how they distributed the weight when they extended the front wheel, explaining that I had a motorcycle, too, and that I had been riding for years. Of course, it wasn't a Harley, but I was a motorcycle enthusiast.

We talked bikes for about ten minutes and all of a sudden the entire situation changed. I was no longer a guy in a fancy suit, but a fellow motorcyclist. I ended up listing the home and getting them happily moved. And I learned an interesting lesson about the importance of making my customers comfortable.

help me understand all the facts about the item I'm interested in so I can make a wise decision. Today, I'd like to earn your confidence in me as an expert on state-of-the-art sound systems. So feel free to ask any questions you may have.

Don't wince at the thought of using these words — they've been proven to work successfully in lowering barriers people put up when dealing with salespeople. Although no one likes hearing canned material, it's only canned if you let it sound that way. In sales, how you say it is as important as what you say. Always remember to speak with a sincere concern for your customers. If you're not truly concerned for them, you shouldn't be in this field.

Knowing How to Approach Prospects in a Retail Setting

Selling in a retail environment is really no different than selling in any other environment — you need to get each customer to like you and trust you enough to ask for help instead of immediately pouncing on your customers with a reflexive "May I help you?" Wouldn't you love to have a dollar for every time you've heard a retail salesperson ask, "May I help you?" when you walked into a store?

As a customer, you may have heard variations of the "May I help you?" greeting, including something like this: "Hi, I'm Bob. What can I do for you today?" What kind of response does Bob hear 99.9 percent of the time he says those words? "Oh, nothing. I'm just looking." If something doesn't work 99.9 percent of the time, doesn't it make sense to try to come up with a better initial greeting?

If you work in retail sales, I have two important suggestions that will increase your sales and the sales of anyone else in your company you share these suggestions with:

- When people enter your establishment, never walk directly toward them.
- When you approach customers, don't rush.

Think about a time when you've been approached by a quick-moving, over-zealous salesperson, and you had to step back away from her. You don't want that to happen to you. Approach your customers as if you are just walking around the store, not making a beeline to them. Smile. Welcome them, and let your customers know you're there in case they have questions. Then get out of the way and let them look around.

Figuring out what to say instead of "May I help you?"

So what can you say instead of "May I help you?" Try saying,

> Hello, thanks for coming in. My name is Anne. If you have any questions, please let me know.

What does this greeting do? It projects a warm, welcome feeling rather than an overwhelmed feeling. You've just invited your customer to relax, and, when people relax, they're more open to making decisions.

Another greeting you may want to try is this:

> Hello, welcome to Standard Lighting of Arizona. I'm happy you had a chance to drop by today. Feel free to look around. My name is Karen, and I'll be right over here if you have any questions.

Pause momentarily in case the customer does have questions. Then step away.

When you step away from the customer, instead of toward her, you distinguish yourself from all the typical salespeople she's ever encountered — and for most shoppers that's a very good thing. When you leave shoppers alone, they walk toward what they want. By observing them from a discreet distance, you know exactly what they came in for. When they finally stop in front of something for a moment, that's when you want to move closer to be ready to answer questions. Don't hang over them like a vulture, though. Just be where they can find you when they look around for help.

Recognizing the signals your customers project

In any place of business where you have a display area or showroom, let your customers look around before you approach them. Being laid back is much less threatening and far more professional than mowing down your fellow associates and careening toward your potential customer like a runaway freight train the moment she walks in the door.

If a customer doesn't look around but remains by one item for a while, then you may walk up and ask a question. Use an involvement question right off the bat because she'll have to answer it with more than a *yes* or a *no*. Plus, you'll discover something that will help you keep the conversation going.

For example: If the customer is looking at a piece of furniture, ask,

> Will this chair replace an old one, or is it going to be an addition to your furnishings?

When she answers, you'll know why she's interested, and you can then begin guiding her to a good decision.

I know of some places of business, such as automobile dealerships or some furniture stores that are so large that people usually *do* need a guide (or at least a map) to find their way around. If you work in such a setting, you have to take your customers to the type of product they want. But, again, step away from them when you get them where they want to be, and let them relax. When they're ready to talk with you, they can still find you quickly, but you haven't invaded their space and taken control of their shopping experience.

In a large retail environment, potential customers may have a challenge locating exactly what they're looking for. In that type of situation, try this:

> Welcome to Furniture Oasis. What brought you in to our store today?

If they are looking for children's furniture and it's in the back of the store, you can guide or direct them to that area. Letting these folks wander on their own, potentially getting lost along the way, is doing them a disservice.

Building Common Ground in Any Situation

When the introductions have been made and you're out of those first ten seconds of a meeting with a prospect, you need to smoothly transition into establishing common ground. How do you do that? By being observant.

If you just walked into Ms. Johnson's office, and you noticed that she has family photos all over the place, ask about her family. You don't need to know details now. Just say, "Great looking family," and let her decide how much to tell you. If you see trophies, comment on them. If you can see that she's a fisherman and you're a fisherman, too, bring up the subject of fishing.

The power of observation is incredibly important to develop as you work on your overall selling skills.

Someone may have referred Ms. Johnson to you. If that's the case, mention the mutual acquaintance — that's usually a great starting point. "Good old

Elena" may have an excellent talent, great family, or wonderful sense of humor. Those are all nice, noncontroversial topics to cover.

In the following sections, I cover ways to reach common ground with prospects or existing customers with whom you may not yet feel entirely comfortable.

By allowing your potential client to first see the human side of you rather than the sales professional side, you help her break through the natural wall of fear that encloses her when typical salespeople walk through her door.

Keep the conversation light, but move ahead

Don't let the conversation part of rapport building become too hard for you. If all else fails, bring up something in the local news. Just make sure it's a noncontroversial subject. Try your best not to bring up the weather — if you start off talking about how hot or cold it is today, your prospect will know you're struggling for something to talk about or that you're nervous.

Another good tactic is to give your potential client a sincere compliment. *Sincere* is the key word here. Sincerity takes you everywhere; blatant, insincere flattery gets you nowhere. A stale line like "Gee, Mr. Gargoyle, I'll bet everybody tells you that you look just like Brad Pitt" does not qualify as sincere.

To keep the conversation moving forward, try an approach called *piggybacking*. In this technique, you simply ask a question, and when your prospect gives you an answer, acknowledge it with a nod or an *I see,* and then ask another question based on the prospect's response. For example, if you meet someone at her office, the piggybacking may go like this:

> YOU: Good afternoon, Ms. Johnson. I appreciate your time. Nice looking family you have there.
>
> PROSPECT: Thank you.
>
> YOU: What grades are your children in?
>
> PROSPECT: The oldest is a freshman in college. The middle one is a junior in high school. And the youngest is a freshman in high school.
>
> YOU: You must be very proud of them. What's your oldest studying in college?
>
> PROSPECT: Business. She wants to work for me when she graduates. I told her I would only hire her if she had straight As. A degree is a degree, but grades will tell me how much someone really learned.

Here's another example:

> YOU: Good afternoon, Ms. Thompson. I appreciate your time. I was wondering how long the company has been in this location? I know I've seen your sign on the building for many years.
>
> PROSPECT: We've been here 25 years.
>
> YOU: That's great. And how long have you been with the company?
>
> PROSPECT: I started ten years ago in the area of inventory control. For the past five years, I've handled all the purchasing.

When you piggyback, don't make a hog out of yourself by asking too many questions unless you think that the other person is agreeable to answering more. The purpose is just to get the conversation going and make her feel comfortable with you.

Acknowledge your prospect's pride

If you happen to be working in a business where you give a lot of in-home presentations, and the people you're presenting to have a nice home, say this:

> I want to tell you that I spend a lot of time in other people's homes, and you should be proud of what you've done here. Your home is lovely.

Look for signs of hobbies or crafts that you can comment on. If a woman is an artist and has her paintings on display, you can say, "You did that? What a great talent to have." That way you're not lying if you think the painting is really poor. Painting *is* a great talent — whether or not your prospect has any is in the eye of the beholder. If your prospect has any hobby she's obviously proud of, give her a sincere compliment about it. People always enjoy hearing compliments.

Avoid controversy

Be cautious that the prospect doesn't tempt you into a conversation about a controversial subject. Some people do that just to test you. Specifically, avoid discussing politics and religion at all costs.

Here's how to get around any topic that may lead you down the wrong path:

> I'm so busy serving clients, I haven't had time to stay current on that topic. What do you think?

By tossing the ball back at the prospect, you've dodged what may have been a fatal bullet, plus you got in a plug for your professional abilities. If the prospect comes back at you with a very strong opinion, you'll know to avoid that subject in future meetings. Or you may feel the need to brush up on it if she's deeply involved, so you'll have a better understanding of this person before you build a long-term working relationship with her.

In any business contact, be certain to never, *ever* use any profanity or slang. It doesn't matter if such language is widely used on today's most popular television programs; it has no place in the business world. You never know the values of the person you're talking with when you first meet her and you don't want to risk offending her. The same goes for off-color, political, ethnic, or sexist jokes. Be sensitive to the values, beliefs, and morals of the person sitting or standing across from you.

Keep pace with your prospect

Taking time to become aware of your normal speed of talking is extremely valuable. And notice the rate of speaking of everyone else you encounter. When you become tuned in to it, it happens naturally.

When you're aware of your speaking rate, you need to know what to do about it. If the person you're trying to persuade talks faster than you do, you need to increase your rate of talking in order to keep her attention. If she speaks much more slowly than you do, slow down or pause more often in your side of the conversation.

Any distortion in your rate of speaking can be deadly. You may lose her if you talk at the rate of a professional auctioneer, or her mind may wander if you're too slow. Try to match your rate of speaking to your prospect's rate of speaking.

Use an agenda

After you establish rapport and it's time to get down to business, it's helpful for both you and the buyer if you incorporate an agenda into your preparations. People tend to get nervous when there's something unknown awaiting them — it's a natural fear. An agenda helps diminish that fear. With it, you tell your prospective clients what you're going to tell them. It's as simple as that.

> Joyce, if you don't mind, let me explain how we'll proceed today. First, I'll tell you about our company. Then, in order to direct our attention specifically to your needs, I'll ask you some questions. Next, I'll show you how our product addresses your specific needs and cover the money aspects so you can feel comfortable about making a decision.

Fear eliminated! Transition to getting down to business — accomplished!

Acknowledge the "we are not buying" pact

When selling to a committee, business partners, or a married couple, chances are good that they made a pact prior to your contact not to buy in haste or at least not to buy today. This is standard practice for their side of the selling table. Rather than pretending this pact doesn't exist, it's incredibly wise for you to get it out in the open and get everyone to admit to it. Then, you can address it during your presentation.

> Before we begin, I'd like to be certain that we're all operating under the same understanding. My guess is that before this meeting took place you agreed not to make a buying decision today. And, that's perfectly understandable. Most of my happiest clients wanted to allow themselves time to think over my proposal. I've done the same thing myself. All I ask is that if you see something here today that is a good fit for your needs that may bring you great benefit and even save you some money that you won't let that pact stand in your way. That's fair, isn't it?

What you have done is to give each of them permission to break the pact if your offering truly is the best solution for their needs. I show you how to use this little strategy to even greater benefit when closing a sale in Chapter 12.

Chapter 9

Qualifying Your Way to Success

· ·

In This Chapter

▶ Thinking like a top detective

▶ Using five quick questions to discover whether to move into a presentation

▶ Asking the right questions to guide buyers toward your product

· ·

*A*t the qualification stage in the selling cycle, you find your potential client, make an initial contact, and receive a commitment to connect in person, online, or via the telephone. The buyer has shown a certain level of interest in your product or service. Now you need to determine not only whether your prospect has a real need for what you're offering but also whether he has the authority and resources to make the decision to buy. All of these factors must be present for you to consider this person a *qualified buyer*. If he isn't, you need to politely withdraw and move on to another potential client.

If you pursue presenting and trying to close an unqualified buyer, all you're doing is wasting his time, getting in a little practice with your presentation, and allowing your confidence to take a hit. That type of situation is part of what has given sales a bad name in the past. Don't go there!

This step in the selling cycle is particularly important for situations in which you don't have a close enough relationship with your prospect to know whether he needs your product or service. And, the person needs to make a financial commitment or a personal commitment in order to go ahead.

So what circumstances would keep someone from being able to make a commitment? If it's a financial commitment, he'd have to have the money or some credit to draw upon. If it's a personal commitment, he may need to check with someone else, like a spouse, before going ahead. It could be a situation, as with insurance, in which the person must qualify in terms of his health. You need to know your prospect's circumstances *before* you go into a full-fledged presentation.

One of the biggest mistakes people make when they try to convince or persuade others is going into a full-blown presentation before they know whether the listener is a qualified decision maker or needs what they have to sell. There's nothing worse for either of the people involved than to be caught up in something that is a total waste of their valuable time. So, for goodness sake, when you see the word *receptionist* on a desk, don't give the person behind the sign your whole presentation. Focus instead on selling him on getting through to the decision maker.

Statistics from my surveys of more than 250,000 sales professionals show that the biggest gap between six-figure income earners and those averaging around $25,000 per year is their skill in qualifying. That statistic alone would make me want to master this area of selling. And all it takes is learning the right questions to ask. I explain what you need to know about qualifying in this chapter.

Taking a Few Sales Pointers from CSI

So how do you get started in qualifying your prospects? You need to ask the right questions. In some cases, you wait and watch for the perfect opportunity to ask. Other times, you have to create the opportunity to ask. Think of yourself as a detective, a gatherer of information to solve the mystery of your prospect's buying needs. If all you had to do was come up with a couple of questions that would always be answered completely and honestly, your life would be simple. But it isn't always that easy. Being able to discover your prospect's needs and concerns, as well as successfully incorporate such information into the opening of your presentation, takes a lot of time and practice before you ever walk through the door of each appointment.

This information-gathering aspect of selling isn't unlike what you may have seen on the popular television program about crime scene investigators — *CSI: Crime Scene Investigation.* These professionals are trained to ask questions in several different ways. If potential suspects come up with a different answer to a rephrased question, the investigators know that the suspect isn't telling the truth or knows more than he's letting on. Such information is valuable for the crime solvers in continuing to seek out answers.

In the following sections, I highlight some of the key strategies used on CSI to solve every case. And they're strategies you can put to work for you when you're trying to get information from your prospects.

Keep out of the limelight

The CSI detectives never presume to know the answers to the crimes they're investigating. They approach each scene with all their senses on high alert. They have the tools they need to gather evidence. They let the crime scene speak to them so they can deduce the right answer — the solution to the crime. When talking with suspects, the detectives ask questions that their observations have already provided the answers to. They're trying to match what science tells them with what the humans have to say.

Likewise, your job isn't to enter your prospects' lives and push anything on them. You're a wise observer seeking clues to what a prospect needs before asking questions. Your prospect believes you know more about the subject than he does or he wouldn't invest his time with you. The potential client needs to share certain information about himself for you to know how to help him. Your goal in qualifying, then, is to involve the prospect in an educational experience where he participates in finding the solution through the use of questions. Each of your questions builds on his answers to the previous ones. You're seeking agreement that your observations are correct.

It's important that you get your points across in an educational style rather than a know-it-all style. A know-it-all may say something like, "Our product is the best in the industry." An educator uses facts to get the same point across like this, "*Car & Driver* magazine ranked this model number one for reliability three years in a row." When you enter the classroom of a great teacher, is the teacher the star? No, he's not. The education — the learning — is the star. The teacher is just the facilitator.

Use nonthreatening language and a sympathetic tone

When CSIs are talking one on one with people involved in the crime, they often include the phrase, "I understand how you feel . . ." and let the suspect in on something personal in their lives that shows they truly do understand. The goal of this line of questioning is to get the suspect to relate to the officer, let down his guard, and be up front about his feelings or information he has about the crime.

Meeting potential clients on their home turf makes them more comfortable. Many business negotiators will tell you that you need to meet on your turf to hold the power — the home court advantage, so to speak. In sales, you're not in a win-lose situation. The goal is to reach a win-win agreement. Making people feel comfortable with you is the first step you take in coming together to determine what the best solution is.

Always take notes

Taking notes is vital, but CSIs don't rush to get every word of vital information. Instead, they jot things down casually. Their notepads aren't large and threatening. They're small enough to fit in a pocket and rather nondescript. The samples they consider for analysis are also miniscule. And they refer back to the information gathered again and again during their investigations. The information they turn up helps direct future efforts with each suspect (which, in selling, is called the *prospect* or, more optimistically, the *future client*).

Take a look at the device you use to take notes. Is it imposing? Do you use a standard form that has 100 blanks that your prospect will feel you must fill in with information about him? If so, it's likely to be somewhat threatening.

When you state a fact back to the prospect, glance or point to where you have it in your notes. This shows that you have the correct information and that you're on top of the details.

Make the people you're questioning feel important

CSIs always remind their suspects how accommodating they are to let them impose on their busy schedules. They thank the suspects profusely for their time and the vital information they provide. No matter how small the tidbit of information, they make those involved feel as if it's the single most important key to solving the case.

Don't just jot down the notes. Make comments on the facts and figures the people provide you with. Compliment them on being on top of things enough to know these details without looking them up. *Note:* If they did look up some of the figures, compliment them on their dedication to accuracy by not calling out numbers from memory.

Ask standard and innocent questions

CSIs rarely come out and ask a suspect "Did you do it?" Instead, they ask what sounds like typical police-type questions about times, people, and places to gather background information and disarm the suspect, such as "Where were you when this happened?" or "What were you doing when the crime occurred?"

In sales, sooner or later, you need to talk about money. Money is an uncomfortable subject for many people. So, you don't just ask, "How much have you got?" Instead, you're more discreet: "Mike, if we were fortunate to find just the right widget for you today, how much did you plan to invest to own one?"

Pay attention to both verbal and nonverbal responses

CSIs notice *how* people tell them what they have to say, not just noting the words they use but paying attention to their body language as well. They know and evaluate not only people's postures, but also what they're wearing, the surroundings they spend their time in, and even the cars they drive.

If someone lives in a $800,000 home and drives the latest Mercedes, it's likely he'll be interested in owning the top-of-the-line model of your product as well. In other cases, if someone is looking at the top-of-the-line model and then steps away when you approach him, it's possible he's hesitant about whether he can afford it.

Build on the answers you get

Rarely do suspects realize that they *are* suspects until they've let their guard down a bit and said something that doesn't jibe with a previous answer. They often find themselves uncomfortable in having to explain the difference in the two answers. They try to give credence to their errors and still keep their innocent attitudes.

Someone may tell you he invested $40,000 in his last series of widgets. You would then assume he'd be comfortable investing in that price range again. If, when you get to your presentation, your bottom line is that same amount and he says he can't afford it, something was missing in the information you were provided. Don't call the client out on the detail — as important as it is — just ask more questions. "Mike, I thought you told me you invested this much the last time. Was I wrong in my understanding that it was an acceptable amount?" This gives Mike an opportunity to explain further without your coming out and saying, "Hey, you gave me bad information!" It could be that Mike did pay that much and was reprimanded by higher ups in the company for going over budget.

If a potential client initially says he has to have a car that seats six, then due to the higher investment, backs off to wanting a model that seats only five, he's potentially embarrassing himself with that discrepancy and may be uncomfortable if you bring it up. A six-seater may be his dream, but he didn't realize that it was out of his range and he only *really* needs to seat five. Just go with the flow of his needs and find him the right vehicle even if it's not the one you originally thought would meet his needs.

Relieve any tension your questions create

Another famous CSI team tactic is to have one of its detectives return to ask just one more question . . . just as the suspect is breathing a sigh of relief and letting his guard down. This usually catches the suspect off guard, and he trips himself up by revealing important information critical to solving the case. I love that part!

Some people just don't handle decision making well. They worry they're going to be lied to or ripped off. So they protect themselves by not giving you all the information you need to help them with their decision. Their thinking is that you can't force them into buying something that way. In reality they're keeping themselves from becoming fully educated about your product. That strategy only hurts them. But, fear is a natural part of selling. So you need to be ready to relieve any tension you may feel arise in your clients. You're not the bad guy they think you are (or that mom and dad warned them about). You may have to re-iterate what your job is all about — helping people make decisions that are good for *them*.

If your potential client has not gone ahead with the purchase, I strongly recommend that you pack up your things and get ready to leave. This usually causes the prospect to relax simply because he starts thinking about whatever it is he's going to do after you leave. Then, use the lost-sale close in Chapter 22. This close is an excellent demonstration of how a CSI would handle the sale if he truly believed it to be a wise decision for the suspect.

Let them know you'll be in touch

Any good salesperson who doesn't make a sale on the first contact will do whatever he can to leave the door open for further discussion with a potential client:

> Mr. Scales, I know you haven't agreed to do business with my company, but may I have your permission to stay in touch with you regarding our

latest developments in case something in the future would be of benefit to you or your company?

Of course with CSI, letting the suspect know that a CSI agent will be in touch is plenty to think about in its own right.

Satisfying NEADS: The Nuts and Bolts of Qualifying Prospects

Good qualifying is a basic of selling that you can't overlook or slough off. Don't set yourself up for failure. Work on your style and questions, and then watch your income and your base of happy clients begin to grow.

The average salesperson today either lets the consumer totally make the decision as to what he wants, or tries to steer the person to what that salesperson likes best. Both of these approaches are wrong. You recognize steering by the use of these phrases, especially prior to qualifying:

- ✔ I know just what you're looking for.
- ✔ This is my favorite.
- ✔ I have the best thing for you.
- ✔ We have the best products.
- ✔ This one looks so good in red.

To help you stay focused on what matters most when it comes to qualifying your prospective clients, I've come up with an easy-to-remember acronym: NEADS. I cover the five parts of the NEADS equation in the following sections, but the acronym itself is what's most important. Granted, my spelling is a little creative, but that spelling helps remind you of how you can determine the needs of your customers. Each letter stands for a question you should ask your prospective clients in an effort to discover their needs.

The success ratio for your entire company would rise if you could get all the salespeople to say to themselves when they meet a customer, "I am concerned about my customer's NEADS. I will discover my customer's true needs and lead my customers to the right product or service for them." Satisfying NEADS helps you accomplish more in your business.

WII-FM: What's in it for me?

An old sales training lesson goes like this: What's everyone's favorite radio station? The answer is always WII-FM. The call letters in this case stand for "What's In It For Me?"

People have a WII-FM mentality, whether they admit it to themselves or not. Human beings are selfish creatures whose natural propensity is to make themselves as comfortable as possible. Be painfully honest: When was the last time you did something for someone else with absolutely *no* expectations of getting anything in return? Now before you tell me what a self-sacrificing person you really are, think about that answer for a second. I'm asking you to remember a time when you did something for someone else without expecting *anything* in return for what you did — no thank-you, no undying loyalties, no promises that the object of your benefactions would someday return the favor, nothing . . . zip, zero, zilch, nada, nienti, goose egg.

If you're like most people (myself included), you'll have difficulty thinking of such a time.

Most people are motivated to do for others only if they themselves expect to receive compensation that they value in return. The compensation may not always be monetary, but people *always* want something, anything, even a crust of bread in exchange for their efforts. Even if the sought rewards are intangible and emotional — compliments, hugs, kisses, pats on the head, a warm smile — a reward is a reward is a reward.

And that's the same philosophy your client holds every time you contact him. He needs to quickly realize the benefit to him for taking your call or setting up a meeting with you. Help him see you as someone who can eliminate a discomfort from his life. To him, you must be someone who can give more than he receives, which is what he expects when he thinks of customer *service.* You contact your customer for one reason: to serve his needs, whether you do it by providing information, a service, or a product. You always answer his question of "What's in it for me?"

N is for "now"

The *N* in NEADS stands for "now" — as in, "What does the customer have now?" Why should you ask this? Because average consumers don't make drastic changes in their buying habits. If you know what your prospect has now, you have a good idea of the type of person he is — and you have a good idea of what he wants to have in the future.

If past experiences dictate future decisions — as they undoubtedly do — then you need to explore your customer's past experiences. You need to know what he has now so that, in your mind's eye, you can see the type of buying decisions he will make in the future.

Show me your current vehicle, home, style of dress, or style of jewelry, and I can probably tell you what your next version of each of those products will look like. I'm not prejudging here. I'm simply observing that most people are creatures of habit. People usually don't make drastic changes in their lives unless they've recently won the lottery or received a large inheritance or windfall.

E is for "enjoy"

The second letter in NEADS is *E*. As I'm using it here, *E* stands for *enjoy*. You need to know what your customer enjoys most about what he has now. What was his major motivation for getting involved with his existing product or service?

To discover what your customer enjoys, you need to structure your questions so you can discover the customer's past. There's a good chance that what he enjoyed about the product or service in the past, or what he enjoys about what he already has, is exactly what he'll want again. That's usually true — unless you can demonstrate a benefit in *your* product or service that is even better than the one he enjoyed when he purchased his present product or service.

A is for "alter"

The *A* in NEADS stands for *alter,* as in, "What would the customer like to alter (or improve) about what he has now?"

Because it's constant, change is a potent force in business. In some ways, everyone is looking for change — more benefit, more satisfaction, more comfort. Your customer's normal urge to improve his present condition is why you want to develop questions to find out what he would like to change. What would he like to be different? When you know your customer's answer to that question, you can structure your presentation to show him how your company can provide the changes he wants in his present product or service.

D is for "decision"

The *D* in NEADS stands for *decision.* Specifically, you need to know who will be making the final decision on the sale.

Many times salespeople meet a buyer looking for a car, a home entertainment system, maybe some furniture, and they meet only that one person. Is it wise for the salesperson to assume that the person he's met will be the decision maker? No. Never assume anything about your potential clients. The customer may be scouting or researching, planning to bring a spouse or parent in when it's time to make the final decision.

So you need to ask qualifying questions to discover whether the person you're talking with is the decision maker. Here are some examples:

Will you be the only person driving the car?

Who, other than yourself, will be involved in making the final decision?

Is there anyone else you usually consult with when making decisions of this type?

What's your usual process for making a purchasing decision?

You've probably heard the standard response to a decision-qualifying question: "I'll have to talk it over with my husband/wife/parents/best friend from college/manager." Many times the salesperson who hasn't properly qualified the prospect will go too far in the presentation before finding out that the real decision maker isn't present. You do nothing more than practice your presentation when you present to non-decision makers.

You need to be equally enthusiastic with everyone you meet. Even though the person isn't the decision maker, he can be an influencer or a champion of your cause.

If the product you're offering is something to be used by a family or a couple, it's wise to at least attempt to present to both parties. One or the other may tell you they're the final decision maker, but in most relationships and for many types of purchases, such decisions require at least input from both parties. If it's impossible to get both people together for a presentation, at least suggest you get the other party on the phone so you can answer any questions he or she has directly.

S is for "solutions"

As a salesperson, you're in the business of creating solutions. And, coincidentally, that's exactly what the *S* in NEADS stands for. You find out what your potential clients need, and then you come up with a solution. With properly qualified prospects, the solution is that they take ownership of the benefits of your products or services.

At my seminars, one casual but effective introduction to the qualifying process that I ask people to adapt to their product or service is this:

As a representative of [name of your company], it's my job to analyze your needs and do my best to come up with a solution to satisfy those needs so you can enjoy the benefits you're looking for.

Taking notes to avoid repeating yourself

To save yourself from needlessly repeating questions, make written notes of your prospective client's responses during the qualification sequence. Referring to your notes to remind yourself what questions you already asked and what the client said his needs were is perfectly okay. Inadvertently asking the same question twice (or more) doesn't inspire confidence in the customer about you or your product. Not only do written notes help you during the presentation, but they also help you to remember what you've already covered when you follow up with the prospect after he's become a regular, happy client. In fact, that's part of how you keep him happy.

Don't forget to ask permission to take notes before you start taking them. Some people get nervous when you start writing down what they tell you. For all you know, they may visualize themselves being grilled in a court of law on what they say to you. If you think you're with someone like that, give him a pad or piece of paper and a pen (preferably with your company name on it), so he can take notes, too. Being prepared for this situation helps you avoid, or at least to handle, uncomfortable situations.

Getting permission to take notes is easy. All you need to say is this: "Over the years, I've found it very beneficial to make notes during meetings with potential clients. Doing so enables me to do a better job. I wouldn't want to forget anything that might prove to save you money or time as we move forward. So, I hope you won't be offended if, while we chat, I make a few notes." Putting it that way gives you an opportunity to admit that you're human and that you're also smart enough to have learned how to do your job well. These little sentences will help put your clients at ease and build their confidence in you.

You serve customers by finding out what they need and then creating the right solutions. When you do this, you create win-win relationships in which people want to do business with your company and get the products or services they need. They give you business and, in turn, you both grow and prosper.

Questioning Your Way to Qualifying Success

Part of qualifying your potential clients includes knowing the right questions to ask. Your goal in qualifying is to get the information you need to have before narrowing down the best solution for your client. The best solution is what you present in the next step of the selling cycle. I cover the NEADS questions as an easy qualifying strategy to remember and use in the preceding sections. However, true professionals in selling invest their time wisely in developing questions that go even deeper into finding out exactly what the client expects your product to do for him.

You can use questions to acknowledge or confirm a statement your prospect made that is important to getting his final commitment — the decision you want your listener to make. For example, if your potential client tells you that gasoline mileage is very important to him in buying a new car, before you present the vehicle you think is best for him, include a question like this:

> Didn't you say that fuel economy was your primary concern?

Such a question starts the *yes* momentum you need to excite the buyer about the product you're planning to present. The *yes* momentum is what every persuader strives for. After you get your prospect agreeing to things, if you simply keep asking the right questions — kind of like following a flow chart — he'll follow where you guide him. Plus, he'll have enough information at the end of your presentation to make a wise decision, which you hope is that he can't live without your product or service.

Questions also create emotional involvement. If you're marketing home security devices, you can ask:

> Wouldn't you feel more confident about entering your home in the evening knowing you would be warned beforehand if there were any danger?

What does that question do? It raises a prickle of alarm on the back of your prospect's neck about the unknown possibilities of walking into an unprotected home. You don't want to frighten anyone into purchasing your product, but you do want to get him picturing himself owning its benefits. That's emotional involvement — and it's a requirement in any selling situation. ***Remember:*** Think of at least two ways to build emotion, through the use of questions, into every presentation you make.

In the following sections, I provide the details you need on how to use questions to confirm a prospect's statements and make an emotional connection.

Before you ask any question, remember this: To sell or persuade, you need to make the other person feel important. Your prospect needs to feel smart, too. So never, never, ever ask a question that your listener can't answer. For example, if you ask someone what the available memory is on his computer and he doesn't know, you've just made him feel uncomfortable. Yuck! Avoid that result at all costs. If he hasn't brought up the subject of available memory, you should ask whether he has the information available on his current computer. Chances are good that he does. If you tell him specifically the information you need, he can get it. But if you assume that he knows it, and he doesn't know it, you've just embarrassed him. And he may find someone else to buy from who is a little more sensitive and able to make him feel important. And where does that leave you? Without the sale.

Tying down the details

I teach many questioning techniques to my students at my live seminars, on my videos, and on my audio programs. One of the most popular techniques is called the *tie-down*. A tie-down does not involve tying clients into their chairs until they say yes. Instead, tie-downs involve making a statement, and then asking for agreement by adding a question to the end of it. Here are some effective tie-downs:

✔ **Isn't it?** For example, "It's a great day for golf, *isn't it?*" When your caller agrees, you set a tee time.

✔ **Doesn't it?** For example, "Jet-skiing at the lake this weekend sounds like fun, *doesn't it?*" When your client agrees, pull out the rental agreement — pronto.

✔ **Hasn't he?** For example, "The previous homeowner has done a great job with the landscaping, *hasn't he?*" When the prospective new homeowner agrees that he likes the landscape, he's just moved one step closer to liking the whole package — house included.

✔ **Haven't they?** For example, "The manufacturers have included every detail about the questions you asked in this proposal, *haven't they?*" Having all the details covered and having the buyer agree helps reduce the possibility of stalling when it's time to close.

✔ **Don't you?** For example, "Cleaning up the lot where your employees park is important, *don't you agree?*" When the person agrees, sign him up for your cleanup service and have him choose a date he wants it done.

✔ **Didn't you?** For example, "You had a great time the last time you went hiking, *didn't you?*" Then pull out the latest style of boot while your client is in a positive frame of mind about the last trip.

✔ **Shouldn't you?** For example, "With so many choices that you enjoy on the menu, you should come here for dinner more often, *shouldn't you?*" If it was an enjoyable meal, suggest a date for a return visit and book the reservation.

✔ **Couldn't you?** For example, "You could let your spouse have a whole day just to relax and rejuvenate, *couldn't you?*" Get a commitment to a spa package!

The goal of using tie-downs is to get your prospect thinking in the affirmative about the subject you've just tied down. While he's agreeing with you, you can confidently bring up whatever it is you're trying to get a commitment on.

Professional salespeople often use tie-down statements such as this:

A reputation for prompt, professional service is important, isn't it?

Who can say no to that? The salesperson who asks such a question has begun a cycle of agreement with the prospect who, hopefully, will continue to agree all the way through the selling sequence.

Giving an alternate

You've certainly seen or heard the *alternate of choice* questioning technique used before, but you probably didn't recognize it as a sales strategy. This strategy involves giving your prospect two *acceptable* suggestions to choose from, and it's most often used for calendar events such as appointments, delivery dates, and so on. Here are some simple examples:

- ✔ **"I can arrange my schedule so we can visit on Thursday at 3:00 p.m. or would Friday at 11:00 a.m. be better?"** Either answer confirms that you have an appointment.

- ✔ **"This product comes in 55-gallon containers or 35-gallon containers. Which would you prefer?"** No matter which container your prospect chooses, he's still chosen to take one of them.

- ✔ **"We'll have our delivery truck at your home on Monday at 9:00 a.m. sharp. Or would 2:00 p.m. be more convenient?"** Whichever option your prospect chooses, you've nailed down the delivery.

You can also use the alternate of choice technique when you want to focus or limit the conversation to certain points. For example, if you're selling playground equipment to a school or homeowners' association, you don't want to open up a debate about placement of the equipment when you're preparing a proposal. You just need to know the specifications required for the materials and equipment desired. In that case, you can ask, "Which do you think would be a better surface under the equipment, wood chips or sand?" It helps you get right to the point of the matter and gives only the two solutions you need addressed.

Alternate of choice questions are particularly effective in surveys. The market researchers are seeking particular information, not general answers, so they build the questions in such a way that the prospect is limited in his responses.

Getting prospects involved

Another questioning technique is the involvement question in which you use questions to help your listeners envision themselves *after* they've made a decision to agree with you. If you're marketing office equipment, you can involve your prospect with a question like this:

> Who will be the key contact for us to train on the use of the equipment?

Now you've got him thinking about implementing training *after* he owns the product, not about whether or not he'll own it.

Similarly, if you want to involve someone in business with you, use a question like this:

> What will you and Janet do with the extra income that our business plan says we'll generate in the next year?

Is your listener thinking about whether to get into business with you? Nope. He's just envisioning spending the money he'll earn *after* he goes into business with you. If what he plans to spend the money on is something he wants badly enough, there's a good chance that he'll find himself *having* to go into business with you to satisfy a need he's been feeling without knowing how to fulfill it. Aren't you the good little helper for bringing him just the right business opportunity?

Chapter 10

Delivering Winning Presentations

. . . .

In This Chapter

▶ Ensuring a good first impression

▶ Following the basic rules of presentations

▶ Making sure the product is in the spotlight

▶ Using visual aids and demonstrations to your advantage

▶ Holding your clients' interest during presentations of intangible goods

▶ Avoiding Murphy's Law in the world of presenting

. . . .

The presentation stage of the selling process is the show — your chance to get your prospective client's senses involved. Major companies prepare for the presentation stage by investing hundreds of thousands of dollars and a great deal of time in creating graphics, models, and samples. Some even invest millions in building entire video presentations with hopes of picking up new clients online that their salespeople may not be reaching.

A presentation can be as simple as giving out a brochure with a quick explanation or as complex as a display at a trade show — complete with bells, whistles, food, clowns, and fireworks. How you present your show depends on what product or service you represent, your company's directives, and the potential investment amount a buyer might make.

In this chapter, I steer you through the potentially frightening territory of the sales presentation (frightening at least until you're trained) — everything from finding the power players in the room to giving a presentation over the Internet. I also give you some great tips for avoiding common presentation pitfalls. So before you give a presentation, read on.

You must have your presentation well rehearsed. Memorize anything that you may be required to say. Practice until you can deliver your presentation smoothly without sounding like you're delivering rote information. How long this takes depends on your product and your own dedication to getting

the job done. Because your presentation engages the clients, you have to be prepared to handle potential breaks in your presentation due to client questions and get smoothly back on track.

Getting More Than a Foot in the Door

Even after you earn the right to give a prospective client a presentation of your idea, concept, product, or service, you're nowhere near done. The decision maker selected you — probably from several other contestants — and is giving you the opportunity to prove that your offering is as dazzling as you and your company say it is. But having an appointment to give a presentation doesn't automatically grant you favored status or guarantee you a warm welcome. It doesn't mean that you will become the prospect's favorite supplier. What many prospects are saying when they let you in the door is, "Okay, wonder boy, impress me!" or "Okay, wonder girl, back up your claims." No pressure here, is there?

In any selling situation, understanding the perspective of your contact person is vital. I cover this point at length in Chapter 4.

Every day, salespeople bombard buyers with overtures for their business. Your contact person may be a real decision maker or someone designated to narrow the field to two or three potential suppliers for the real decision maker to talk with. Many times when a large purchase is required, a purchasing agent brings in several competing companies to give presentations to a committee. If you've done your homework well, you'll know exactly who will be present and why each person is there.

Think of this as the opening to all of the *Mission: Impossible* films. The first aspect of the mission is to identify the players and what's in it for each of them. This way, should you decide to accept your mission, you'll know who needs more persuading and how to go about doing just that. In the following sections, I provide pointers on how to start your presentation on the right foot.

Find the power players

When you begin an in-person presentation, thank and acknowledge the person who invited you, make eye contact with each person in the room, and see if you can tell which member of your audience is the power player. There's one in every group (including families), and she may or may not be the person you've already been talking with. Just watching how the other members of the group treat each other should clue you in. Workplace behavior isn't much different from what you see in a documentary about the social habits of wolves. Just as in wolf packs, the subordinates in most workplaces usually defer to the power player when important issues arise.

Another hint for identifying the top dogs in a workplace: They often take the best seat in the house during presentations. The best seat is usually at the head of the table or at the 12 o'clock position at a round table, with you at the 6 o'clock position. Or the power player may sit closest to the door in anticipation of an interruption for a vital call or message. You won't be able to make a perfect call every time, but as you hone your skills at the people game, you'll start picking out the power players in minutes.

Some power players don't play the game the way you'd expect and may sit unobtrusively in the back of the room. By watching everyone else's body language, though, you should still be able to recognize that person.

Be quick or be sorry

In today's world of the ten-second television commercial, few people bother anymore to develop their ability to concentrate. In fact, the average person has a short, downright gnat-like attention span, which means that you must compress the heart of your presentation down to a matter of only a few minutes. After those few minutes, spend the rest of your time involving your buyers directly in the presentation through questions, visual aids, or a hands-on demonstration. (I discuss these topics in more detail later in this chapter.)

To help your potential clients focus on your presentation and to help yourself stay on track, state your objectives prior to beginning your presentation. Limit your objectives to three. For example, you might say the following:

> Today I would like to cover three things. First, I would like to better understand your business. Second, I would like to demonstrate a product I think you will find beneficial to your company. And finally, if you see the value in what I am presenting to you today, I would like to discuss the action steps required to help you benefit from it as soon as possible.

I've long taught my students that they should practice, drill, and rehearse their presentations to get through the nitty-gritty in just under 17 minutes. Go past 17 minutes, and your prospect's mind wanders and her eyelids droop. Besides helping to keep your prospect awake, brevity and conciseness demonstrate concern for her valuable time. She may not realize that she appreciates your concern for her time, but on some level she will appreciate it — and the concern will make a difference.

This 17-minute time constraint may challenge you if your product is, say, a complicated mechanical system. If that's the case, you may want to plan for a short break or a summary or question-and-answer period after the first 17 minutes are up. Letting your potential client stretch her legs or be actively engaged increases the level of concentration she gives you. When the blood stops circulating in your extremities, paying attention is difficult. The mind can only absorb as long as the body can endure.

The magic 17 minutes do not begin the moment you enter the room or while you're building rapport. The 17-minute period begins when you get down to the business at hand and cover the finer points of your product's features and how those features can benefit your client. It also does not include the time you invest in answering questions, overcoming concerns, or closing. It's just the amount of time to target for the actual product benefit presentation. You need more time with complex products, but even then you should refine your presentation to only the most critical elements in order to develop the interest of your clients.

Break well and prosper

If you choose to schedule a break, or even if an unplanned break occurs, here's a vital piece of advice you must take to heart: Always do a brief recap before starting back into your presentation. A *brief recap* is just a restatement of the major points you've covered so far, a quick way to bring everyone back to where you were before the break. Any break in the action allows your listener's mind to wander. She starts looking at her watch, she thinks about lunch or her next appointment, or she wonders what the rest of the office is doing. She may even leave the room to make a call. If she does leave, her mind focuses on the person on the other end of the call, not on your presentation. And you'd better believe that the emotional level your prospect was at when the break began will not be the same when she comes back. Before you can move on with your presentation, you must take a moment or two to bring her back to where she was.

Studies prove that, after any interruption, it takes ten minutes to get back to the same level of concentration and emotional involvement you were at before the interruption. Just thinking about all the interruptions you have in a normal day makes you wonder how you ever get anything done, doesn't it?

Knowing the ABCs of Presenting

The general guidelines for giving effective presentations are simple. They're the same ones you learned in English class for writing a good story: Tell your audience what you're going to tell them, tell them, and finish by telling them what you've told them.

This method serves the same purpose in oral presentations as it does in written ones. It helps the person on the receiving end understand and remember the story you told. And when you're selling, you want your presentation to be a memorable occasion for the decision maker. Master the four basics of presentations — speaking on your customer's level, pacing your speech, using the right words to create ownership, and interpreting body language — and you're on your way to earning favored status in the mind of every buyer who hears your presentation. (These tips work even if you have to give a presentation on the phone or online.)

Being multilingual (even if you're not)

Know enough about your potential client — going into the presentation — that you can speak with her on her level. What does it mean to speak on someone else's level? Consider this example:

> Suppose you're in your 30s, and you're trying help an older couple who want to replace a 20-year-old appliance. What do you say to them? Well, with these buyers you'd probably talk about dependability and the new features that your product displays. You'd also point out the benefits that would accrue to the couple if they owned those features. The benefits would be lower utility bills with increased efficiency of new appliances, longer food storage time (which means less waste and greater convenience of getting at things), whether it has an outside drink door, and so on.

> Now cut to a different scene: You're trying to sell the same refrigerator to a newly married couple for their first home. Do you talk to them the same way you did to the older couple who were replacing an old appliance? No, with the younger couple you accent the features and benefits that apply to their situation and satisfy their present needs. The features are the same, but the benefits are seen in a different light when viewed from their perspective. They may want something less expensive because that's all they can afford. But if you can show them the overall savings of getting a bigger or better fridge now, as opposed to the replacement costs down the road, you'll be farther ahead because they'll be more comfortable making the investment when the decision is rationalized for them.

I call this versatility of message being multilingual. You speak senior citizen. You speak gen X *and* gens Y and Z. You speak single parent. You speak high end. You speak economy. Being able to converse with someone at her level — whatever that level is — pays big.

If you want to test this theory, try talking at your normal business level to a 5-year-old and see how long you keep her attention. Then talk with her on her level and watch the animation in her face as she realizes that you've just entered her world.

To become multilingual when you sell a product or service to different businesses, pick up industry magazines, visit websites, and use other respected sources to familiarize yourself with their language — their world. For instance, suppose you're trying to sell insurance to an architect; why not visit the architect's website? If you can speak with the architect on her level, she will like you. *Like* builds to *trust* and *trust* helps to develop *commitment*. The same applies to whatever industry your potential client is in. If you can at least ask intelligent questions about her industry, she'll be more likely to open up to what you have to say about yours.

Also, within a committee or family, you may have decision makers with different interests. For example, if you're presenting to a committee in a business situation, you may have a finance person, a technical person, and an executive in the room. Each has a different language she uses in evaluating products or services from her perspective. Know who is in the room and be prepared to speak to each.

Recognizing the posted speed limit

When you give a presentation to a prospect, you need to be sensitive enough to recognize the proper demeanor to have with each client. This part of your presentation is kind of like what stage actors do: They play off of the attitude and enthusiasm of the audience. If you're too energetic for your audience and speak at too fast a rate, they'll be turned off. Then again, if you're too mild mannered for them and speak too slowly, you may lose them as well.

The ideal approach is to pay attention to the rate and pitch of your buyer's speech and then closely match it. When this happens, on some subconscious level, your prospect gets the message that you're like she is. Plus, she'll understand you better. Be careful if the other person has an accent different from yours. If you adopt her accent, she'll think you're mocking her or that you're insincere. Also, if her pacing is very slow, you can speak at a level slightly above hers.

An average person can comfortably comprehend speech at a rate of 160 words per minute. That's the rate at which most audiobooks are recorded. Borrow one from your local library and listen long enough to catch the pacing of one so you will know how to moderate your own speech. Some research indicates that adults can listen with full comprehension at 300 words per minute, but don't count on it. As with anything involving human beings, err on the side of moderation, and you'll be comfortably correct most of the time.

Forcing yourself to get down to another person's level may have an adverse effect on your entire presentation. It may literally throw you off course. With a little practice, though, you'll develop a good sense for what's right.

Using words that assume your client will buy from you

Speak as though your prospect already owns what it is you're selling. Don't say, "If you join our neighborhood safety awareness group . . ." Instead, say, "When we meet, you'll enjoy the value of participating in our neighborhood safety awareness group." Giving your prospect the ownership of your idea, product, or service helps to move her closer to making a decision. This is called *assumptive selling*.

Another example is to talk about what life is like *after* your prospect owns your product, as in "After the system is installed, you'll enter your home after work every day knowing that you saved energy without having to turn the thermostat up or down."

Assumptive selling is not the same as *suggestive selling* — when you order nothing more than a chocolate shake but your friendly McDonald's server oh-so-sweetly asks if she can get you an apple turnover today. With suggestive selling you're offered something you haven't yet asked for or about. Assumptive selling is operating as if you have made the decision to own a product or service you expressed an interest in.

Deciphering the human body's grammar, syntax, and vocabulary

You don't necessarily need to learn to speak Spanish, French, or Russian to conduct business (although in the global marketplace, it wouldn't hurt you to learn at least one other language). What I'm talking about here is body language. The study of body language has been around for a long time. In fact, most people are aware of body language, but they don't consciously read it and benefit from it.

Here are just a few examples of the kinds of messages body language communicates (and how to read them):

✔ **Leaning forward:** If you lean forward when you're talking to someone, you're showing that you're interested and paying attention. When you recognize that positive sign in other people, keep moving forward.

In fact, you may be able to pick up the pace of your presentation a bit if your entire audience is leaning forward.

✔ **Leaning back or glancing away:** When you lean back or glance away from someone who's talking, that means you're losing interest in what she's saying or that you're uncomfortable with what was just said. What do you do if you recognize this body language in your audience? Pause if you're in the middle of a long monologue, summarize the last couple of points, and ask your client a question. Or, if it's a group presentation and you see several of your clients displaying this body language, suggest a short break or a question-and-answer period.

✔ **Crossed arms:** If you cross your arms when you're listening to someone, this indicates that you doubt what the other person is saying or that you're not truly interested in hearing what she has to say. When you receive this sign from your audience, move to a point-proving demonstration, chart, graph, or diagram. Or, ask a question such as "On a scale of 1 to 5, with 5 being very important, how valuable is this point to you?" If it's not valuable, skip ahead in your presentation to the next topic.

Just as important as knowing how to read the language is knowing how to speak it. When you understand positive body language cues, practice them as a part of your presentation. They can be as critical as the words you say. If you want to successfully persuade your prospects, you need to be able to give positive, warm, honesty-projecting gestures, such as the following:

✔ **Sit beside the person you're trying to persuade instead of opposite her.** You're not on an opposing side. You're on your prospect's side.

✔ **Use a pen or pointer to draw attention, at the appropriate times, to your visual aids.** Some people hesitate when they use a pen or pointer, and that hesitation says that they're uncomfortable. (You always want to avoid any suggestion of discomfort during demonstrations.) This is something you should practice as part of your rehearsal for presentations.

If you wonder about the effectiveness of this technique, watch magicians. They would never be able to keep their magic if they didn't master the ability to draw your attention to (or away from) what they want.

✔ **Use open-hand gestures and eye contact.** Open-hand gestures (such as exposing your palms or pointing with your whole hand rather than an index finger) and lots of eye contact say that you have nothing to hide.

Don't use the palm out (or pushing) gesture unless it's when you're trying to eliminate a prospect's negative concern. Even then, push to the side, not toward the prospect.

These are just a few of the basics of body language, but the whole field of study on body language can help you so much more. When you begin paying attention, you'll find that many other body language cues will become obvious to you. I highly recommend that you research what's available at your local library or online if body language piques your interest, including *Body Language For Dummies* by Elizabeth Kuhnke (Wiley). When you find out a little bit about body language and start studying the body language of others, you'll quickly see how to benefit from it.

Getting comfortable with virtual presentations

When you can't possibly meet in person with your prospective client and you have to conduct business over the telephone or via webinar or screen sharing, you need to be aware of certain strategies to apply.

Phone presentations

Because you can't see your clients when you're on the phone, you may have trouble knowing whether they're being distracted or interrupted. Even though you can't read body language over the phone, you can definitely listen to voice inflections (just as your clients listen to yours). You can tell fairly easily whether someone is paying attention by counting the length of pauses between their comments, and the number of *uh-huhs* or *hmms* you hear. Also, pay attention to any background noise on the other end of the line. If you hear barking dogs, doorbells ringing, or small children, chances are good that you don't have this person's full attention.

If you're in doubt as to whether your prospects are on the same page with you, ask a question. Don't, of course, ask if they're paying attention. Instead, ask how something you just covered relates to their business or what they think of it. Restate that point or benefit clearly so they're not embarrassed if they really weren't paying attention.

Another strategy to use when you're giving phone presentations is what I call the *pregnant pause.* If you briefly pause during your presentation, the pause will make your prospects wonder what happened and draw their attention to what you'll say next, thus drawing them back to the point at hand.

The product needs to be the star of the presentation — especially if you're not meeting in person. If at all possible, be sure to send a sample product or, at the very least, an attractive visual of it to the client so she can see what you want her to see during your presentation. An even better option: If your client has Internet access, try to arrange to give your presentation via a

Web conferencing service (see the next section), or at the very least, have her log on to your company's website and direct her where to look, what to click, and so on.

Video or Web presentations

If you're asked by a prospective client to join her for a presentation via videoconference or through an online service such as Skype, GoToMeeting, or other Web conferencing service but you're not savvy to these types of communication tools, you need to find someone who is and take a lesson. These services aren't difficult to work with, but the logistics of setting the stage just right can be tricky.

For example, when videoconferencing with a service such as GoToMeeting, Skype, FaceTime, or JoinMe, you may use an eyeball type of camera attached to your computer. You may even be doing this from home. When you participate in videoconferencing, you need to be aware of what else is in the picture with you. Check your camera and be sure that it doesn't allow your next potential major client to see a torn poster hanging on the wall behind you or a neglected plant. Believe me, these kinds of objects can harm your credibility. Be certain you have an attractive background even if you have to borrow something to put up behind you. If you do decide to place a plant behind you, beware of putting it (or any other object) in a position in which it may look like it's coming out of your head (in other words, anything positioned behind you should not be at the level of your head).

Take note of how your local newscasters appear and act on camera. They are in the talking-head type of shot, which is what you'll be in — your head and shoulders will be in the frame, but not much else. Newscasters make great eye contact with the camera — they smile into it, smiling with their eyes.

If your presentation online requires you to show slides or other visuals, maintain as much control of how the flow goes as you can. For example, you can control a slide deck from your computer while it's being viewed online from someone else's computer. In PowerPoint, you can save your work as ready-to-view HTML documents. Clients and coworkers can then launch the presentation in a browser, even in full-screen mode. They can view slides in any order or repeat important slides at their convenience. *Presentation on demand* is another feature within PowerPoint that allows people to rerun your presentation at any time that's convenient for them. Visit www.microsoft.com/office/powerpoint for a tour of the latest features you may benefit from. Even better, do the same research for the top three most popular programs for creating slides. That way you won't be caught unprepared if your client uses something different than what you use.

Letting the Product Be the Star

One key in presenting or demonstrating anything — a new hobby, a multimillion-dollar piece of high-tech equipment for a Fortune 500 company, or anything in between — is really pretty simple: Let the product shine; let it be the star. You're just the host who introduces the key players (your product and your prospect) to each other and then fades into the background to let them get acquainted.

Even though one of the players may be an inanimate object, even an intangible one, you need to think of that object in terms of the future primary relationship between the product and its new owner. And you need to let the possibilities for that relationship develop (with your encouragement, of course) while keeping the entire process under control.

Getting out of the picture

As a salesperson, you are not unlike the matchmakers of old. You may help me find a mate, but after the two of us meet, you step out of the picture. Of course, you may occasionally monitor the progress of our relationship, but you won't be coming to live with us.

Even though the product must be the star, never forget that your prospective client needs to always remain the focus of your presentation. Never give so much attention to the product and what it can do that you ignore what it will do *for* the person sitting there with you — your prospective client.

If you start putting your hands on the product or turning your eyes, back, or chair more toward the product than the people, you risk losing their attention. It's better to allow the clients to get their hands on the product even if it means they turn their backs on you. You remain the director of the presentation, assisting them in their experience with the product.

Staying in control

Don't let your prospects see what you want them to see until you're ready for them to see it. The product has to be the star, but you need to be the guide — or the bodyguard — letting the audience close only when it's appropriate.

If your demonstration involves the use of a piece of equipment, don't let your prospective client come in and begin punching buttons or demanding answers to a lot of questions — and taking control of the presentation away from you. Just tell the buyer that she has great questions and that you'll cover most of them in your presentation. Then ask that she hold her questions until after the demonstration. When she recognizes that you've planned something special for her, she'll probably settle down and let you do your thing.

Keeping control can become a challenge when you have several things to display. If your demonstration falls into this category, I recommend that you bring something (like a cloth) to cover your display items, uncovering only those items you're prepared to discuss. Or, if you can, simply leave anything not pertinent to the moment out of the buyer's line of sight. If you're using a video or computer screen, be sure to have an attractive screensaver that you can go to when you need your prospect's attention focused back on your planned presentation. Otherwise, your buyer will probably try to read ahead on the screen instead of listening to what you're saying.

The primary need of all humans is the need to be comfortable. If your potential client isn't comfortable with what you're offering, she'll never part with her money for it, give her commitment to it, or follow through with it. So, your number one goal in any presentation is to get the prospect to an acceptable comfort level with your offering.

Mastering the Art of Visuals

The majority of people learn and understand best when they involve as many of their senses as possible; however, each person usually has one dominant sense. Some people learn best by closing their eyes and listening. Others have a strong need to touch and feel things. Most people, however, gain the best understanding by seeing things.

I'm sure you've heard the phrase "seeing is believing." That phrase comes from the desire of most people to be shown the proof that what they're being told is real, or at least that it can come true. Take a moment to see the difference between *telling* someone about a new product and letting her *see* it, either in picture form or through a product demonstration. Obviously, letting the prospect see it involves more of her senses. And that's where visual aids come into play.

Visual aids should show three things to new clients:

> ✔ **Who you (and your company) are.** Visual aids should identify your company and the industry to which it belongs. If you are worldwide suppliers of your particular type of product, put that information in your visual aids. The story of your company builds credibility.

✔ **What you've done.** If the current must-have app uses software developed by your company, brag about it in this portion of your visual aids. Be careful not to belabor the point, though. Being proud of your company is one thing; being a bore is another thing altogether (and something you obviously want to avoid). This is also when to mention or show your company's rating from an independent source.

✔ **What you do for your clients.** This is the part your prospective client is most interested in. This is where you tune in her favorite radio station, so she can hear the answer to her most pressing question, "What's In It For Me?"

The best visual aids include all three of these key points. If they don't, be sure to try to verbally incorporate these points into your presentation.

In the following sections, I describe two types of visuals and how to use them: the kind supplied by your company and the kind you make yourself.

Using the visuals your company supplies

If you represent a company's products or services, you've probably been exposed to their visual aids. These are usually slick, high-quality sheets with graphs, charts, diagrams, and photos or video presentations or slide decks that you facilitate. Such visual aids often contain quotes from various well-thought-of authorities about your product or service or at the very least testimonials from satisfied clients. For organizing and storing printed visual aids, some companies provide you a great-looking binder that also stands up like a miniature easel.

You may work for a company that's more high tech than this. For example:

✔ You may get computer-generated graphics that appear on a projection screen and include music and professional announcers. For computer presentations, you need a laptop or tablet computer and multimedia projector.

When you prepare for one of these high-tech presentations, be sure that your prospective client has a white board or screen for you to project your images onto. Presenting your product professionally is tough when all you have to work with for a background is wood paneling or flowered wallpaper.

✔ You may also work with videos for your presentations. Videos often include recorded testimonials from actual customers your prospect can relate to. When your prospect sees someone just like herself who is benefiting from your product or service, the relationship between your prospective buyer and your product grows a little stronger.

Whatever your specific visual aids depict, the important thing to remember is this: Your company invested in the creation of your visual aids for a reason. And that reason was not to make your life more complicated by having to carry all this stuff around and keep it updated. Instead, your company did it because many, many years' experience proves that visual aids are very effective when they're used properly.

So what's the best way to use visual aids provided by your company? Most likely, it's the way your company recommends. Few companies succeed in business by putting out garbage as visual aids and then leaving their salespeople to figure out how to use them. Typically, companies rely on a task force of some sort that includes top salespeople, manufacturing people, and marketing people. All their suggestions usually have to be approved by a director or manager of the marketing department — someone ultimately accountable if the brochures, videos, or sample products do the job of moving product into the hands of consumers (or if they don't).

If for some reason you don't like or have trouble using the company's visual aids, talk with the people who train you on how to use them. If their suggestions don't satisfy you, talk with a top salesperson, someone who does use them effectively. You may even want to go on a sales call with that salesperson to watch how she handles things. After you master her suggestions for using the visual aids as well as possible, if you still think you have room for improvement, ask to meet with the people who put them together. They'll probably be glad to offer you constructive suggestions and, hopefully, listen to yours.

Developing your own visual aids

If you have no visual aids to work with, put some thought into what you can develop on your own. Involvement of the senses in attempting to persuade others is critical. In fact, I recommend that you involve as many of a prospect's senses as possible.

For example, say you want to sell your family on vacationing in the woods when you know they'd rather go to the beach. You may want to rent a video on all the outdoor adventures available to them in the woods. Many vacation spots offer free videos as promotional items in information packages. Or you can get a video on nature in general, with flowing waterfalls, gentle breezes blowing in the trees, canoeing, horseback riding, whatever appeals to your audience (in this case, your family). Such a video involves two senses: sight and hearing. And what's that I smell out back — smoke? If possible, you may even have a little campfire going in the yard while the family watches your video. Or prepare some hot dogs and s'mores ahead of time so that they get their sense of taste tied in to the joy of that vacation in the woods. Invest in hiking boots, lightweight backpacks, or canteens filled with spring water in order to get the sense of touch involved.

All these things (the video, the campfire, the food, the equipment) are sensory aids vital to your presentation if you're serious about persuading your family to go on this type of vacation. When they accept ownership of all these feelings, it'll be an easy sale (unless you have a family member with a phobia of bugs or wide-open spaces).

The same strategy applies to formal business sales presentations: The more senses you can involve, the better. Start with developing aids that focus on sight and hearing, such as the ones that I describe in the preceding section — charts, graphs, computer graphics, videos, and the like. To strengthen the impact of the visual aids, find ways to get additional sensual involvement (no, I don't mean *that* kind of sensual involvement). You can involve your prospects' sense of touch just by handing them things. Smell and taste are a little tougher, especially if you're selling an intangible object like a service. With intangibles, you may want to paint visual pictures that bring those senses into play. (I discuss product demonstrations and how to talk about intangible goods in "Presenting Intangible Goods" later in this chapter.)

For example, say you're selling a cleaning service to a working mother. You may not necessarily want to have her smell the cleaning agents you use — but you can talk about how fresh the home will be after your professional crew completes its duties. And to get a homeowner prospect's senses completely involved, always refer to her residence as her *home* — not her *house*. (A *house* is made up of lifeless bricks and boards; a *home* is made up of the people who live there and the events of those people's lives.) Bringing a small box of candy or mints as a new-client gift involves the sense of taste in your presentation, even though it doesn't directly apply to your service.

Demonstrating Products to Your Prospective Clients

When you demonstrate a tangible product, you have to be like a game show host. You want a lot of excited contestants, and the way people get excited is through involvement. Who cares if Alex Trebek knows all the answers to the questions on *Jeopardy!?* He's a nice person and all, but the fun is in playing the game.

Selling is not a *spectator* sport; it's an *involvement* sport.

One of the greatest fears all clients have in selling situations is that they'll trust what the salesperson tells them, buy the product or service that's for sale, and then, after they own the product or service, find out that it doesn't meet their expectations or their needs. The best demonstrations give people the opportunity to prove to themselves that what the salesperson is telling them is true.

How long this takes depends on the product you're offering. A kitchen knife can be demonstrated in seconds. A software application may require longer. Your presentation should be geared to taking the least amount of your potential client's time as possible. If you go longer, it's because she's really interested, want to see it again, ask questions, and so on.

If you have a challenge with your demonstration — something goes haywire or malfunctions — be prepared to take another approach to demonstrating it. After you master the initial presentation of your product, start asking other salespeople about how they handled situations where things just didn't go right; then build those strategies into your preparation. It's wise to analyze your presentation with questions that begin with, "What do I do if . . ." and do your best to cover all your bases during preparation.

For example: If you sell copiers and you don't have prospective buyers push the buttons, make double-sided copies, change the paper, and open and close the machine, you're not selling. You're showing. Let your prospective clients perform the functions, and they will feel involved.

It won't matter to the office manager that you've won all the time trials at your office for making the most complicated copying challenges come out perfect. Instead, what matters is how simple it is for everyone on your prospect's staff to meet those challenges — and you should build into your demonstration the proof that they can do so. During your demonstration, your prospect and her staff members should be able to make normal copies simply and to find out something about a new feature that's going to make her job easier. Your key contact person should see exactly what all the warning lights are on the machine and what to do about each one. (Don't go overboard here, though. They may begin to wonder about the quality of the machine if there are so many warnings. Just assure them that if anything is amiss, the machine can diagnose itself. Then, she just needs to follow the instructions for whatever button lights up.)

Here's another example: The best computer salespeople stand or sit at their client's shoulder, giving instructions on how she can do whatever it is she just asked about. A good salesperson makes sure the client's hands are on that equipment. That way, the buyer has a positive experience with the product and builds confidence in the capabilities of it. What's really happening is that the client is learning something new and building confidence in her own ability to use the computer. She may even be overcoming a fear of computers altogether. And if she overcomes that fear and gets comfortable using the product, you can bet she'll be much more likely to want to own it.

Presenting Intangible Goods

If the item you're selling is intangible — insurance, financial services, banking services, wireless phone service, education, and so on — your presentation will differ from that of salespeople offering tangible items. When potential clients cannot see, touch, hear, taste, or smell what you're selling, you need to develop ways of keeping their attention during your presentation.

Fortunately, many companies employ software that can provide immediate analyses of individual needs. For example, if you sell financial services, you may be able to plug Jim and Sally's number of years to retirement and existing savings into a calculator to project what their incomes will be at retirement age. Playing with the numbers in various scenarios can be fun for them and definitely keeps them involved.

If you don't have anything other than paper (brochures, flyers, proposals, and so on) to work with, there are specific strategies to consider:

- ✔ First, don't hand your prospects anything to read until you want them to read it. Their attention will be on the printed piece, not on what you're saying about its contents. If your printed piece contains several points that you want to address separately, hold the brochure in your hand and point to each area with your pen as you discuss them. When you're ready to move away from the brochure, you can then fold it back up and set it aside telling them you'll gladly leave it behind with them to review again. This way, you keep control of it rather than having them pick it up again and get distracted from what you're saying.

- ✔ If there's not a comparison chart available that shows how your products or services stack up against the competition, create one. You want to be certain that any information your client gathers is perceived correctly (as in comparing apples to apples). Let her know you created the comparison chart, but list your sources in a footnote at the bottom so she can see that you didn't just make up the information.

When talking about intangible services, you have to work at creating mental pictures in the minds of your potential clients. You don't have anything physical to show them, but you can create images in their minds of how much better their lives will be after they own what you're offering. For example: They'll have greater health if starting a new exercise program or joining a gym. Get them thinking about feeling better, stronger, and more energized. Help them *feel* the satisfaction of having their clothes fit better and *hear* the compliments they'll receive from others. For insurance, focus on the peace of mind they'll have knowing they're properly protected. If you're selling retirement programs, help them *envision* what their future lifestyle can be like through the commitment they're making now. Constantly take what the intangible *is* and help them see what they can *be, do,* or *have* when they own it.

Avoiding the Crash-and-Burn Scenario of Presentations

If I were to tell you all the horror stories I've heard about failed sales presentations, I'd need a whole day of your time. The unfortunate thing is that those same salespeople could have avoided the challenges they faced had they taken a few simple precautions. But fortunately for you, hearing so many of these horror stories has helped me develop effective suggestions for avoiding your own demonstration missteps. In the following sections, I cover just a few things you may not think of, but all of them should become a vital part of your preparatory checklist when you're getting ready to make a presentation.

Understand your need for power

If your demonstration requires the use of electrical power, do your best to find out in advance exactly where the available electrical outlets are. If you're running the show on your computer battery, check and double-check that it's fully charged prior to your presentation — and bring a spare, fully charged battery with you, just in case.

A woman I know of invested hours in preparing her computer-generated demonstration with high-quality graphics, customized charts, graphs, and diagrams. Her only problem: The power cord she brought to her presentation was too short. She had to place all her equipment right next to a wall, which was about 20 feet from her audience. As a result, she lost vital eye contact and other rapport-building closeness with her audience, and probably the sale, too — all because she brought the wrong extension cord.

Be sure your visual aids are in order

Food stains and bent corners on your presentation materials give the impression that you don't care about details. And if your materials are confiscated by a roving band of evil, invisible little gremlins who mischievously rearrange your slides into a state of utter chaos, your audience will be less than thrilled. So before your presentation, be sure to review each and every piece of equipment or presentation material that your audience will see. You'll sleep better knowing things are in order.

Never use your materials immediately after someone else has been through them without checking them. Misplacement of contents is rarely intentional, but it does happen.

Test everything ahead of time

You may have a very dependable demonstration model of your computer software. In fact, it could be one you've used for several weeks or months without any challenges. But on the day of your big presentation, Murphy's Law may strike. You remember Mr. Murphy. He's the poor bloke who deduced the most prevalent law in the known universe: If anything can go wrong, it will. Having a bad cable for your equipment or your computer can wreak havoc on the best-laid plans. Not having Wi-Fi available or having a weak Internet signal in the location where you're meeting is always a possibility. So always arrive early enough to test your equipment onsite. And test it early enough that, if you find something isn't working, you can adjust for it.

Customize as much as you can

Don't you love it when someone gives you a generic presentation that you just know she's given, word-for-word, to at least 40 other people before? I didn't think so. No one does. By making the extra effort to customize your materials, you appear competent and knowledgeable about your customer's specific needs. And that's just the kind of person she's looking for.

Don't customize by skipping over materials in your generic, full-blown presentation. People will feel slighted by the absence of this information. Instead, remove pages or delete slides you won't need. Page past graphics on your computer screen that are unnecessary. If you can't delete them, go ahead and show them. Just make sure you offer a brief explanation that you know those particular graphics don't apply to your present audience's needs and that you won't waste their valuable time going over them in detail.

Bring a protective pad

If you're scheduled to make a presentation in someone else's office, don't take a chance that any of your equipment will mar her furniture. To prevent damages, always check the bottom of your equipment before placing anything on a potential customer's furniture, and have protective padding on hand. Rough edges can easily leave scratch marks.

I know of a salesman who, when it was time to fill in his order form, placed it on the client's table and, because it was a three-part form, printed heavily on the paper. The only problem was that the table was made of a fine, soft wood. Because the salesman didn't have a pad of paper under the form, his heavy printing etched itself into the tabletop. Needless to say, his lasting impression wasn't favorable.

Being prepared for the worst . . . and hoping for the best

Jim is a manufacturer's representative for a line of products sold to automotive service shops. He travels around the country a great deal servicing his clients' needs. Once or twice a year, Jim coordinates large-scale presentations of the latest innovations in equipment from his company. He invites two or three representatives from each of his best, noncompeting clients' companies. Jim puts weeks of work into each presentation, including building models, coordinating slides, conducting interviews with end-users — in other words, doing whatever it takes for his presentation to succeed.

Jim is so detailed in these presentations that he's often invited to company headquarters to show other representatives his presentation methods. Jim's customers always enjoy his presentations, and he often leaves with much larger orders for his products than he would if he were to meet with customers one-on-one. In addition to placing orders for the latest and greatest products for their stores, his various clients can compare notes with each other on the latest industry trends. The Big Presentation is a win-win event for everyone involved.

At one of Jim's presentations, however, he stayed at a new hotel. He heard it had a great reputation and thought his repeat attendees would enjoy the change of scenery. All was going well until the alarm clock failed to work, and he overslept on the morning of his presentation. Waking up with only ten minutes to go before show time, he quickly showered, dressed, and dashed to the meeting room. He was going to be able to start on time, thank goodness. However, about ten minutes into his well-planned presentation, the light bulb in his projector burned out. Being the detail-oriented person he is, Jim had put a new light bulb in the evening before, but he didn't count on a new bulb being bad. It took him half of a very embarrassing hour to find the correct staff people to locate a replacement bulb so he could move on with his presentation.

Luckily for Jim, his clients already knew his track record, and they all ended up having a good laugh about it later in the day. However, if Jim had been giving this presentation to new clients, his credibility could have fallen so much that he would've had to spend many hours following up in order to gain their business — if he ever got it at all.

The best thing of all in this incident is that Jim took the time to analyze what went wrong and how he could prevent it from happening again. He's a professional who sees every experience, whether good or bad, as a learning experience. Today Jim's checklist for presentations includes at least two extra light bulbs, knowing the name of the audiovisual person who can help in case of an emergency, and carrying a backup alarm clock — a key-wind alarm clock, at that, to beat power failures.

Chapter 11

Addressing Client Concerns

*U*nless you sell balloons at a parade, few customers contact you, make an impulse purchase, and go away happy. What really happens is that nearly all buyers have concerns. What concerns do they have? Potential clients always have questions if they have any interest at all in what you're offering. Some of those questions can include the following:

✔ Will the product or service do what you say it will?

✔ Will you really be able to make my required delivery date?

✔ Have I negotiated the best investment?

✔ Am I making a good decision?

✔ Is it something I need right now or should I wait?

All these little doubts and fears creep up on potential clients when they feel the urge to invest in your product or service or to commit to your idea. The concerns that arise when a potential client feels moved to make any commitment that involves his time or money are completely natural. In some cases, there may not be fear, but rather a desire for a clearer understanding of what your product will do for them.

Unfortunately, most people new to persuading think that a "No" or a sign of hesitation means "Good-bye, Charlie." The seasoned persuader, however, knows that clients can have good reasons to hesitate. The best reason of all is that they feel themselves leaning toward "Yes." So your client's hesitation can simply be a sign that he wants to slow down the selling process so he can absorb all the information you're giving him. Or hesitation can mean that the client needs *more* information before he feels comfortable making a decision. In such a case, the client objects in order to show you that you need to back up and resell him on a certain point. When a potential client hesitates or gives you a stall, just think, "He's asking for more information."

If you get nervous or afraid when you hear an objection and start beating a hasty retreat for the door, you're leaving empty-handed. And if you try to overcome your client's objection and he doesn't like the way you handle it, you're going to be heading for the door anyway, and he'll have it open before you get there! So why not experiment with ways to address your client's concerns or handle his objections? The worst that can happen is that you won't get what you want and you'll be free to move on to the next likely candidate. The best that can happen is that your client sees how competently you handled his concern and that his concern wasn't strong enough to keep him from going ahead with your offering.

Until you come to expect client concerns, you won't know how to handle them. And until you know how to handle client concerns, you won't come close to reaching your highest earning potential in sales. So go into every presentation anticipating concerns, and you'll come out ahead. This chapter gives you the help you need in addressing client concerns.

Reading Your Clients' Signals

Prospective clients give you three important pieces of information when they voice objections or raise concerns during your presentation:

- ✔ **They're interested but don't want to be thought of as an easy sale.** If you've properly qualified the potential client (see Chapter 9 for more information), you know what he has now, what he enjoys most about it, what he would alter, and that he is the decisionmaker. Armed with that knowledge, if you're confident the prospect would benefit from your offering, chances are he's interested, but he just doesn't want you to think of him as an easy sale. In that case, you want to slow down the pace, encourage questions, and generally get him relaxed and chatting before you ask him to make a decision.

- ✔ **They may be interested, but they aren't 100 percent clear about what's in it for them.** If your prospect is already asking lots of questions and looks somewhat perplexed or doubtful, he's interested, but he just doesn't have a clear enough picture of what's in it for him. This situation is especially common when the prospect doesn't have previous experience with a similar product and you're educating him from ground zero. To respond to this kind of prospect, you have to cover the features and benefits in a bit more detail — asking questions along the way that help you create the right word pictures in your presentation. (See Chapter 10 for more information about winning presentations.)

✔ **They may not be interested, but they can be if you educate them properly.** If you face this kind of questioning client, you must first earn his trust so he'll give you the time you need to educate him on your product. You also have to build the prospect's curiosity about the product, service, or idea so he wants to know more.

When the fish aren't biting, change your bait

Most persuaders find it hard to influence people who voice no objections and raise no questions. In other words, the most difficult people to persuade are like dead fish: Their eyes wiggle every now and then, but they don't respond.

In negotiation situations, you carry the presentation forward by directing and redirecting your course of questions and information based on the feedback your prospect gives you. If he tells you nothing, the communication often stalls. When that happens, you have to guess which direction to follow next — and guessing is very

bad because when you guess, you're no longer in control. Guessing is like casting your line with no bait on it.

The people who don't get verbally or physically involved in your presentation likely have no intention of going ahead with your proposition. Those who *do* bring up challenges for you to address are, at the very least, interested. If they're really tough to convince, they'll probably become your best customers when you finally do convince them. So the next time you hear an objection, be glad. Getting objections and getting past them are necessary steps in the selling cycle.

All three situations tell you one thing: The prospect needs more information. By backing up and clarifying exactly what it is the prospect is objecting to, you find out just which direction to take for your next step.

Addressing Your Clients' Concerns with Some Simple Strategies

Objections from prospects are just part of the business of selling. What's important is that you know how to handle them. Fortunately, you can use some key strategies to address your prospects' objections so that they come away with more information *and* more respect for you and your product. In this section, I show you how.

Distinguishing conditions from objections

If your customer's objection is "I'm totally broke," and you're selling a luxury item, chances are pretty good that you've just heard a condition, not an objection. And there's a big difference between the two.

A *condition* is not an excuse or a stall. It's a valid reason that the prospect cannot agree to what you're proposing. If you're trying to exchange your offering for your potential customer's money, and the customer has no money and has no credit, just thank him for his time, get permission to stay in touch should things change in the future and move on. With so many potential clients out there who have no conditions, you have no good reason to beat your head against the wall with those who *do* have valid conditions.

Always leave people who voice valid conditions on a positive note, though. You never know how that person's situation may change down the road. He may win the lottery in the next 24 hours. Old Aunt Thelma may leave him an inheritance. He may borrow money from his rich grandpa. Or, better yet, he may convince Gramps that your offering would make a great birthday or Christmas gift for him.

Remember: If he wants what you have to offer badly enough, he'll call you. And you can rest assured that his calls won't go to someone else with whom he doesn't have a positive relationship. After all, why would he call a stranger when he can rely on a salesperson he knows to be knowledgeable, competent, and considerate?

Bypassing your clients' concerns completely

If you know that your potential client wants and needs the product or service you're offering but feels a natural inclination to object — in these situations, you can often bypass the objection altogether. Simply say, "That's a good point, Mr. Smith. I believe it will be addressed to your satisfaction by the end of my presentation. May I make a note of it and come back to it later?" If he gives you permission, he'll pay attention to the rest of your presentation for a satisfactory answer. Or, he may see enough benefit during the balance of the presentation that the value outweighs his concern and it becomes a moot point.

If you're new to persuading, don't ignore any objection without testing the waters to see how big a concern it truly is. Sometimes just acknowledging the concern is enough. Your prospect will be satisfied that you're really listening, and then he'll move ahead.

When your prospect raises a concern, it doesn't necessarily mean "No way." It may simply be a way for the prospect to say, "Not *this* way." If that's the case, you just need to adjust what you're saying and take another path to the same destination.

Helping your clients see that they're trading up

If your prospective client has money, credit, or both, but he just doesn't want to part with it now, you haven't convinced him that he'd be better off with the product than he would be with his money. This is where you need to work on building the value of the benefits of your product or service.

If an investment you're offering requires the person's time, "No time" is not a valid condition (as described in the sidebar "Distinguishing conditions from objections"). It's an objection. Everyone has the same 86,400 seconds in every day. How people use them is their choice. If you want someone to invest his time with you, you have to show him enough benefits for him to want to spend his time on your offering nowinstead of on what he's already planned.

Beating your clients to their own concerns

If you know that your prospect is likely to voice a particular concern, beat him to it. By being in control and bringing the issue up when you want it brought up, rather than when your prospect thinks the time is right, you can brag about it and turn it into an advantage.

For example, if you know that your product costs more than others on the market, you can be fairly certain that your prospect will be concerned about that cost. But you can beat the prospect to that objection by explaining upfront that your product requires a higher investment because it contains only the highest-quality ingredients. And those high-quality ingredients make people feel better, make the product last longer, or perform in a superior manner. Those benefits are worth bragging about *before* your buyer gets busy laying bricks for that wall of defense against the investment.

The following sections describe specific tactics you can use to beat your clients to their own concerns.

Addressing specific concerns about money

Here is a specific script for how you can handle an objection to your product's investment:

> CLIENT: Tom, I'm sure I can find this product, or one just like it, for a lot less money.

TOM: Well, Jim, I understand your concern. You know, I've learned something over the years. People look for three things when they spend money: the finest quality, the best service, and of course, the lowest price. I've also found that no company can offer all three. They can't offer the finest quality and the best service for the lowest price. And, I'm curious, for your long-term happiness, which of the three would you be most willing to give up? Fine quality? Excellent service? Or low price?

This client is going to have a tough time coming back at you and saying, "Well, poor quality and crappy service are okay as long as they're cheap."

Here's another way to handle a concern about money. Your choice between the two methods is going to be a judgment call. When the customer raises the concern, if you think that he has developed a certain belief in you — in your competency — then you may prefer to use this approach:

CLIENT: Tom, I'm sure I can find this product, or one just like it, for a lot less money.

TOM: Jamal, I could have chosen to work for any company in the area in my particular industry. After careful research, I chose my company because I wanted to be able to sit with my clients and look them in the eye and say, "You are doing business with the very highest quality company in the industry." I know you appreciate quality and, because of that, those few extra pennies you'll invest per day to enjoy *the finest quality* will benefit you in the long-term scheme of things, don't you agree?

With this approach, you enhance the credibility you've already established. In effect, you're telling your client that you're not an amateur. You have a concern for your own reputation, as well as your clients' satisfaction and you plan to be in the business awhile.

Bringing up and bragging about concerns

Having product that's backordered can be a serious challenge if you let it be one. But bringing it up and bragging about the fact that the product's popularity, quality, or other great benefit is the cause puts backordering in a different light — a light that many customers will accept.

Take advantage of this tactic with concerns that you know are most often heard about your product or service. If people object to the cost, have a testimonial at hand from a happy client who had the same concern and now feels his return on investment was well worth it. Many companies post such testimonials on their websites. You can easily impress your prospect by calling up the website on your laptop right then and there to address the prospect's concern. Let him read it rather than telling him about it. In fact, asking your prospective client to take a look at your company's website prior to your presentation is always a good idea. Send the prospect an email with your Web address and a few links to areas within your site he may find helpful.

This method of beating prospects to their concerns — by bringing them up, bragging about them, and then elaborating on them — has proven successful for many of my students who used to see common challenges as stumbling blocks. Now they see them as springboards to success — and you can, too.

Understanding the Do's and Don'ts of Addressing Concerns

Before you get too deep into dealing with your prospect's concerns, you need to be aware of some basic do's and don'ts of this important step in selling. In this section, I fill you in on a couple of each that will guide you through any selling situation.

Do acknowledge the legitimacy of the concern

Dismissing your prospect's concerns as unimportant can cause those objections to get completely blown out of proportion. In many cases a simple "I see" or "I understand" is acknowledgment enough. In other cases, you may do well to say, "Let me make a note of that so we can discuss it in depth after we cover the benefits you've indicated you need most," and then jot it down. Jotting down the concern validates the concern and shows professionalism on your part. Your presentation may cover the concerns the client had or create so much value that those concerns become nonissues.

If you need to circle back around to the questions or concerns that you set aside during your presentation, state them back to the client in his own words. "Now, John, you mentioned that you're concerned about taking your people out of the field to train on this new software." If John is now really excited about the benefits of the software, his concern about this may no longer be an issue. You see, you don't have to go back and answer every concern. In some cases, you just need to bring it up. The client may already have an answer for it with the information you presented after he expressed it.

Do get the clients to answer their own concerns

The most important "do" of addressing concerns is: Get the other person to answer his own objection. That advice may sound tricky to follow, but here's why it's so important: You're trying to persuade your prospect, so he'll have reservations about anything you do or say. Why? Because anything you say must be good for you, too. Until the prospect realizes that you're acting in his best interest, he will doubt you.

When *you* say it, a prospective client tends to doubt it. When *he* says it, the buyer believes it to be true. And *that's* why you want to get your prospect to answer his own objections — because he's much more likely to believe *himself* than he is to believe *you*. All you need to do is provide the information that answers his concern and let him draw his own conclusions. You let him persuade himself.

You may need to nudge a client a little by asking a question to get him to state the desired answer: "How do you see that feature impacting your company's level of efficiency, Josh?" It's much more powerful when he answers than if you just say, "That feature will increase your company's efficiency by 20 percent." See the difference? Take advantage of the strategy, and you'll close more sales because your clients will be convincing themselves.

This technique often works well when you persuade a married couple (children, take note). When one partner objects to something, don't respond immediately. *Average* persuaders are quick to defend their offering. But there's a better way: Learn to sit tight. Many times, one spouse jumps in with the next comment, and you have a 50/50 chance that the originally silent spouse will answer the objection for you. If the second spouse agrees with his partner's objection, then you know you'll have to work a little harder to overcome it. The point is that these two people already have a positive relationship (you hope) and trust each other's judgment. Being quiet while they think it through can cause the objection to evaporate into thin air right before your eyes.

When something important to you is hanging in the balance, being patient is difficult. During such moments, seconds feel like hours, and you can quickly become very uncomfortable. To keep yourself from jumping in too soon, try this trick. Silently count to 20 or 30. Or you may want to count the seconds by saying to yourself, "one-thousand-one, one-thousand-two, one-thousand-three," and so on. (Just remember to count to *yourself,* not aloud.) Some salespeople recite a short poem to themselves to kill that time. Just don't let your mind wander off from the matter at hand. Whatever method you choose, just be careful not to let them see your lips move.

What you never want to do when you're waiting for a response is look at your watch or at a clock in the room. Even a slight glance at a timepiece can distract the prospects because they're already looking at you, waiting for your next move. So practice waiting until you're comfortable with it.

Don't argue with your client

Although not arguing with your client may seem obvious, when you're negotiating with someone, emotions can take over, and things can get out of hand. Arguing or fighting an objection or concern raises a barrier between you and the person you're trying to persuade. You're trying to persuade your prospective buyer to something, not go ten rounds with him. If you keep the perspective that objections are simply requests for further information, you shouldn't have much of a challenge with this advice.

Don't minimize a concern

To the person you're persuading, every point he raises is valid. Remember to put yourself in his shoes. How would you react to someone who acts as though your concerns are stupid or unimportant?

Handling Concerns in Six Easy Steps

In the following sections, I give you six steps for handling objections or addressing concerns that almost always work in your favor. If you practice and apply the following steps properly, they'll take you a long way toward achieving your goal of selling others, even when they raise objections or concerns. (They also work pretty well in diffusing unusually tense situations, so heed them well.)

Before you begin the six-step process, take note of the following general pointers on objections:

✔ Sometimes you hear more than one objection or concern from a prospect. If you start running through all six steps with each objection you hear, you can spend a lifetime trying to persuade. Experience helps you tell which concerns you need to address and which you may be able to bypass (see the section "Bypassing your clients' concerns completely" earlier in this chapter).

✔ If a concern or objection is raised during a group presentation and you have to do a bit of research and get back to the questioner, be certain you have the contact information (specifically, an email address) for each person in the group. Never rely on one person to relay vital information in the manner that you know to be best for moving the selling process forward. Send the exact same email message to each person and let everyone see that they're part of the group email. If each person receives it individually, they could all wonder what else you may have shared with the others.

✔ Include the link to your company's website for each member of the group to peruse. Often in a committee decision-making situation, only one or two members get the whole package of information. They then break it down for the balance of the decision makers. This may be the way the *company* wants the process handled, but what *you* want is to get as much information as possible equally distributed.

Outsmart your client's last objection

Construction work was my first job. It was tough, physically demanding, and ultimately — for me — unfulfilling work. In my part of the country, real estate was booming, so I studied and eventually got my license. My next step was to sell myself into a job with a local company. I had two strikes against me at this point: My only means of transportation was a motorcycle, which made it tough to drive people out to view properties, and even worse, I didn't own a suit and didn't have enough money to invest in a good one.

After being turned away by several real estate companies, I finally talked with a man who told me he probably could help me work around the motorcycle challenge, but having a suit was critical. It dawned on me then that this was his final objection. I asked, "If I have a suit, then will you hire me?" To my surprise, he said yes and told me to show up in a suit at the next company sales meeting. He didn't specify what *kind*

of suit I needed, though, so I took the liberty of cleaning up and wearing my band uniform. You see, when I was 16, I played in a band. We were greatly influenced by the Beatles, and our band uniforms were silver lamé. Technically, my band uniform was a suit.

I walked into that sales meeting just as he was informing everyone that they had a new agent on board. You should have seen his face when he realized that my suit was my old band uniform. It got a lot of laughs, and the guy agreed to let me stay on if I could produce. I was the only motorcycle-riding real estate agent in a band uniform in the country at that time, and my nonconformity turned out to be an advantage. People talked about "that crazy kid, Hopkins." It was free advertising.

Identifying and outsmarting my prospect's last objection to what I was selling was a turning point in my life. It can be in yours, too.

Step #1: Hear them out

When someone trusts you enough to tell you what's bothering him, do him the courtesy of listening. Don't be quick to address every phrase he utters. Give him time; encourage him to tell you the whole story behind his concern. If you don't get the whole story, you won't know what to do or say to address his feelings. Don't interrupt either; you may jump in and answer the wrong concern.

Step #2: Feed it back

By rephrasing your client's concerns, you're in effect asking for even more information: "So what I'm hearing you say, Alex, is that you aren't 100 percent sure this new system will resolve the challenges for every department. Is that right?" You want to be certain that he's aired it all so that no other concerns crop up after you've handled this one. You're saying to him, "Go ahead. Lay it all on me. Get it off your chest." In doing this, you're asking him to trust you.

Step #3: Question it

This step is where subtlety and tact come into play. If a potential client objects to the amount of space your product will take up, don't say, "What's wrong with it?" Instead, gently ask, "Would you feel more comfortable with a smaller model?" Or, "Is that the only thing that's holding you back?" If it is, he'll tell you why. Maybe he's concerned about appearing ostentatious. If so, you have to further build his confidence by stressing the benefits the product provides.

Step #4: Answer it

When you're confident that you have the whole story behind your client's concern, you can answer that concern with confidence. If the prospect's concern is cost, you can engage in the following dialog:

> SALESPERSON: I can certainly appreciate your feelings. But I think we ought to keep that $1,000 in the proper perspective. Over the years, most of my happiest clients received true enjoyment/value from this product for at least five years. This fact really makes that $1,000 only $200 per year, doesn't it?

> PROSPECT: Yes, it does.

SALESPERSON: If you're like most people, you'll receive the benefits of this product for 52 weeks per year, which means that $1,000 breaks down to about $3.85 per week. Then, of course — and this may sound ridiculous — it finally boils down to about 55 cents per day. Do you think you should avoid enjoying all the benefits we've discussed for 55 cents per day?

PROSPECT: Well, when you put it that way, it does sound a little silly.

And you've just gotten the prospect to answer his own concern.

Step #5: Confirm your answer

After you answer the objection, confirming that your prospect heard and accepted your answer is important. If you don't complete this step, the prospect very likely will raise that concern again.

You can confirm your answers simply by completing your answer with a statement such as, "That answers your concern, doesn't it, Bob?" If Bob agrees with you that your comment answered his concern, then you're one step closer to persuading him. If he isn't satisfied with your answer, now is the time to know — not later, when you try to get his final decision to go ahead.

Step #6: By the way . . .

By the way are three of the most useful words in any attempt to persuade or convince another person. You use the phrase to change gears — to move on to the next topic. For example:

By the way, what delivery date works best for you?

By the way, how would you like to receive your monthly statements, via email or at your postal address?

Don't just keep talking. Take a conscious, purposeful step back into your presentation. If it's appropriate, turn the page in your presentation binder or move on to the next slide or video. Point to something other than whatever generated the objection. Take some sort of action that signals to the other person that you're forging ahead.

The lady doth protest too much

If prospects bombard you with objections, you may want to ask a few questions to get them to express their *real* objection. If people protest too much, they're either not interested and don't have the guts to tell you so, or they're hiding the real reason they aren't going ahead. For some people, liking your offering but being unable to afford it is hard to admit. So instead of admitting that they can't afford it, they come up with a hundred other reasons why your product, service, or idea isn't right for them. Eventually, you may need to say something like this:

Mrs. Johnson, obviously you have quite a few concerns about our product. May I ask, what will you base your final decision on, the overall benefits to your family or the financial aspects of this transaction?

This way you're asking, as is your right, for the real objection to your product or service while still being nice, warm, and friendly (and the most common final objection is the money). *Remember:* You can't move beyond this step in the selling cycle until you identify and handle that real final objection.

Chapter 12

Closing Sales

· ·

· ·

Closing is the fun part of sales: the moment when you tie it all together; the moment when what your client needs and what you're selling become one. If you adopt this book's philosophy of selling, you come to know that, in effect, you work on closing the sale from the moment you first contact any potential client. That's just a given of the world of selling. But unless you hone your *instincts* for closing into finished *skills,* you're just winging it. And in this chapter, I help you hone to your heart's content, giving you specific strategies for closing sales. After you get past your own version of first-timer's jitters and you've done it a few times, I'm confident you'll agree that closing sales is downright fun.

Closing the sale starts at the beginning of the transaction, when you first make contact with your potential client. You close on meeting with you. You close for the date, time, and location of your meeting. You close on receiving information or other contact from you and so on. If you're weak on making original contact, on qualifying, on handling objections, on presentations, or on any other area of the sales process covered in Part III of this book, or if you're generally weak in asking pertinent questions, I don't care how great a salesperson you think you are, you're costing your prospect, yourself, and your company a lot of money, time, and aggravation. No one closes every sale, but just think how much better you can become when you put your best effort into it. A perfect ending needs a perfect beginning.

Knowing When to Go for the Close

The crucial question in any selling situation is, "When should you close the sale?" A certain electricity is in the air when the buyer is ready to go ahead. Here are some positive buying signs to watch for:

- **The buyer has been moving along at a smooth pace and suddenly slows the pace way down.** She's making her final analysis or rationalizing the decision.

- **She speeds up the pace.** She's excited to move ahead.

- **The prospect suddenly starts asking lots of questions.** Like anyone else, she asks questions only about things that interest her.

- **She asks questions about general terms of purchase before she settles on one particular model.** Some people immediately start asking questions about initial investment, delivery, and so on. They feel safe doing this because they know you can't sell them everything. But if they ask these questions after you know exactly what they want, it's a good sign.

If you notice any of these positive signs, test the waters. If you think that your prospect is ready to close the sale, ask a confirmation question to make sure you're reading her buying signs correctly: "Gwen, can you see yourself out on the lake in this boat enjoying the solitude of early morning fishing?" When you ask this question (from which you expect an answer confirming that the prospect wants to go ahead with the purchase), one of two things will happen:

- The prospect gives you a yes or an answer that indirectly confirms her desire to go ahead with the sale.

- The prospect gives you an objection or asks for more information to enable her to make a decision.

Don't start talking before she answers. You want to be sure to get either a confirmation to go ahead or an objection. If you get the former, you can go ahead with the close (see the next section for more about confirmation questions). If you get the latter, you need to answer the prospect's questions and address her concerns before attempting to close. (See Chapter 11 for more information on dealing with customer concerns.)

Recognizing That Sometimes All You Need to Do Is Ask

Salespeople are often uncomfortable if they have to go beyond putting their offering out there. If a prospect doesn't quickly see the value and jump right in to own it or to participate in some way, a salesperson may start to lose confidence. And this wavering of confidence weakens the salesperson's desire to close the sale. In other words, the salesperson doesn't ask for the order, call for a decision, or otherwise try to get a commitment from the buyer.

My company, Tom Hopkins International, Inc. conducted a survey and asked people who were not persuaded to buy why they didn't go ahead with whatever it was they were offered. Interestingly enough, the most common answer was that (drum roll, please) *they were never asked.* The prospects were contacted, a product or service was demonstrated to them, and their questions (or objections or concerns) were answered. In some cases, they were convinced of the value of the offering and probably would have gone ahead, but nothing happened — the salespeople didn't ask them to make a commitment or to part with their money, so they didn't.

When you ask your potential client for her business, what you're doing is using a question to confirm what the prospect has indicated that she wants. This type of question is called a *confirmation question.* In the following sections, I give you several ways to confirm your prospect's level of interest.

The bottom line with this most bottom of all lines in selling is this: If you want the sale, sooner or later you need to ask for it. Don't ever let the fact that you didn't ask someone to make a buying decision be the reason a potential buyer doesn't own your product or service.

Take your client's buying temperature with basic questions

One way to determine whether your prospective client is ready to make a decision involves basic *testing questions.* These questions come in a variety of styles, such as yes/no questions and open-ended questions. The style you choose to use depends on how you feel about each situation. With yes/no questions, you just test whether your prospective client is ready for the next step in the selling process. Use open-ended questions if you feel you need more information or clarification from the prospective client about what she's thinking at this point in the sale. With these types of questions, your goal is to get her to open up to you about her level of interest or what may still be nagging at her or holding her back. For example:

> Janice, do you see why we're so excited about what this new model is doing for our clients?

If Janice isn't excited, you still have more selling to do. Any hesitation on her part after you ask this question tells you that you've missed something. It may be wise to do a brief benefit summary of all the points Janice has agreed to up to this point to reaffirm her excitement. Pay close attention to her reaction to the benefits you mention. She may need further clarification on something. It'll show in her demeanor.

Here's another example of a "testing" question:

> Marta, tell me, how are you feeling about all of this so far?

Listen carefully not only to what Marta says but how she says it. You'll hear uncertainty in her answer as she tells you where she is currently standing about making a decision.

Ask assumptive questions

Sometimes salespeople wait so long to ask for the sale that the right time to ask passes them by. To get past this timing challenge, figure out how to take a prospect's buying temperature (see the earlier section "Knowing When to Go for the Close" for more about timing your close). You do this by asking a question like the following (this strategy is commonly referred to as the *trial close*):

> Not to assume too much, but if everything we've discussed here makes sense, how soon would you want to begin benefiting from your new software?

Soften this type of question by beginning with "Not to make assumptions, but ..." (If you were asking a personal question, you would start with, "Not to be personal, but ..." Sure you're being personal, but by stating it that way, you show respect for the prospect's privacy and give her an option not to answer if she's uncomfortable. You never want to purposely make a customer uncomfortable, but you will face selling situations in which you need to ask questions of a personal nature.) If the prospect answers such a question enthusiastically, in the affirmative, she's probably ready to go ahead. But if such a question brings up another concern or hesitation, then she's probably not ripe yet to make a commitment.

Give your client alternatives

The *alternate advance* involves giving your potential client two choices — but either one advances the sale. This way, no matter which option your buyer chooses, the sale moves forward because the buyer isn't given the option of saying no. Giving your buyer positive choices helps her focus better on what would be best for her — and that's what you really want, isn't it?

> SALESPERSON: Ms. Hall, which delivery date would be best for you the 8th or the 13th?
>
> MS. HALL: I'd need to have it in my warehouse by the 10th.

What happened in this exchange? As long as you can meet that delivery date, Ms. Hall owns it. If Ms. Hall is uncertain, she'll raise an objection here or try to change the subject.

Here's another example of the alternate advance:

> SALESPERSON: Joyce, will you be the one trained on the use of the new system or would you want someone else to be involved?

When Joyce tells you whom to train, you know that she's going ahead with the sale.

Jump to an erroneous conclusion

The *erroneous conclusion* is an intentional error you make to test how serious the prospect is about going ahead with the sale. If the prospect doesn't correct you, you may have missed some information along the way (perhaps during qualifying) that would have told you she wasn't serious. If she does correct you, her buying temperature is heating up. In this kind of test, all you want to do is take your prospect's buying temperature to see if it's warm enough to go ahead.

For example, a salesperson is selling home improvements to John and Cathy in their home, and during her demonstration Cathy tells John, "Honey, my mother is coming in July. If we decide what we want today, we need to have it finished by then." Many salespeople would ignore that remark or regard it as an interruption. But the champion salesperson hears that comment and remembers it. Later, when it comes time to close, the salesperson may smile at the wife and have the following exchange, using an erroneous conclusion:

> SALESPERSON: I can see that you're kind of excited about this addition. Now, your mother is coming in August, isn't she?

CATHY: No, in July.

SALESPERSON: So the first week in June would be the best time to get started?

CATHY: Yes.

SALESPERSON: Let me make a note of that.

The salesperson *knew* that Cathy's mother was coming in July, but she asked whether her mother was coming in August, because she knew Cathy would correct her if she were serious about getting the work done. Then, when Cathy offers the correct answer, the salesperson can segue right into the best time to begin with the home improvements, getting one step closer to that final close.

You can use the erroneous conclusion test close on almost anything. For example, Cathy may have said to John during the presentation, "I think I'd like a bay window on the south wall." Later, the salesperson can use that line for an erroneous conclusion test:

SALESPERSON: Let's see. You said you wanted the bay window on the east wall . . .

CATHY: No! I want it on the south wall.

SALESPERSON: Yes, that's right. Let me make a note of that.

The purpose of this method is not to tell a lie or trick the customer — I would never recommend that. It's simply a test for you to determine whether the prospect is sincere in moving ahead. After all, the prospect wouldn't correct you if she weren't interested. But if you're at all uncomfortable with this method, don't use it. A secondary warning here is not to use this method more than once in a sales presentation or your potential client may begin to doubt that you know what you're doing.

Toss them a porcupine

If I were holding a prickly porcupine right now and tossed it at you, what would you do? Instinctively, you would probably either jump out of its way or catch it and quickly toss it back, kind of like a game of hot potato. You can use a method of questioning called the *porcupine method* in much the same way. When your prospect asks you a question, you just ask another question about that question.

Here's an example of the porcupine method in action at a car dealership. A young woman is walking through a car lot looking at convertibles. Suddenly she stops, points at a car, and says, "This is the convertible I'm interested in. Do you have it in red?" The average salesperson would answer her by saying, "If we don't have it in red, I can call around and get one for you in a hurry." When a salesperson gives an answer like that, is she looking to help herself or the customer? She's looking to help herself by making a sale as soon as possible. Plus, the response the salesperson has given is a pushy statement.

Unlike the average salesperson, the champion salesperson answers the customer's question this way:

> SALESPERSON: Which shade of red do you prefer, Red-Hot Red or Cranberry Red?

How is the customer going to respond to the salesperson's question? She's already said that she's interested in the convertible and she wants it in red, so she'll most likely choose one color or the other, and the salesperson can note that on her paperwork. The salesperson is now one step closer to getting the customer's autograph on that dotted line and having her drive away happily in her new Red-Hot Red convertible.

The real power in selling is in pulling with questions, not being the stereotypical pushy sales person. Poor sales people talk and tell. Sales pros ask questions to draw information out of buyers — information that tells them the best solution to offer.

Using Closing Questions and Statements

Closing is where you make it all happen, where all your hard work pays off and you — and your client — reap the rewards. Unless what you're selling is the latest, greatest, everyone-has-to-have-it whatchamacallit, you're likely to hear the word *no* quite frequently. In fact, the average consumer says *no, nada,* or *pass* to a new product or service approximately five times before giving it serious consideration (by that I mean saying *yes*). If you, as a salesperson, know only one or two ways to ask for a buyer's business, you'll run out of closing material before she runs out of no-sale material. In the following sections, I describe several statements you can use to close a sale effectively.

Always have something handy to capture important notes — and always let the prospect stop you from writing your notes. Letting your prospect stop you doesn't hurt — it helps. Your desire to take good notes shows the prospect that you're a professional salesperson who knows how to get things done. When she stops you, she's telling you that you need to keep selling.

The basic oral close

When you're talking with your prospects in person, you have the perfect opportunity to close the sale through your conversation. Here's an example of a simple closing statement using the alternate choice questioning strategy:

> Chester, Mary, I'm excited for you to have all new kitchen appliances at one time. Would you prefer to finance the purchase or use a credit card?

If you know everything is right and that all the cards are on the table, go ahead and ask for the order. Don't keep selling — that's one of the biggest mistakes novice salespeople make. They don't always recognize when they can close; they simply continue to talk, re-demonstrate the product, or even change the subject while searching for a reason to remain in the company of their prospects.

The basic written close

If you use order forms in your selling, this closing method works especially well: Walk into the meeting with your buyers with a leather binder. Have an order form under a cardboard protector. That way, you can flip to it instantly when the time is right. Here's how the situation may play out:

> PROSPECT: Does it come in blonde wood?
>
> SALESPERSON: Is blonde the best color accent for your furniture?
>
> PROSPECT: Yes. I think that would look fantastic.
>
> SALESPERSON: Let me make a note of that.

Then you write down the prospect's preference on the order form. Be careful, though. Some people panic when they see you filling out a form:

> PROSPECT: What are you doing? I haven't agreed to anything yet.
>
> SALESPERSON: Mary, I like to organize my thoughts to keep everything in order. I do that on the paperwork so I don't forget anything — especially anything that may save you time or money.

Keep filling out that order form. By the time you finish your conversation, the form will be almost completely filled out. In most cases, the forward momentum you develop while completing the form is enough to get it approved. If the buyer gets used to seeing you write on the order form, you're almost home.

The reflex question

Go into every closing sequence by asking a *reflex question* — a question your prospect can answer without thinking. The purpose of the reflex question is to create even more forward momentum toward the closed sale. By this point in the selling cycle, you should have earned the right to use your prospect's first name, but if you're not sure if you've earned that right, you probably haven't. **Remember:** Never jump into the familiarity of using that first name unless you're certain it's okay.

If you have a prospect's first name and your paperwork requires a middle name or initial, you can ask a reflex question like this to get a reflex response:

SALESPERSON: Marcy, do you have a middle initial?

PROSPECT: It's K.

And you're back to completing the paperwork in greater detail.

If you're dealing with a corporate executive, a good reflex question is to ask for the company's complete name and address. If the executive hands you her card and lets you copy all the information, you get to move ahead. Congratulations!

Other reflex questions may be to verify today's date or a required delivery date ... anything that goes on the paperwork. If the client has already made up her mind to purchase, she'll rattle off these answers for you. If the client has any hesitation, these questions should trigger her to stop the forward momentum and ask more questions.

When the paperwork is ready, you scan it for accuracy, turn it to the clients with pen in hand, and say:

> Chester and Mary, you seem very excited about this new suite of furniture. With your approval right here, it will be my pleasure to welcome you to our family of happy clients.

The sharp angle close

In some situations, your buyer will, in essence, throw down the gauntlet and challenge you to give her exactly what she wants. The key here is to accept the challenge — but with the understanding that if you can come through, you win by getting the sale, and she wins by owning the product or service just the way she wants it. This method is referred to as *sharp angling* your prospect into ownership. I go over the basics and the timing of this method in the following sections.

The basics of the sharp angle close

To use the sharp angle method, your prospect must first express a demand or desire that you can meet. For you to use your prospect's own demand as your way to get to yes, always remember that sharp angling involves two pivotal points:

✔ You must know what benefits you can deliver.

✔ You must know when the delivery can be made.

For example, your prospect may ask you an assumptive question of her own, a question that assumes that she will buy your product or service. What should you do in response? Answer with a question that shows that, in her own mind, she has bought your product or service:

> MS. STEWART: If I decide I want this boat, can you handle delivery by Memorial Day?

> SALESPERSON: If I can guarantee delivery by Memorial Day, I bet you can guarantee me that you'll be prepared to have a great time enjoying the holiday on your new boat, can't you?

The salesperson is still guiding her prospect, Ms. Stewart, toward what she wants to do: Buy a boat.

> MS. STEWART: I'd want delivery no later than May 15. Can you handle that?

The average salesperson would be tempted to jump in and say yes, whether or not she could "handle that." Pay close attention to how a champion salesperson takes advantage of this same opportunity:

> SALESPERSON: If I can guarantee delivery by May 15, are you prepared to approve the paperwork today?

Or, if the salesperson really doesn't know if she can make delivery on that date, she may want to respond this way:

> SALESPERSON: If, in checking with my company, I can guarantee delivery by May 15, are you prepared to approve the paperwork today?

Then you remain silent until Ms. Stewart answers. Remaining silent is the key here. The first person to speak owns the product. It will either be you keeping the product in inventory or Ms. Stewart keeping the product at her home or business. So unless you need to keep inventory up rather than making sales, keep your lips sealed.

The timing of the sharp angle close

Be aware that sharp angling can be hazardous to your selling health: A dangerous part of the sharp angle is that you may be tempted to apply it before you've gathered enough qualification information or before you've built enough rapport. I recommend that you do *not* use the sharp angle too early in the selling process. If you sharp angle too soon, you may offend some people, because the method may not come across smoothly and can be interpreted as overly aggressive. But once the prospect's thinking and the rapport you have with her are in good shape, the sharp angle is a wonderful way to get agreement.

The following over-simplified exchange shows you how to time your use of the sharp angle:

> PROSPECT: Can you get it for me in red?
>
> SALESPERSON: Are you ready to go ahead today if I can?
>
> PROSPECT: Yes.
>
> Or:
>
> PROSPECT: I may be, but first I need a lot more information.

Before you ask, "Will you go ahead if I can?" you must be absolutely sure that you can deliver your product. Saying you can deliver the product won't do much good if you can't. Overselling and overpromising are the two worst enemies of a professional salesperson. Always be honest, and your reputation will bring you more business.

One of the reasons trained salespeople outsell average salespeople is that the professionals know more about their products and what their companies can deliver. How do you get this information? The answer depends on your product, the company, and your attitude. Salespeople often make enemies in production departments and on shipping docks by promising clients things the company can't deliver. When the client gets angry over a missed delivery date, the production department or the shipping dock usually takes the blame. Know what your company can deliver. And always thank the people in your company who help you get your job done, especially if fulfillment requires extra effort on their part in order for you to keep your sale.

The higher authority close

Every happy client is a potential higher authority for another potential client. This closing method keeps that fact in mind and is very effective if you know it thoroughly and set it up correctly. No matter what your product or service is, all you need to do is adapt the wording to your own style of selling.

The *higher authority* must be exactly that — someone who is respected by and known to the prospect. The prospect doesn't have to know the higher authority personally, but she must know of the higher authority's existence and position. If you sell industrial equipment, you want a prominent decision maker at a well-known company; if you sell advertising, you want a high-profile businessperson. The following sections describe the steps for using this close successfully.

Don't settle for just one higher authority — you can wear out any one person when you rely on her too much. When you do your job with the utmost professionalism, most clients are happy to help you out. It's an ego boost for them to be considered a higher authority.

Select your higher authority figure

You should constantly be on the lookout for higher authority figures. For example, imagine that you're the sales-record smasher for BuiltGreat Computer Systems. A prominent businessperson in the area invested in a computer system for her company, Steel Plastics, Inc., and she's very pleased with the system's performance and increased productivity. This businessperson, Katharine Steel, is an ideal higher authority figure for anyone interested in your computers.

Recruit your higher authority figure

On one of your visits to Steel Plastics, Inc., after they have had plenty of time to know the system inside and out, ask Katharine Steel if she'd be willing to share her knowledge of your product with other businesspeople. Katharine agrees because you've done a solid sales and service job for her on a good product, and you've assured her that you'll call only when you need help with an occasional prospect who may be in a similar situation. In other words, you promise not to bother her if you're working on selling a two-computer system to a small business.

Remember to give Ms. Steel a small gift of appreciation proportionally appropriate to the size of the sale. If she helped you close a $500 sale, a gift card to a nice restaurant may be appropriate. If the sale was $50,000, a gift card to a spa day may be more in line. You're the one who knows Ms. Steel's likes and dislikes. Be aware that in some industries and with some companies, it may be inappropriate for their people to accept such gifts. Choose appropriately.

Schedule your higher authority figure for the sales situation

You're out to update the computer system at Triple A Advertising with your newest system. George Phillips is the decision maker there. While planning your appointment with George, you decide that you may need the higher authority figure confirmation, so you call Katharine Steel to determine if she'll be available to take a phone call while you're with George Phillips. With Katharine's cooperation, you complete your plans for a powerful presentation to George at Triple A.

Use the higher authority figure confirmation effectively

You know that George will have concerns about your system similar to those that Katharine had. (Will the software that makes your systems superior be the right one to increase productivity for Triple A? Is your service department as good as you say it is?) And in planning your presentation, you know that George will have specific technical questions. The primary purpose of your interview with George Phillips is to isolate the specific technical and other reservations he has about your equipment and company. After you clarify these questions for him, and after you agree that these are all reasons why he questions the idea of installing your system now, you're ready to bring in a higher authority — Katharine Steel.

Be sure to make the list of George's reservations specific, and to get George's agreement that these are all the reservations he has. Write them out on a piece of paper. After you clarify and write down the causes of George's reservations, you're ready to appeal to a higher authority:

> YOU: Do you know Katharine Steel of Steel Plastics, Inc.?
>
> GEORGE: No, but I know of the company.
>
> YOU: Katharine is the owner, and she's a client of mine. George, so I can relieve your mind of some of the questions you may have about the system or our services, would you be offended if we called Katharine and asked her your questions? You see, she had the same concerns you did before she invested in our system.

When Katharine is on the phone, tell her, "I'm here at Triple A Advertising with George Phillips, and he has some questions about BuiltGreat." Then hand the phone to George and let him take it from there. He has the list of questions in front of him, so he'll miss none of his objections when he talks to Katharine.

Close after the call

After Katharine Steel has discussed the technicalities and reassured George that the BuiltGreat computers are performing well in her office, George's objections have vanished. When the phone call ends, you're in a position to smile and ask, "By the way, which delivery date is most convenient for you: the 1st or the 10th?"

If something keeps Katharine from taking George's call, even though you set it up with her in advance, you may not be able to close the sale that day.

Try to set up a specific time to contact her again, when you can be present with George, or try to arrange a conference call among the three of you.

Take a copy of George's objections and hot buttons with you to the re-contact meeting so that, at the start of the re-contact, you can get back to where you left off. Remember to do a brief recap with George before you get Katharine on the line.

Some salespeople turn away from the higher authority confirmation because they think that all competitors hate each other and won't cooperate. But in general, most people at competing companies are friendly with each other. If you happen to run into a case of bad blood between competitors, simply back off.

Overcoming Your Client's Stalls and Fears

When you're closing sales, you may come across situations in which closing isn't quite as simple as the example I provide in the previous section — situations in which your prospects stall or hide behind a wall of fear. So in the following sections, I show you exactly how you can help the potential client work through that stall so she has no more objections or concerns . . . and you can close the sale.

Empathy is understanding another person's feelings, thoughts, and motives — and it's extremely important in the world of selling. When you have empathy for your prospect, you put yourself in her shoes. You know and feel what your prospect is feeling — which means you know exactly how to proceed based on the information the prospect has given you. Until you develop empathy for your customers, you probably won't make it in selling. Your prospects need to sense that you understand and care about helping them solve their problems, not think that you're just out looking for a sale. As a professional salesperson, you must truly believe that you can satisfy the prospect's needs. You must see the benefits, features, and limitations of your product or service from your prospect's view; you must weigh things on the prospect's scale of values, not your own; and you must realize what is important to the prospect. Your prospect must always be the star of the show.

Taking a lesson from Benjamin Franklin

This decision-making strategy — in which you make a list of the positives and negatives surrounding a choice — was developed by the great Benjamin Franklin, and millions of people have used it successfully for years. Everyone can understand its effectiveness because it's so simple, basic, and easy to understand that it rarely fails to get the point across.

Here's an example of a situation in which a salesperson may want to use this approach with Kevin and Karen Smith in a real estate office:

> SALESPERSON: Do you think that the home on Third Street may be the best decision for your family?
>
> KEVIN: [hesitant, noncommittal] Well, you know that a home is a pretty big investment. I don't know that I'm ready to make a decision on this right now.

The salesperson has asked a lot of questions up to this point, and now she's ready to put the answers to work for her in order to close the sale. She can see that Kevin and Karen really don't want to make the final decision. They're impressed with the home, they need to get the family moved quickly, and the numbers work out. But they're trying to avoid committing to the home. In other words, they are behaving like typical buyers — fearful of finally making a decision. This is a perfect opportunity for the Benjamin Franklin decision-making process that I describe in the following sections.

Starting the process

You begin this strategy by relieving any pressure that your clients may be feeling. Relax your posture and slow things down. Then, you open their minds to using this strategy to help them see things more clearly:

> SALESPERSON [calm, determined to help Kevin and Karen to make the decision they want to make, to help them make the best decision for them]: Could it possibly be, Karen and Kevin, that the problem is that you haven't had a chance to weigh the facts involved?
>
> KEVIN [nodding, open to reason]: Yeah, I don't think we've really gotten to the heart of this thing yet.
>
> SALESPERSON: Well, a decision is only as good as the facts on which it's based, don't you agree?
>
> KAREN: [seeing the wisdom of the salesperson's reasoning] I think that's probably true.
>
> SALESPERSON [reflective and sincere]: You know, it's interesting. A while back I was reminded of a man we Americans have long considered one of

our wisest men — Benjamin Franklin. What Ben used to do when he was uncertain about making a decision was to take a sheet of paper and draw a line right down the middle. On one side of the page he would write all the reasons in favor of the decision, and on the other he would write all the reasons against the decision. Then he would simply add up the reasons on each side and see which decision was the best. It's a funny thing. One day I decided to try Ben's system, not only in my professional life, but in my personal life as well. Pretty soon, my whole family was using it to make all kinds of decisions. Would it be okay with you if we tried it now just to get a feel for the facts of your decision?

The important thing here is to keep going with the flow of the conversation. After you master this strategy, you'll know how to weave this story into any conversation.

SALESPERSON: Ben Franklin said that if a decision was the right thing to do, he wanted to be sure to go ahead with it. If it was wrong, he wanted to be sure to avoid it. So why don't we analyze the decision and "get down to the heart of it," as you put it?

KEVIN AND KAREN: [as one voice] Okay, yeah, let's do that.

SALESPERSON: Great. So the reasons *for* the decision go on one side, and all those *against* the decision go on the other side. Then you can add up the columns, and the right decision should be clear. We have time, don't we? It'll take us just a couple of minutes.

KEVIN: Yeah, okay.

Listing the pros

The salesperson has a long list of things Kevin and Karen like about the home because she's made notes on every positive comment they've made since they drove into the neighborhood. If Kevin and Karen run out of positives off the tops of their heads, the salesperson can remind them of those on her list.

When you make note of each item, do it with a check mark. But don't write down their actual reasons. You're just tracking how many there are now. If you start writing each one out, this strategy takes longer, and the prospects start weighing each reason against the others.

SALESPERSON [waits a beat for Kevin's agreement, then draws a line down the center of the page she holds in front of her]: Okay, let's start it off here. Let's think of the reasons favoring the decision. You agree that the home has all the features you were looking for, isn't that right?

KAREN: Yes, it does.

SALESPERSON: And we've already established that, with the right financing, you can actually have a smaller monthly investment than what you have on the home you're in now.

KEVIN AND KAREN [as one voice]: Right.

SALESPERSON: You said you wanted to be close to the elementary school, and this home is just three blocks away. That's certainly a plus, don't you think?

KEVIN AND KAREN [as one voice]: Absolutely.

SALESPERSON: Let's go on. You thought the professional landscaping in the backyard was impressive.

KAREN [looking at the salesperson, but seeing the future]: Yeah, the kids would have a lot of fun in that yard.

SALESPERSON: Wouldn't they? Let's write that down. And what about the outside of the home? When we first pulled up, Karen, remember how you got so excited?

KAREN: It really is a beautiful home.

SALESPERSON [counting the positives]: Let's see; that's five. Can you think of any others?

KEVIN: Well, we really liked the extras in the kitchen.

SALESPERSON: All right. We'll put that down.

KEVIN: I like all the big trees on the property.

SALESPERSON: Okay. We'll put that down, too.

KAREN: Oh! We both liked the sunken bathtub in the master bedroom.

SALESPERSON: Great. Is there anything else you can think of?

Set a goal for between six and ten items on the plus side. If you haven't reached at least six at this point, refer to your notes and remind your prospects of other items to add to this column.

Noting the cons and adding the totals

After your goal of six reasons *for* the decision has been reached, continue:

SALESPERSON [objective, fair]: Now, how many reasons can you come up with on the negative side?

KEVIN [with a heavy sigh]: Well, let's see. The down payment is a concern. It's almost all we've saved.

SALESPERSON: Okay, what else?

KEVIN: We were really interested in finding a home that had solar heating.

SALESPERSON: Those are both valid points, Kevin. Can you come up with any others?

After a pause, it's obvious that Karen and Kevin aren't coming up with any more concerns. They've just told the salesperson, bottom line, exactly what will keep them from owning this particular home. She doesn't even have to answer those objections at this point, because what she's looking for is a clear desire on the part of Kevin and Karen to own this particular property. When that decision is made, she'll work on the financial details of how they can own this home, so she says:

SALESPERSON: All right. Why don't we just add these up?

She shows them the list, and together they count aloud. Afterward, she announces the results: ten yeas, two nays.

SALESPERSON: Karen, Kevin, don't you think the answer is rather obvious?

Expect to wait through a long silence after you pose this question. The key here is to shut your mouth and not do or say anything that takes away from your request for a decision. Your prospects will do one of three things:

- ✔ They will try to stall, put off making the decision by asking for more time or asking a question to change the subject.
- ✔ They will decide to go ahead.
- ✔ They will give you an objection.

In this situation, a silence pervades the room for some time while Kevin and Karen think this over. Finally, Kevin replies with a stall:

KEVIN: I'll tell you something. We're the kind of people who really need to think it over.

When you're faced with a stall like this, consider using the story in the next section to move past it.

Getting past a vague stall to a concrete final objection

So how do you handle a situation in which the prospect absolutely insists on thinking it over? Continuing the story from the preceding section, where Kevin and Karen are thinking about investing in a home, here's how the salesperson proceeds:

> SALESPERSON: That's fine, Kevin. Obviously, you wouldn't take the time to think it over unless you were seriously interested, would you?
>
> KEVIN [reassuring, but committed to the stall]: Oh, we're interested. We just really need to think about this before we decide.
>
> SALESPERSON: Because you're interested, may I assume that you will give it very careful consideration?
>
> KAREN: Of course we will.
>
> SALESPERSON: You're not telling me this just to get rid of me, are you?
>
> KEVIN [polite, but committed to the stall]: No. I'm not trying to get rid of you. We like the house, but we have to think it over.
>
> SALESPERSON [trying to keep communication open]: Just to clarify my thinking, what is it about the house that you want to think over? Is it the value of the home? The neighborhood?

Ask about the benefits of the home that you know your prospects liked. Every time they say no, they're that much closer to yes, aren't they? Kevin and Karen have answered no to every benefit, so what do they want to think over? In most cases, the decision comes down to money. Either the home is too expensive, they won't be comfortable with the large initial investment, or they may be worried about their credit and getting qualified for the loan.

> SALESPERSON: Well, could it be the financing or even the initial investment that you want to think over?
>
> KAREN [as though offered a life raft]: Yes. We may have another baby, and I'm not sure if we should make a financial commitment like this right now.

Now the salesperson has a concrete idea of what specifically is the hurdle between her and the close. This is how all selling situations should be handled: in a relaxed, friendly, gentle, and professional manner. It's not only what you say but how you say it that creates a successful sales environment.

Sometimes even the warmest presentation, delivered with genuine care for the customer's needs, can be met with "We're the kind of people who really need to think it over." And always remember that the "I want to think it over" line is a stall. You use it yourself when you're on the customer side of a selling situation, so why shouldn't you expect to hear it from others when you're on the persuading side of things?

Responding to "It costs too much"

When you isolate a money objection as the obstacle to final agreement, one particular technique is ideal: You and the client can see the big dollars they're afraid of in much smaller, easier-to-handle numbers.

To show you this technique at work, here are Karen and Kevin in the real estate office again:

> KAREN: I just feel that this home costs too much.
>
> SALESPERSON [ever in search of specific obstacles to "yes"]: Today, most things seem to. Can you tell me about how much "too much" you feel it is?

Salespeople tend to look at the total investment when they hear "It costs too much," but this tendency usually spells trouble. Instead of addressing the total cost, go for the *difference* between what the amount is and what your buyer expected to pay. If your prospect plans to spend $20,000 for a car, and the car she's looking at is $22,000, the problem isn't $22,000, it's $2,000.

Going back to our real estate example:

> KAREN: We really wanted to spend around $190,000, and I don't feel that we can go as high as $215,000.
>
> SALESPERSON: So, Karen and Kevin, what we're really talking about is $25,000, aren't we?
>
> KEVIN: $25,000. Right. That's exactly what I'm concerned about.

Now the salesperson has gotten Kevin and Karen to admit that the real problem they're having is over $25,000. And she's ready to move to the story in the following section, where she shows them just how little money that really is.

Reducing an expense to the ridiculous

When you know exactly what amount of money your prospects are concerned about, you can work with them to help them see how they can handle the amount and have what they really want — the product or service — at the same time. Start by handing them your calculator. Giving them a calculator is a good way to get them involved as you work out the finances. Here are Kevin and Karen again, in the real estate office:

> SALESPERSON: [asking what Karen already knows] Karen, do you think it would be safe to assume that this would be your dream home and you could be happy here for a long time, assuming everything else was right?
>
> KAREN: Probably. I think it would be a great place to raise the kids.
>
> SALESPERSON: Okay, so let's just say that you're going to live in this beautiful home for 20 years. Would you say that's about right?
>
> KEVIN AND KAREN: Twenty years … yeah, that'd be about right.
>
> SALESPERSON: Let's divide that $25,000 by 20 years, okay? We get $1,250 per year, don't we?
>
> KEVIN: Yes.
>
> SALESPERSON: And would you say that you would actually be in the home 50 weeks a year, allowing for 2 weeks of vacation each year, of course?
>
> KEVIN: That sounds about right.
>
> SALESPERSON: Dividing our $1,250 per year by 50 weeks. That makes the difference in the investment $25 per week. So now we have 7 days in each of those weeks, and when we divide $25 by 7, what do we get?
>
> KAREN: [catching an early glimpse of the ridiculous] $3.57.

The salesperson has gotten Kevin and Karen to see that they're really upset over just $3.57 cents per day. Pretty ridiculous, isn't it?

Making the indirect comparison

When you make an indirect comparison, you help your prospects rationalize having the product, service, or idea you're offering simply by sacrificing, for now, some small luxury that they would certainly give up in order to have a much larger gain. Here's how the salesperson in the previous example uses this strategy with Kevin and Karen:

> SALESPERSON [giving them something to compare it to]: Kevin, do you and your family drink much soda?

> KEVIN: Sure. You know how kids are. We probably go through at least one six-pack a day.
>
> SALESPERSON: How much are sodas these days?
>
> KAREN: Around $4 a six-pack.
>
> SALESPERSON: Karen, Kevin, wouldn't you agree that the benefits and the enjoyment you will get out of this wonderful home are worth $3.57 a day? Do you think that we should let $3.57 stand in the way of all the family memories you will make there, for less than it costs your family to have soda every day?
>
> KEVIN: When you look at it that way, I guess it doesn't seem to be such a significant amount.
>
> SALESPERSON: Then we've agreed, haven't we? Now, let's get to work to get you out of your existing house and into this *beautiful home* by the *holidays* so you and your family can begin *building memories* right away. By the way, would the 10th or the 12th be the better closing date for both of you?

Notice the *italicized* words. These keywords create pleasant pictures in the prospects' minds. For the sake of this example, assume that Kevin and Karen said they wanted to be in the home by November 1. That gives the salesperson the license to address the upcoming holidays, a time of year that almost always creates warm feelings in buyers.

Citing a similar situation

What better way to ease your prospects' fears than a story of another couple who had all the same concerns and indecisions, but who still decided to buy and now are glad they did? Here's an example of a story you can relate to your clients, based on their fears and hesitations:

> Marcus, Beth, I know you're hesitant about the financial commitment of buying a home when you have your first baby on the way. You know, I had another family looking for the perfect home just about a year ago. We searched and searched, and they just couldn't decide on a home.
>
> One day we looked at a beautiful home, and they got very excited about it. I asked them if they thought that this was the home for them, and they agreed that it was a great house. I also asked if they wanted to begin the process of owning that great home. Bob thought we should go ahead, but Jill was afraid that the home might be a bit larger than they really needed. She thought they could get by in a smaller home, and she wasn't sure that she wanted to move before their baby came.

Well, they decided to go ahead and were amazed at how much space the baby things took up. After they moved in, Bob and Jill were so glad that they decided to invest in the bigger home when they did.

Now, you'd like to be all settled in at your new home before your baby comes, wouldn't you?

Make notes about the stories you have to tell about your other satisfied clients, and then use these stories when new prospects experience the same situation, as inevitably happens.

Noting a competitive edge

If you're faced with a prospect who just doesn't want to make a decision about your product, service, or idea, you can tell a competitive-edge story to help her along. These stories don't need to be elaborate, and they're not meant to talk your prospects into anything they don't want or need. The stories just remind prospects (mainly ones who are in business, as opposed to individuals) that they have competitors. So if you're not telling them anything they don't already know, what's the appeal in competitive edge stories? In a word, *survival*.

Use a calculator when you crunch numbers

Champion salespeople always do their selling math with a calculator. No matter how confident you are in your mathematical abilities, always use a calculator. Know your formulas and figures so that you can quickly provide any numerical information that your potential client may request.

A prospective client who sees you punch numbers into your calculator — or one who runs the figures herself — probably won't question the figures. But if you start furiously scratching numbers on paper with a pencil, the prospect gets uncomfortable sitting and watching you. Even worse, if you rattle figures off the top of your head, your prospect may doubt you. Instead of paying attention to your presentation, she'll be looking over your shoulder to double-check your math.

Not using a calculator raises doubts about your mathematical abilities. Plus, your prospect may wonder, "If she's this careless with figures, where else will she be careless?" You don't want to do anything at this stage of the relationship to make your prospect start wondering if she should be working with you at all. You want her entirely focused on the math at hand as you show her how she really can afford the product she wants so badly.

A little competitive-edge story like this, for example, works well:

> Ms. Ramirez, remember that many of your competitors are facing the same challenges today that you are. Isn't it interesting that, when an entire industry is fighting the same forces, some companies do a better job of meeting those challenges than others? My entire objective here today has been to help provide you with a competitive edge. Gaining a competitive edge, no matter how large or small, makes good business sense, doesn't it?

Prospects are all alike in one regard: They need help making decisions. Think about it. How many things have you been talked into owning that you really didn't want? Probably not very many. Few people get talked into buying something they don't really want. If it's a major purchase, you usually have a hard time selling your prospects on it even if they *do* want it.

Problems arise when unscrupulous salespeople lie about what a product is and what it will do. Through deceit, these salespeople violate the buyer's trust and the buyer ends up owning something other than what she thought she was getting. The jails are full of salespeople who have done things like this. They let greed get in the way of their service to customers. Such an approach to selling is the direct opposite of the kind of selling I advocate. If you put customer service ahead of money, you will *always* come out on top.

Is closing good for your customer?

Are closing questions, assumptive statements, and sales-time stories in the best interest of your customers? Based on my experience, the answer is an unequivocal "yes." I've done a lot of selling, and I always take my customers' interests to heart. I know that they'll get the truth from me, as well as great service. But I can't guarantee them truth in selling and excellent service if they go someplace else.

All along, from my early days in selling to today, I've tried to help every consumer have a positive image of the sales industry. I knew that positive image would be there if I gave my customers professional service, and I've always been one to provide it. That's why I worked harder than many of my associates to consummate sales that I knew were in the best interest of my customers. This obviously would not include selling them anything they didn't want. However, if all things were right, I would do everything I could to help my customers get over the hills of fear and procrastination. I felt it was my obligation.

Remember: If you properly qualify people (as I describe in Chapter 9), you know whether they truly have a need or desire for your product or service. If their lives will be better because they own your offering, you should do your best to persuade them into having it.

Think about it: Drawing on your own experience, have you appreciated the professionals who have helped you make buying decisions? Have you been happy enough to recommend those people to others? Of course you have! We all have. To become a champion salesperson, you should set a goal to become someone people will not hesitate to recommend. Become someone people seek out as an expert in your field. And then everyone — you and your customers — wins.

Chapter 13

Getting Referrals from Your Satisfied Clients

For many seasoned salespeople, referrals are a major source of new business. Clients who come to you from an existing client's recommendation are usually more inclined than cold-call clients to want to own your product, service, or idea. Why? Because they already have positive feelings about you and your offering — and the source of their positive feelings is someone they already know and trust. This is what we refer to as a *prequalified* lead. Prequalified, referred leads are usually slam dunks: The prospective client is already sold on you because the person who referred you to him thinks you're a true pro. So with referrals, you enjoy tremendous credibility right from the start.

In fact, when it comes to qualified referrals, studies show a 60 percent closing rate. Compare that impressive figure to a closing rate of 10 percent with non-qualified non-referrals, and you can see just how much harder you have to work on cold calls. Don't get left out in the cold. When you can figure out how to be successful at getting referral business, leaving all those choice clients for your competitors to pick up just doesn't make sense.

Salespeople universally agree that referrals are easier to convince than non-referrals. But some salespeople think getting referral business is next to impossible, so they refuse to give referral methods much attention. Such salespeople take the attitude that attaining referrals is just a haphazard, sometimes-it-happens-and-sometimes-it-doesn't way to prospect. Don't buy into such thinking for a second. Professional salespeople consistently benefit from referral business — so consistently, in fact, that they shoot holes in this theory every day.

Effective ways to benefit from referral business are what this chapter is all about. Here I provide you with a proven, highly effective referral system that can help you produce a much greater number of referred, qualified leads. The system may not work 100 percent of the time, but even if it works only 50 percent of the time, it will generate many more selling situations with clients who look forward to finding out about you and your offering than what you're getting now.

Never take a referral for granted. As with any other sales technique, method is not the only factor to consider when you try to get referrals. You must show referrals the same positive attitude, the same high energy level, the same respectful manner, and the same quality presentation that you show to cold calls. Referrals are only *partially* sold on you or your product. The important thing is that they're willing to give you the chance to convince them of how they'll benefit from your offering.

If you're successful at convincing them, referrals will just keep on coming. Before you know it, you'll create an endless chain of happily involved clients who are more than willing to contribute to your success. Happy clients love to think that they're partially responsible for your success, and encouraging their continued participation and interest in promoting your career certainly doesn't hurt.

Remember, when you make a referred client happy, you've impressed two people — the referral, and the person who did the referring. All this happiness converts to even more leads for you because you did the job right.

Understanding Where, How, and When Referrals Arise

With qualified referrals providing you a closing ratio of a whopping 60 percent on average, you can't afford not to know how to identify and obtain such a substantial increase in your sales potential. That's why it's surprising so many people take part in referral-building activities without recognizing — and taking advantage of — the opportunities. If only they had read a good overview that would help them recognize referrals when they see them — an overview just like the one you're on the verge of reading right now, for example.

What if getting referrals isn't all that important to your particular selling situation? Rather than seeking them out for yourself, consider garnering leads for your clients or other members of your team if you have one. Becoming a source of referrals for others increases your value to all those you work with and eventually result in sales that translate into increased income. One way or the other, then, whether as a source of prospects for your own business or as general public relations, referrals play a key part in your success in sales.

Figuring out where to get referrals

Referrals are like flies: They're always buzzing around you. But unless they land in your soup, you don't always notice them. The key to success in getting referrals is to become like flypaper and catch all referrals that fly by. The following sections describe several great sources of referrals.

From family and friends

Perhaps the easiest and most accessible referrals are those that your family and friends can give you. If you're of the mindset that you don't want to "burden" those close to you by asking for their help, you'd better rethink just what it is you're selling. After all, if you really believe in your product, service, or idea, don't you want the people closest to you to enjoy its benefits, too? By assuming that your offering will burden others, you may be cheating them out of all the enjoyment that it can give them.

Why not keep Grandma in the loop about what you're doing? She may not be an ideal candidate for your product, but she certainly may know others who are. Besides that, Grandma is likely to keep her loving grandchild in mind as she goes about her daily routine. If you're lucky, she'll become a downright excellent qualified lead collector. Spread the word to other family members, close friends, and acquaintances (as I describe in Chapter 7), and you'll be racking up referral business in no time.

Through networking

Networking at business conferences, clubs, professional organizations, and religious gatherings is a way to increase your number of referrals. But the gatherings don't have to be formal affairs. Getting referrals can be as simple as mentioning to others what you do or something exciting that has happened during your busy week of selling. When you're excited, other people will be, too. People are attracted to energetic conversation and happy dispositions — so be a people magnet.

If you're having a particularly great week, share it with the world. Let them enjoy the positive vibe created by your success! Don't brag. Just allow yourself to be exuberant about your accomplishments. Exuberance is contagious. If your week has been particularly trying or difficult, on the other hand, consider asking for the advice of the people you respect. Most people are generally kind and helpful. In order for them to help you, you'll have to have the opportunity to tell them your story. Of course, your story involves your product offering. You can use this as a way of getting others interested in what you are selling, too. The next time they see you, they'll want to hear your appreciation of the positive effects their advice had for you.

So what have you done? Through your willingness to share your concerns and victories, you have involved others in your career: Other people now have a vested interest in your future success.

From happy customers

Make sure that your products and service are beyond reproach, because negative news spreads like fire through dry country meadows. Slip up just once, even just a little bit, and the once comfortable visits with your clients and their associates become awkward — maybe so much so that you avoid old clients altogether.

For example, avoid promising the moon and the stars within a two-day delivery period unless you can also wave a magic wand and make it happen. It's so easy to get carried away and tell your client what he wants to hear even when you know your information is inaccurate. In the long run, not only will you lose the disillusioned client, but you can also kiss goodbye all the wonderful referral opportunities he could have steered your way.

Satisfied clients tell at least three people about their experience with you. Dissatisfied clients tell at least 11 people. Negative stories generate more sympathy than positive stories do. So don't allow the flames of discontent to spread far when a challenge arises. If a poor reputation precedes you, you'll have to work harder to get the first sale (if you even get a real opportunity to do so) and prove your value before asking for referrals. Honesty and integrity must be first and foremost in your mind if you intend to succeed in business and in life.

If you leave your customer's office with a sale but no referrals, you have unfinished business to attend to — kind of like having a great dinner, but leaving before dessert. It's never too late to get referrals, but when you leave empty-handed, you also deprive your clients of an opportunity to do good or to brag. It's true! What's the first thing you want to do when you shop non-stop for days and then eventually, finally, find a great bargain? You want to tell people about it! What's the first thing you want to do when you own a beautiful new car? Show people! What's the first thing you want to do when someone comments on what a terrific new whatchamacallit you have? Let him know where he can get one just like it for a great price! Don't cheat your happy clients out of all their fun by not giving them the referral tools they need to help others help you.

From other salespeople in your field

Thinking of other salespeople in the same or related fields as your enemies is neither necessary nor productive. Believe it or not, thinking of them as a possible source for referral business is much more profitable. For instance, if you are in the healthcare field and you meet a sales representative who is extremely successful selling surgical equipment and you're selling diagnostic equipment, that sales person may be able to provide referrals or at least be willing to swap referrals with you.

If your relationship with other salespeople is based on mutual respect, you'll find other salespeople sending clients your way whether you have a formal arrangement to do so or not. Perhaps another salesperson's company is smaller than yours and unequipped to handle clients beyond such-and-such magnitude. Bingo! He sends the Big Clients to you. Or maybe a contact insists on having a feature that your competitor's product doesn't have — and another prospective client trundles down the turnpike headed right your way.

Of course, returning the favor is only common courtesy. It's not unusual for salespeople at car dealerships or insurance agencies to recommend another salesperson who is better suited to meet a particular customer's needs. Professionals who have the needs of the client at heart and know they would do the client a disservice by handling those needs ineffectively work this way. They also know the value of giving good customer service to their fellow salespeople.

Through public-speaking engagements and teaching opportunities

Public-speaking engagements and teaching opportunities are great for referral business, especially if you're the professional chosen to give the presentation or to teach. (You may find this type of opportunity through a homeowners association, retirement community, or other groups that bring in outsiders to speak at their meetings.) When this happens, you're automatically considered the expert in your field. But to earn the reputation you've been awarded, you'd better be prepared and handle your presentation well. Compare it to giving your best sales presentation to an audience of 50 or more potential clients all at once. Pretty important, isn't it?

I recommend participating in these situations only for those who can carry it off effectively. Too many people get carried away with the moment of stardom and forget that they're there to build their businesses, not to audition as a replacement for David Letterman. (If you're scheduled to give a presentation before a large crowd, check out *Public Speaking For Dummies* by Malcolm Kushner, published by Wiley. I also recommend the video *How to Master the Art of Speaking,* available from my company, Tom Hopkins International.)

I once went to a conference where the speaker provided cards on which participants wrote their names and others to contact who would also benefit from attending the conference. Each referral was put on a different card along with comments on why the participants believed that their referrals would enjoy and learn from the conference. The speaker encouraged us to fill out as many cards as we liked. We then put the cards into a large barrel. Each day of the conference, a member of the speaker's entourage pulled a card from the barrel to see who would win weekend getaways, free admission to advanced seminars, audio or video recordings, or books that were being sold at the conference. At the end of the conference, the speaker had the makings of another conference. What a system!

Knowing how and when to get referrals

Getting referrals is simple! You get referrals by asking for them. You'd be surprised how many salespeople feel awkward asking for referrals. How do such salespeople solve the problem of their awkwardness? They avoid the referral part of the selling situation altogether — and in the process cost themselves and their companies big bucks.

Or some salespeople try to get referrals by asking their clients, "Can you think of anyone else who may be interested?" And the clients can think of no one who may benefit from the salesperson's offering. Such a salesperson concludes that asking for referral business didn't really work for him.

In reality, it wasn't that it was impossible for these two groups of salespeople to get referrals. Instead, it was impossible to get referrals using the methods they were using. Instead of analyzing their methods and trying something different, they stopped asking for referrals altogether.

So, specifically now, when *do* you get referrals? You prepare to get referrals the moment you make contact with someone. From the first words they utter, you should look for areas in which you can help the client isolate names and faces that he can give you later (the names, that is, not the faces). Always listen carefully, not just to what will help the present client, but also to what will help the present client's referrals — your future clients — who may also need your services.

Good referral business comes from clients with whom you have good relationships. This doesn't necessarily mean that they own your offering. For example, you may have built a good relationship with a past or potential customer who for some reason is unable to own your product at this time. If you've kept in close contact and done a good job in building rapport with the customer, though, he more than likely would be willing to steer you toward a business associate who can benefit from your product or service. All you have to do is ask.

Be cautious about asking for referrals before you close the sale with your present potential client. Asking before you have their autograph on your paperwork or their credit card approved is like putting the cart before the horse. It appears that you're no longer interested in him, just in what he can do for you. And that's not professional selling.

There is one specific time when your chances of getting referrals are better than most: just after you have successfully closed a sale and the customer is excited about owning your offering. At that moment, the client is usually more than happy to give you referrals — names of other people who need what the client now owns. Just after the sale occurs is a time when enthusiasm is high and resistance is low.

But don't just plunge in and say, "Do you know anyone else who may want my whatchamacallit?" If you ask that way, your client probably won't be able to come up with a name. He's too distracted by his new purchase. You have to _prepare_ him in the art of giving good referrals. I cover this important topic in the next section.

Getting Referrals in Six Easy Steps

This section's easy, six-step process to obtaining referrals will give you so much more success in developing your referral business that you will make it an automatic part of every selling situation. Begin by setting a goal for how many referrals you want from each contact. Start with a goal of just one referral, and work your way up to a place where you know the steps so well and they flow so naturally that you'll get at least three referrals with every contact you make. Some of my students are getting as many as five or ten referrals from every client by implementing this simple strategy.

Memorize these six steps to getting referrals. The better you know them, the better you'll mine the rich lode of referrals that's just waiting for you in your current clientele.

1. **Help your client think of specific people he knows.**

2. **Write down the referrals' names.**

3. **Ask qualifying questions about the referrals.**

4. **Ask for the referrals' contact information.**

5. Ask the client to call and set up your meetings with the referrals.

6. If the client shows nervousness or refuses to call, ask if you can use the client's name when you contact the referral.

I cover each step in more detail in the following sections, examining this referral system so you can make it an integral part of your successful selling plan.

Step #1: Help your client think of specific people he knows

When you ask for referrals, you can't give your client the whole world to think about. Instead, use the information you've gathered about him, such as friends and family or other business associations he has. Help your client focus on a particular group of faces. Centering on one or two faces is impossible when his thoughts are bouncing off the wall with his new offering — which means your job is to get him focused again.

Refocus your customers by using a method like the one shown in the following hypothetical situation:

SALESPERSON: Bill, I can see you're excited with your new car, aren't you?

CLIENT: Oh, it's sweet. I can't wait to drive it off the lot!

SALESPERSON: You were a tough negotiator, Bill. I guess it feels good to know that you received significant savings on the car, too, doesn't it?

CLIENT: Yeah! I didn't expect to be able to afford a car this nice!

SALESPERSON: So tell me, Bill, where do you plan to drive your new car this first week?

CLIENT: Well, I'll be going back and forth to work, of course. And I play baseball in a city league every Thursday night. I can't wait to drive up in my new car.

SALESPERSON: I wish I could be there to see your face, as well as the faces of your co-workers and teammates. Bill, is there anyone at your workplace or on your baseball team who may be in the market for a new car?

By mentioning work and baseball, the client focuses in on those people he is closest to and with whom he'll be in contact that very week . . . while his excitement over his car is still fresh. And the salesperson has helped him do that.

Step #2: Write down the referrals' names

After your client has thought of specific people he knows, take out a small notepad or your note-keeping electronic device and record the names of those referrals. (Be sure to ask Bill how to spell the names of the people at work and on the baseball team who are in the market for a car.) Keep your notes handy so you can jot down the information your client gives you. Plus, you'll need those notes to qualify the referrals (see the following section).

Step #3: Ask qualifying questions

While your client is busy answering questions about the referrals, jot down notes to help you remember specific things about them. Some information you may want to know when you contact the referrals from the example that I provide in the preceding section includes

- ✔ What brought Sally to mind when I asked who you know that may be interested in getting a new car?
- ✔ What kind of car does she drive now?
- ✔ Do you know whether she would be the primary driver of the car?
- ✔ How many are in her family? (You need to know what size car she may need.)
- ✔ What did she say when you told her you were looking for a new car?

When you get in touch with Sally, you'll be able to begin a conversation with her based on Bill's answers to your questions. When you've taken a few notes, move on to the next step.

Never assume that what your client tells you is 100 percent true about the referral's needs. He may not know all the answers to your questions and guess at some of them. And never tell the referral that your client told you all of this information about him. Just have your notes handy to use as you qualify him further during your contact.

Step #4: Ask for contact information

Asking for the contact information of the referrals is more difficult because your client may not know this information offhand. But don't let that deter you. You can't just settle for the name because there may be several people with the same name in the phone directory when you try to look it up later.

And, these days, many people aren't in a phone book because they use their cell phone exclusively. Knowing how to contact the referral is critical to successfully selling him.

When asking for referrals, have your client go to his contact list either on his computer or cell phone. As he scrolls through looking for the person he mentioned, it's likely he'll come across someone else he hadn't thought of who may also need what you offer.

Step #5: Ask your customer to call the referral and set up the meeting

This step is where most novice salespeople balk. They won't even try it. But keep in mind that this question is simply setting the stage for the final step. Few clients will be comfortable calling to set up a meeting for you. But they'll be so relieved that you offer them Step #6 that they'll jump on it. If you had gone directly from Step #4 to Step #6, you may not have gotten the same response. There is a method to my madness here. Here's how it works:

> SALESPERSON: Thanks so much for the referrals, Bill. You know, since I won't get to see your excitement when you show off your new car, would you mind calling Sally and sharing your good news with her? Then we can work on arranging a time for me to meet with her.

If your customer is fine with that, then good: Start dialing. But if he hesitates and acts uncomfortable, take the pressure off immediately by moving on to the next step.

Step #6: Ask to use the client's name when you contact the referral

Your client may not know the referral all that well, or he may feel uncomfortable making the call. If this is the case, let him know you understand his hesitation, but ask if you can bother him for one more favor. Ask for his permission to use his name when you contact the people he referred you to. He'll probably be relieved to be let off the hot seat and be more than happy to give you permission to use his name.

Setting Up Meetings with Referrals

When you call someone and you already have an "in" with that person's close, personal friend or respected business associate, you have common ground. You also have the benefit of knowing some pertinent information that may be relevant to getting the appointment.

Before you call such a referral, review the information you wrote in your notes (see the previous section, "Step #3: Ask qualifying questions") and decide how to set the stage for this selling situation. If you properly qualified the referral, you know enough about him to ask just a few additional questions to get him interested in your offering and want to meet with you.

Through testimonials from your mutual business associate or friend, you can tell the referred lead what your client (and their friend) thought was most attractive or appealing about your offering. Chances are good that your referral will be just as interested in those same special features as his friend or associate was. If he's not interested, keep asking questions until you discover what about your offering does interest him. Here's an example:

> SALESPERSON: Hello, Sally, my name is Allen, and I work at B & B Motors. I just helped Bill Robinson get his dream car, a new 370Z. He mentioned that you may be in need of a new vehicle yourself, and I promised him I would call you and let you know about the special offerings we're having on our Nissans this week. He just bought a beauty and told me you two had been talking together about needing a new car. Tell me, Sally, what are you looking for in a new car?

> REFERRAL: Well, I'm not really ready to buy yet. I've just been looking around.

> SALESPERSON: What have you seen so far that you like the best?

> REFERRAL: Well, what I like and what I can afford are two different things.

> SALESPERSON: I hear you. Bill said the same thing. That's why he wanted me to call you and let you know about our special promotion that's going on now. You know, you aren't too far from our dealership. I work late tonight, so I'm available around 6:00 this evening. I know Bill said you shared his love for sports cars. Is that right?

> REFERRAL: Yes. But the ones I've seen are so expensive. I think I'm just going to wait a while.

SALESPERSON: I'll tell you what. Why don't you come on over after work. Tell me your situation and let me share with you what we're doing. Because of the success of the promotion, our dealership is serving munchies in our lobby in appreciation of our loyal customers. So don't eat first. You can munch out here while we talk. Is 6:00 good for you, or would 6:30 be more convenient?

REFERRAL: Actually, 6:00 is better for me.

SALESPERSON: Great, I'll see you then. Just come to the front desk and ask for Allen Brice.

Not only did this salesperson use the qualifying questions from his referral notes, but he further qualified Sally by asking more questions. He was more likely to get the appointment because Sally knew that Bill had purchased a similar car and perhaps had similar financial concerns — and she knew that the salesperson was able to work out a way for Bill to own his dream car. The salesperson's ability to help Sally's friend Bill encouraged Sally to find out if the same would be possible for her.

What do you think the chances were of getting the appointment if the salesperson had been making a random cold call? You're right — they fall in the slim-to-none category.

Aiming to Get Referrals Even When the Going Gets Tough

Just like you won't get a sale every time, you won't get a referral meeting every time. But you should always try to get referrals, even when you don't persuade or convince the potential client to get involved with your product or service. Now may not be the right time for that prospect, but that doesn't mean that he doesn't know anyone else who may be ripe for getting involved with the product, service, or idea you represent.

Getting a meeting with a referral may require some time and persistent follow-up. People who are referred to you don't have a relationship with you. So you need to build that relationship by keeping your face and name in their minds and in front of their faces all the time.

Often, the ability to get the referral appointment depends on the success of your follow-up program — if, of course, you use one at all. It's disheartening to go through all the work to get referrals, only to lose them because you lack an organized follow-up system.

In Chapter 14, I show you how getting referrals and setting up meetings are closely linked with practicing proper and creative follow-up methods. When you follow up on those who offered the referrals, they're happy to refer you again when the situation arises. When you follow up on the referrals themselves, you give yourself greater opportunities to increase your profitability. How? By improving your closing rates through cultivating an effective referral business. Remember that referrals offer a 60 percent closing rate.

You may not get a meeting with every referral. But then you don't need to in order for referrals to become a highly productive way for you to find new business. Selling is a numbers game. Everyone you meet is likely to know someone else who may benefit from your product or service.

Part IV
Growing Your Business

Five Follow-ups You Need to Make

- **Referral contacts:** Referrals are a great source of business. A referral is not a guaranteed sale. But contacting a referral is definitely easier than starting from scratch.

- **Current clients who are happily involved with your product or service:** You need to contact these people in appreciation of their continued loyalty — to you, your company, and your product or service — and to continue to serve their needs. A good time to follow up with loyal clients is when one of their referrals becomes a client.

- **Current clients who would benefit from new and improved versions of your product or service:** Reminding clients when it's time to consider updating the product you helped them acquire is just good customer service — and it's often a good source of additional sales.

- **Difficult-to-reach prospective clients:** Some prospects are hard to reach, so you need to follow up with them several times before finally making a connection. Consider contacting them twice in a week, and once each of the following weeks as the maximum.

- **People in your network:** These may be people who are not clients but who are willing to help you with introductions to potential clients, advise you in your career, or otherwise provide you with assistance. I suggest as a rule of thumb you be in touch with them six times per year.

For more strategies on how to make the most of your time visit www.dummies.com/extras/selling.

In this part . . .

✔ Maximize the benefits of keeping in touch with clients and understand how your clients would like you to follow up with them, be it by phone, email, or social media.

✔ Embrace social media and undertand how to use it to present, keep in touch, promote your product.

✔ Apply sales pointers such as building on answers you get, making potential clients feel valued, and relieving any tension that may arise.

✔ Avoid common time traps and invest rather than spend the time you have. Keep organized in your work, planning, and workspace.

Chapter 14

Following Up and Keeping in Touch

*P*racticing consistent and persistent follow-up is proven to be one of the most important factors in successful selling. That's why developing an organized, systematic approach to follow-up, while individualizing your chosen methods with your own creative flair, works to your advantage.

With advances in technology, some professional salespeople are practicing highly structured, thorough follow-up methods. They're not only following up with qualified leads and company leads but also reaching out to people considered *marginal inquiries* — that is, people who may not represent a sale but can open doors to other potential clients. If you want to compete with the big boys and girls in the world of sales, you must make follow-up an important part of your regular selling routine. In this chapter, I let you know with whom to follow up and when. I describe what type and level of service clients expect from your follow-ups, and give examples of effective follow-up methods. I also fill you in on the importance of sending thank-you notes and let you know how to get the best results from your follow-ups.

Be a follow-up fanatic! Even if you haven't found the most creative or memorable way to follow up, practicing follow-up with zeal is better than doing nothing at all. Allow yourself a few mistakes and plenty of time to organize and maintain your chosen follow-up schedule. Expect *gradual* increases in the number of *yes*es you get. Be diligent about follow-up with your prospects, your customers, and yourself. And above all, think of follow-up as the best way to travel the path of sales success.

Knowing When (and with Whom) to Follow Up

The kind of follow-up you do depends on the kind of person you're following up with. The following five groups of people are the foundation of your business. Keeping in touch with them regularly helps build your future.

- ✔ **Referral contacts:** There's no point in asking for referrals (see Chapter 13) if you don't follow up with the referrals you get. Referrals are a great source of business. Studies show that experienced salespeople spend half the time selling a referred, qualified lead than they spend selling a nonreferred, nonqualified lead — with a much higher closing rate. *Remember:* A referral is not a guaranteed sale. But contacting a referral is definitely easier than starting from scratch.

- ✔ **Current clients who are happily involved with your product or service:** You need to contact these people in appreciation of their continued loyalty — to you, your company, and your product or service — and to continue to serve their needs. A good time to follow up with loyal clients is when one of their referrals becomes a client. Sending a thank-you note will likely result in even more referrals. (I discuss thank-you notes in detail in "Remembering the Importance of Thank-You Notes and Gifts" later in this chapter.)

- ✔ **Current clients who would benefit from new and improved versions of your product or service:** Reminding clients when it's time to consider updating the product you helped them acquire is just good customer service — and it's often a good source of additional sales.

- ✔ **Difficult-to-reach prospective clients:** Some prospects are hard to reach, so you need to follow up with them several times before finally making a connection. Consider calling twice in a week, and once each of the following weeks as the maximum. This should keep you viewed as being persistent instead of being a pest. That first week, the person you're trying to reach could have been away from the office at a conference or on vacation. (Hopefully she would have told you that in her outgoing voice mail message.)

Persistent salespeople are rewarded. Some clients may not be as difficult to reach as they are difficult to close. You need a plan for following up with people who expressed an interest in your product but for whatever reason can't make the buying decision yet.

- ✔ **People in your network:** These may be people who are not clients but who are willing to go to bat for you to get you introduced to potential clients, advise you in your career, or otherwise provide you with assistance. I suggest as a rule of thumb you be in touch with them six times per year. These connections may or may not be evenly spaced. It could be that you and the others in your network volunteer for a particular event in your area each year and see each other three times because of that. In a case like that you contact that person three other times during the year, perhaps evenly spaced.

Even the briefest contact or smallest sale can lead to a whole new list of potential referrals for new business. Treat everyone you contact as if they control 1,000 new leads for your product or service. This is important no matter how your current selling career is going or what's happening in the economy. You can't sell if you're not talking to people.

Paying Attention to What Your Clients Want from Follow-Ups

To adopt effective methods of follow-up, you need to know the concerns clients have about the level of service they expect and the frequency of your follow-up. After all, you're only able to serve your clients well when you know what they want. Here's a list of clients' most pressing concerns about the selling and servicing of their accounts:

- ✔ Receiving a call that a salesperson promised to make
- ✔ Knowing contact numbers and the best available times to keep in touch with the sales and service people
- ✔ Being able to reach someone whenever the need arises
- ✔ Having the ability to talk to someone in authority
- ✔ Knowing that the salesperson and the salesperson's company appreciate their business
- ✔ Spending minimal time on hold in order to speak to a real person
- ✔ Being kept informed of ways to keep costs down and productivity up
- ✔ Being informed promptly of potential challenges and getting any problems resolved quickly
- ✔ Receiving acknowledgment of recognized challenges and accountability for errors
- ✔ Being addressed politely and receiving personal attention
- ✔ Being given realistic and honest information as it applies to delivery or problem-solving issues

By making follow-up and service a regular part of your day, you can efficiently address all these client concerns and maintain an edge over your competitors, who may not be as determined to follow up as you are. When you provide excellent service and follow-up with your clients and prospects, you earn the reward of serving the lion's share of all the clients who need your offering.

Recognizing How to Follow Up

If you want your clients to remember you and your offering, you must offer them a memorable experience. If you see follow-up as boring, tedious repetition, you can expect your clients to feel the same way: bored and tired of your constant contacts. So make sure that your methods of follow-up — and the messages you give through them — provide valuable information and add up to a rewarding and memorable experience for your clients. The following sections describe the most common follow-up methods.

A key question to ask every client and potential client is this: "How do you prefer that I keep in touch with you?" Your goal with follow-up is not to work on a schedule that suits you, but to meet your clients' needs in whatever format they desire.

In person

Depending upon what you sell, it may be appropriate for you to occasionally pop by and visit with your clients in person. An example is if you sell office or warehouse equipment. It's nice for the clients to talk to you face-to-face and beneficial for you to see your products in action. Seeing how your products are used by real people helps you better understand their needs. For instance, maybe you got your clients involved in a particular product because of what they told you during the qualification process that I describe in Chapter 9; however, when you see how they're using the product, you can offer additional suggestions for increased productivity or ways to cut costs with the product that they hadn't realized. Such suggestions help you develop long-term relationships with your clients.

Other benefits of an in-person follow-up are that you get direct, valuable feedback to pass along to the product developers at your company and that you can see if your clients are approaching maximum capacity for your product and have a need for something newer, bigger, or faster. Being proactive with follow-up prevents the competition from getting a foot in the door.

If your clients prefer in-person contact, ask if it's okay for you to pop by when you're in the area or if they prefer you set a specific time to visit. Some people don't care when you stop by as long as you *do* stop by. It could be that the decision maker doesn't need to see you but wants you to meet with some of the users of the product. Other clients may want to have regularly scheduled follow-up meetings.

This strategy applies to both business and consumer sales. If you help home-owners create their ideal backyard environment with a pool, landscaping, built-in barbecue, or so on, it may be prudent to meet with them at the home. You want to see how they're enjoying it, what questions they have, and to pass along ideas for enhancing their experience even more.

Phone

Telephone follow-up is perhaps the most common, most economical, and most difficult method of follow-up to turn into a memorable experience. Why? Just look at all the ways your clients can miss you. People can avoid your calls by using screening devices such as answering machines, secretaries, or voice mail. If your phone calls are being screened, you have to get creative to instill enough curiosity in the people you're trying to reach to make them want to talk with you. Even if the people you're calling aren't trying to avoid you, they may just be very busy, and what you're offering may not be the most important thing in *their* day — even though it is to you.

Reaching someone by telephone can be difficult if you aren't creative in your efforts. For example, when you try to reach that high-powered executive on the phone, you may have to go through a company receptionist, a private secretary, and sometimes even a business partner before you get to the decision maker. But the real frustration comes only when, at the end of this gauntlet, you discover that you've gone through it all just so the decision maker can advise you to leave a message on her voice mail or to send an email message! If you aren't prepared with a creative and tempting message, how often do you think the important decision makers will return your call as it lines up with the dozens of other sales calls they receive on a daily basis? If you said, "Not often," you're right. Now do you see the value in giving your follow-up your own little flair?

To make your phone calls memorable, prepare a message that will get the person's attention and pique her curiosity. The people at the top are always looking for ways to improve profitability and productivity or to carve out a greater percentage of market share. If you believe that your offering will help the person you're trying to reach, give her a teaser in the message that will make her want to put your name at the top of her callback list. A message such as this one, for example, helps you cut through the clutter and connect you with the people in charge:

> Hello, Mary. It's Erica Post at 555-0000. I'm sorry I missed you, but you may still have an opportunity to find out about our new program to increase quality production while decreasing company expenditures in labor and stored inventory. Look for the informational packet I'll send to you on May 22. Expect a call back from me, Erica Post, to discuss how you and your company will benefit from our latest offer. Or, for immediate information, call me tomorrow morning before 11:00 at 555-0000.

One short phone message such as this one accomplishes several objectives:

- ✔ **It piques the customer's interest by teasing her with possibilities of how to help her company.**

- ✔ **It tells the executive that you can provide individual as well as company benefits.** Mentioning the benefits to the individual is a good habit to get into, whether your offer of individual benefits occurs during follow-up or you incorporate it right into the fabric of your presentation. Stroke the ego of a high-powered executive. Show her how she'll look good to the corporate elite, and she'll be that much more willing to own your offering.

- ✔ **It gives the potential client a specific time to call if she wants to hear more.** By being specific, you can schedule your time to remain in your office to receive returned calls. This follow-up technique helps you avoid playing the annoying game of telephone tag with people you really want to reach. If the customer is too busy (or has not been tempted enough) to return your call at the suggested time, you've at least given yourself the opportunity to contact her via direct mail or email. And guess what follows the mailing? You guessed it — another phone call!

The same strategy works when you call consumers. Adjust your message to build their curiosity about benefits specific to them.

Direct mail

Direct mail is a common method of follow-up, but your mailings don't have to be ordinary. Personalize your follow-up to make it memorable for the person you're contacting. For example:

- ✔ Include premiums with your mailings. *Premiums* are offerings that benefit customers when they respond to a mailing. They may include a special promotional discount on your offering or a coupon to use the services included in your mailed package. Sometimes a mailing includes nothing but a premium. When the premium is the only thing in a mailing, the follow-up's only purpose is to build goodwill with your customers.

If you use this method of follow-up, let the recipient know that you will call her in a few days for her feedback. Your notice about the upcoming call gives you *another* opening to contact her with effective follow-up — it's a win-win situation. Your client feels valued, and you can expect a warm welcome when you contact her in hopes of keeping or receiving her business.

✔ Insert *For Your Information* (FYI) materials with a message of how your clients can benefit from them. FYI materials may not have anything to do with your personal offering, but they let your clients know that you're thinking of them.

So what qualifies as FYI material? Maybe you recently came across a press release relating to your client's field of expertise. If you did, let your client know about it. Sending the release may be of no direct, immediate benefit to you. But it informs your clients of events that may profit them and lets them know you're thinking about them.

The more spontaneous your FYIs are, the more effective they will be. Instead of having your secretary type a formal cover letter for your FYIs, just jot a little handwritten note and attach it to the mailed material. Your note can be as simple as a few lines to let your client know that you were thinking about her. Don't forget to include your business card with the note and maybe a little teaser about what's new with your product or service to get her to call.

Networking within your company to find more ways to follow up

Top-producing salespeople have found ways to follow up that are both effective and creative. It may not be too effective to ask your competitors for their methods of follow-up. But other salespeople in your company may be doing creative things that they are more than willing to share with you.

At your next sales meeting, make a point of discussing different methods of follow-up. This is called *networking,* even though you're doing it right at home within your own ranks of salespeople. And don't forget to follow up your discussion on follow-up by taking some follow-up action!

Before you toss all those collected business cards from all those business meetings into the circular file or tuck them away in a file you'll never see again, take the time to go through the cards and write a note about how much you enjoyed the person's input or conversation at the business meeting. If you've been thorough enough to jot down a word or two on the back of each card to remind you of your conversation, you'll have something specific to address when you do your networking follow-up.

You'd be surprised how many people have a really positive response to this type of follow-up. Many even go out of their way to contact you with future needs! If you follow up shortly after you attend the business breakfast or networking event, you'll more easily recall what everybody said. When you enter each person's contact information into the software you use to keep track of them, be sure to include any notes of conversations so you remember her when she calls.

Email

Email is a wonderful tool to use for follow-up if your client uses it regularly — and these days, who doesn't? You can send a note with an attached URL (website address) of an article or piece of information that the client may find useful in her business, or at the very least, interesting about her hobby. If the article is a long one, summarize in your message why you thought she'd find it interesting.

Whenever there's a new development in your industry or within your company that may impact this particular client, drop her an email about it. If the new development has nothing to do with the client's needs, however, don't waste her time with it. I believe the general populace of the world feels guilty in some way that they're not reading as much as they should. There's an abundance of knowledge available, and too many people berate themselves if they haven't read the ten best-selling business books and the latest edition of at least three newspapers in order to feel they're on top of things. So keep your email messages to clients brief and to the point, and they'll be much appreciated.

By the way, it never hurts to include an offer to serve the client's needs should a question arise. Always, *always* keep yourself open to hearing from your clients.

This strategy also applies to consumers. Let's say you helped a family acquire a new furnace or air-conditioning unit. When they got it, they received the instructions about checking the unit and changing the filters. Now, your company offers a service that ships filters to your clients' homes when it's time to change them. They never have to worry about forgetting again. You now have a valid reason to contact them with the concept and opportunity. You can include a link right in your message to where the client can join this service. In this case, you're following up and potentially selling another service all at once.

One of the best advantages of using email as a follow-up is that many email programs have a feature that sends you a message when your emails have been read. That way you know your message was received.

Text

Many people run all the details of their business and personal lives from their mobile phones. They may be on the go a lot and not have immediate computer access all the time. Whereas some folks receive their email messages on their mobile phones, others do not. As a professional salesperson you need to be flexible. As I mention earlier in this chapter, a key question to ask every client and potential client is this: "How do you prefer that I keep in touch with you?" If a client's life revolves around her mobile phone, the answer may be "by text."

Sending messages via text is a great tool for people who are busy and want only basic information, but want it *now*. If your clients prefer to be contacted that way, invest a little time in learning some basic text shortcuts and etiquette. Although I don't recommend you use text abbreviations, especially LOL (laughing out loud *or* lots of love) in business situations, you need to know what they are in case your clients use them. (There are too many abbreviations to mention here; check out `www.netlingo.com/acronyms.php` and `http://didyouknow.org/shortcuts/` for lists.)

You do, however, need to be brief when sending a text message. Just always be professional. For example, what you may speak in words, such as "I can arrange my schedule to meet with you at 1:00 p.m. or a bit later at 3:00 p.m. if that's better for you" may translate to "I can meet @ 1p or 3p" in a text message. Ideally, this short-form message would be to someone who already knows that you are professional and won't judge you based on this short message. Sending the same message as "cn mt u @ 1 or 3" is much less professional.

If you have a message of exceptional importance to deliver, begin by using the method each client prefers, but consider following up that message with a different format. For example, if your client prefers you contact her via telephone and you end up leaving a voice mail message, also send the message via email or text to increase the likelihood of it being received.

Remembering the Importance of Thank-You Notes and Gifts

Everybody likes to be appreciated, and I think you'll agree that there's precious little positive stroking in this world. So use your follow-up system to let your customers know that you appreciate their business and all the referrals they've sent your way. I call this *warm-and-fuzzy follow-up,* and it comes in a form that should become a permanent part of your sales repertoire as soon as possible — as in sometime yesterday. So what form should this take? The deceptively modest thank-you note. In the following sections, I describe some of the most appropriate times for sending thank-you notes and explain when and how you can move beyond notes and send thank-you gifts.

Knowing when you can send a thank-you note

I've made it easy for you to get started with the thank-you note habit. Here are ten instances in which thank-you notes are appropriate, followed by the exact words you can use for the occasion:

- **For telephone contact:** "Thank you for talking with me on the telephone. In today's business world, time is precious. You can rest assured that I will always respect the time you invest as we discuss the possibility of a mutually beneficial business opportunity."

- **For in-person contact:** "Thank you for taking time to meet with me. It was a pleasure meeting you, and I'm thankful for the time we shared. We have been fortunate to serve many happy clients, and I hope to someday be able to serve you. If you have any questions, please don't hesitate to call."

- **After a demonstration or presentation:** "Thank you for giving me the opportunity to discuss with you our potential association for the mutual benefit of our firms. We believe that quality, blended with excellent service, is the foundation for a successful business."

- **After a purchase:** "Thank you for giving me the opportunity to offer you our finest service. We are confident that you will be happy with this investment toward future growth. My goal now is to offer excellent follow-up service so that you have no reservations about referring me to others who have needs similar to yours."

- **For a referral:** "Thank you for your kind referral. You can rest assured that anyone you refer to me will receive the highest degree of professional service possible."

- **After a final refusal:** "Thank you for taking the time to consider letting me serve you. I sincerely regret that your immediate plans do not include making the investment at this time. However, if you need further information or have any questions, please feel free to call. I will keep you posted on new developments and changes that may benefit you in the future."

- **After a prospect buys from someone else:** "Thank you for taking the time to analyze my services. I regret being unable at this time to help you appreciate the benefits that we can provide you. We keep constantly informed of new developments and changes in our industry, though, so I will keep in touch with you in the hope that, in the years ahead, we will be able to do business together."

✔ **After a potential client buys from someone else but offers you referrals:** "Thank you for your gracious offer to give me referrals. As we discussed, I am enclosing three of my business cards, and I thank you in advance for placing them in the hands of three of your friends, associates, or relatives whom I might serve. I will keep in touch and be willing to render my services as needed."

✔ **To anyone who gives you service:** "Thank you for your continued and professional service. It is gratifying to meet someone dedicated to doing a good job. I sincerely appreciate your efforts. If my company or I can serve you in any way, please do not hesitate to call."

✔ **On an anniversary:** "With warm regards, I send this note to say hello and, again, thanks for your patronage. We are continually changing and improving our products and service. If you would like an update on our latest advancements, please give me a call."

As you can see, you have many reasons to say, "Thank you." A thank-you note or two to the right person at the right time can go a long way toward building your success. How? Suppose receptionists or assistants who think they don't get enough recognition *do* get recognition from you. Will they remember? Of course they will. Will they feel good about you? Yes. Will they be more receptive to your calls and questions? Probably. ***Remember:*** You can never go wrong by thanking someone.

Take advantage of technology to help you start and stay on top of a thank-you note process. One I highly recommend is SendOutCards.com (`https://sendoutcards.com`). You can not only send cards but customize them with your own photos and copy in your own handwriting font and include gifts.

Going beyond notes with thank-you gifts

There may be instances for which a thank-you note doesn't seem to be enough and you want to send a gift. For example, if someone has gone *way* out of her way to help you, and if you think she deserves a little gift or an extra-special thank-you, and if a thank-you is appropriate, then by all means send that person a thank-you gift right away.

So now you may be wondering this: What are some appropriate gift ideas? If a customer likes classical music, consider sending her a set of tickets to a performance. You may want to send a gift card to a movie theater to a secretary or assistant. You can thank clients with a round of golf at their favorite course, or give the secretary and her guest a gift certificate for lunch to show your gratitude for her extra effort to arrange the appointment you worked on for a month.

In some businesses, it's not appropriate to send gifts due to rules or regulations in those industries. In other instances, sending gifts is most appropriate. If you don't know whether a thank-you gift is appropriate, ask your manager or a more seasoned salesperson her opinion. You may even want to consult Miss Manners, Emily Post, or Dear Abby.

Many gifts to clients are tax-deductible to your business. Ask your accountant about this. Your thank-you gift can be even *more* beneficial for you.

Mother knows best

I learned the value and power of thank-you notes early in life. When we Hopkins kids were young, our parents occasionally went out with friends for dinner. As most kids do, I often tried to stay awake until my parents came home. On those times when I did manage to stay awake, invariably I saw my mother sit down at her little desk in the hallway as soon as she got home and begin to write.

One time I got up and asked her what she was doing. Her answer could have come straight out of Emily Post: "We had such a wonderful time with our dear friends this evening that I want to jot them a note to thank them for their friendship and the wonderful dinner."

My mother's simple act of gratitude — expressed to people who already knew that she and my father appreciated and enjoyed their friendship — helped to keep my parents' friendships strong for their entire lives.

Because I understood that building relationships is what selling is all about, I began early

in my career to send thank-you notes to people. I set a goal to send ten thank-you notes every day. That goal meant that I had to meet and get the names of at least ten people every day. I sent thank-you notes to people I met briefly, people I showed properties to, people I talked with on the telephone, and people I actually helped to own new homes. I became a thank-you note fool.

To this day, on a plane on the way home after a seminar I write thank-you notes to students, to my staff, and to the wonderful people I meet at hotels and in taxicabs (even to the flight attendants). And do you know what happens when I go back to those cities? They remember me. They remember that I cared enough to thank them for a job well done or for sharing their time with me.

I believe so strongly in the power of thank-you notes that you will find one on the back of every seminar workbook I print.

Maximizing Results from Your Follow-Ups

Maximizing results is a great goal to have in handling any contact, not just a follow-up. To do so requires efficiency, a well-laid plan, and good records. In this section, I cover just those aspects of follow-up so you can get the best results from your efforts.

Imposing order

Follow-up sounds so simple when somebody advises you to send a letter or to just pick up the phone and make a call, but establishing an effective follow-up system involves much more than that. An effective follow-up plan requires you to master and implement the Rule of Six, a rule of selling that can increase your sales volume many times over: To make the sale, you should contact prospects a minimum of six times within a 12-month period.

Think of all the contacts and prospects you have — and multiply that number by six. When you look at follow-up that way, you can easily see how some salespeople get overwhelmed with follow-up. In fact, many champion sales-people hire assistants whose main function is to do prompt and effective follow-up.

If you're new to sales, you probably won't be able to hire someone to take care of your follow-ups. So you need to work extra hard to provide prompt follow-up to referrals, prospective clients, loyal customers who now own your offering, networking possibilities, and just about everybody you come into contact with during a normal business day (as if there is such a thing as a *normal* business day!).

For your follow-up to be effective, and because follow-up is a constant in the selling process, you must organize your follow-up time and program to ensure that your business stays productive. You can set up your follow-up system in several different ways — choose the method that works best for you. For example:

- ✔ You can use something as simple as 3-x-5 index cards to keep track of your follow-ups, such as when you contacted the person and the basic details of what information was covered. Or you may want or need to use customer relationship software.

- ✔ If you have a lot of people to keep track of, use a sales force automa-tion software program designed to store the maximum amount of information in the minimum amount of space. By setting up a database specially designed for follow-up, you can save time and energy that you can then devote to face-to-face selling. Some of the most popular programs include Sage ACT! (www.act.com) and SalesForce.com (www.salesforce.com).

If you already use a system, invest some time in learning how to maximize the *tickler* or *reminder* features. If you don't have one, be certain these features are easy to manage in any program you decide to use. (Check out Chapter 6 for more information on taking advantage of technology.)

Whichever way you choose to organize your time and the follow-up information you collect, your method should enable you to systematically and periodically keep in touch with all your contacts.

As you schedule your follow-up time, keep your customers informed of the best times to contact you. Be sure that you are accessible at the times you tell them to contact you. Just by being there, you eliminate telephone tag or the nagging fear that the contact you've waited for all week will come when you're out on an appointment.

Let your customers know your work schedule (as much as possible), and they'll appreciate being able to reach you when you say you'll be available. Keeping your announced office hours is just another way to let your clients see how efficiently you run your business and, likewise, how efficiently you would (or do) service their needs. (Head to Chapter 16 for more pointers on planning your time efficiently.)

Gauging your nuisance quotient

Whether you receive a *yes* or a *no* from people to whom you present your product or service, you should include them all in your follow-up program. Why?

✔ With those who become clients, service is key, and you can't serve them if they don't make a connection with you. Surprise, surprise — not many of them will reach out to make that connection. The job is up to you.

✔ For those people who choose to purchase from someone else or not to make any purchase at all, you need to get their permission to stay in touch with new developments that may apply to their situation.

In the following sections, I explain when and how often to contact people in your follow-up program and describe actions to take when someone still says no to your product or service after follow-up.

Knowing when and how often to make contact

With your clients, you want to stay in touch fairly often, depending upon the product or service they acquired. If they're purchasing office supplies from you, you may need to be in touch weekly. If the purchase was a Lear Jet, you may only need to be in touch once every other month or so.

Your clients may need a comfort contact every now and then to feel you're really there for them. Your non-clients, on the other hand, may feel you're scratching your nails on their blackboard if you call too often. You'll master gauging this with time and experience.

If you're a beginner, ask each person how often she would like to hear from you. Don't say, "How often shall I contact you," though. She may answer with, "Don't call us. We'll call you." Instead, suggest it this way, "With your permission, I'd like to follow up with you in about 30 days just to see how well the product is meeting your needs and find out if you have any questions. Would that be all right with you?" The client may suggest you call sooner or that she will have a better idea of how things are working out in 45 days. You can gauge your nuisance factor based on her response.

One of the most important tidbits of sales wisdom is this: Avoid harassing your customer. Sometimes knowing when keeping in touch with your client has crossed the line to downright bothering her is difficult. But you defeat the entire purpose of follow-up if you fail to recognize the signs of annoyance a customer is sending your way. If a customer hangs up on you, that's a pretty good sign that you've failed to recognize her annoyance. How many hang-ups do you get on a given day?

Be sensitive to your clients' needs. Don't call them on a Friday before a holiday and try to sell them your new offering over the phone. This kind of call is not follow-up; it's irritation. Similarly, don't call at lunchtime or at the very end of the day and expect a long, drawn-out conversation with your client's undivided attention. Her mind is set on beating a path to the door, not on listening to your offering.

Keep your follow-up short and sweet, and do it at times most convenient for your prospects' schedules. Interruptions are sometimes unavoidable, but when too many interruptions occur, give your clients the opportunity to get back with you at a time better suited to their busy schedules.

Treading carefully with someone who says no after follow-up

If, after all the follow-up, you still get a *no* from a client, leave the contact or meeting on a positive note. If you know that her answer was not based on your poor performance, you may still be able to get a referral from her or do future business with her when her situation changes.

Be polite! Find out when she expects her situation to change and ask permission to call back again. She may be receptive to hearing what you have to say a few short months down the road when she is ready to own your offering. If you leave her with a positive feeling and continue to build rapport through constant and persistent follow-up, the only thing stopping her from owning your offering is time — and that, too, shall pass.

If your customer admits that she bought from your competitor, don't you think you need to discover why she chose your competitor over you? If this situation arises, don't get angry with your prospective client. Instead, make her feel important by asking her if you can take up just a few more moments of her time to get her advice on how you can improve your sales skills or your product or service.

If you've invested a lot of time in a customer who decided not to take you up on your offering and has instead gone with someone else, she may even feel obligated to speak with you. These interactions can be the best learning experiences you have. Not only do you find out what you may need to improve, but you gain new insight into your competitor's offering or into what your competitor says about you and your company. Think of these times as invaluable opportunities to become a better salesperson. And don't forget to take this opportunity to follow up with a thank-you note to the customer for her advice.

If you're diligent in following up with buyers who choose not to own your offering, you may just sneak them away from your competitor the next time they get the itch to own. By keeping in touch with them even better than the salesperson with whom they chose to do business, you make the customer wish that she had done business with you. Let her see your organization and care for her well-being through your effective follow-up — and when she needs a new-and-improved version of what she now owns, she'll probably think of you first.

Being disappointed and letting your clients know you're sorry not to have the opportunity to do business with them is okay. Let them know that you're not giving up and that you still hope to win their trust. And for the customers you obtained because of your effective follow-up, remain just as consistent and persistent in the service you provide. Make sure they know that you're concerned about meeting their needs and that you put their needs before your own.

Keeping track of your successes

Be sure to keep thorough notes on all your follow-ups and the success you have with your current follow-up methods. When you do something great that gets excellent response, write it down in a *success journal* (a place where you can keep track of everything that works for you — follow-up or otherwise). Be specific and detailed, and describe the selling situation in which you implemented the successful follow-up method. The more information you record, the more likely you are to repeat the experience in the future.

When customers tell you what you need to work on, put those comments into your success journals, too.

If you take all this time to write down what you do well, in addition to what you need to improve on, be sure to take the time to review your journal periodically and evaluate whatever changes you make.

You may need to solicit the help of another professional salesperson in your office to hold you accountable for making the changes you know you need to make and to help you implement such changes. When your colleague sees you kicking back and relaxing, she should have your permission to give you a gentle wake-up call, a reminder of what you said you wanted to do to improve your sales results.

Sticking with the follow-up program

How well your prospects respond to your follow-up depends entirely on the effectiveness and efficiency of the method of follow-up you use. If you follow up quickly and regularly (and with a bit of flair), you can expect higher percentages of response from your prospects. Of course, the response you get also depends on whether you're working with prospects who can truly benefit from owning your product or service.

Don't get discouraged if some prospects don't respond at all. Sometimes, no matter how good your follow-up, you get zip, zero, zilch for your efforts. If you take the goose egg more times than not, you may benefit from evaluating your methods of follow-up and putting another kind of zip into your messages.

Knowing which methods work best for you and which types of clients respond to one method of follow-up as opposed to another can take time. So be patient. Don't give up if, after your first few attempts at follow-up, you get disappointing results. Instead, keep seeking ways to improve your follow-up program. Contact other professional salespeople who are willing to listen, look at your follow-up program, and offer advice. Good follow-up techniques can sometimes take as long to master as good selling techniques. It doesn't happen overnight.

Chapter 15

Using the Internet to Make More Sales

In This Chapter

▶ Enjoying the benefits of social media

▶ Prospecting, presenting, and staying in touch online

▶ Working effectively with social media

▶ Avoiding the trap of too much technology

. . . .

*S*ocial media consists of a group of fantastic tools for you to use in preparing for and making sales. When used properly (with the help of the information in this chapter), it's an excellent resource that allows you to take advantage of resources that may otherwise be beyond your means. With the resources available to you through social media, you can even grow your business when there are challenges in your industry or in the global marketplace.

Think about the time, effort, and financial means it would require for you to have access to the most up-to-date information on any potential client if it weren't for the resources available through social media. I strongly suggest that you quickly adopt the social media tools as your best friends — second only to the pen, mouse, or touch screen with which your client approves the paperwork that closes the sale.

Understanding Social Media's Positive Impact on the Selling Profession

Although it's the cause of distraction for some people in business, social media truly is an empowering tool for sales professionals. As you find out in the following sections, it allows you to stay well informed about industry news, and find out about a client's potential need faster than ever. Having access to the social media is like having a souped-up reference library literally at your fingertips; you can look up nearly every topic, company, or product you can think of. You can find unique ways to locate potential clients. And, you can increase your own level of expertise in your particular field of sales.

Always consider the source and date of information you see online. If the information was posted by a corporation or reputable organization, it's likely valid. But if you're not familiar with the source of the information, be aware that it may not be the most reliable. Most social posts include the date and time of day when they were posted, so you know how current the information is.

Do your best to limit your nonbusiness social media time to 30 minutes per day or less. Set a timer if you must, but don't get sucked into reading random posts that look interesting now, but may curtail your productivity during prime selling hours.

It's better than the newspaper ever was

Through social media, you can read all the latest news for your industry. Look for your industry association as a group on LinkedIn or seek out their Facebook fan page. If the association has an Instagram account as well, follow it. This is where they're likely to post information they feel is important to share with the world — as well as posting it on their own Internet website. If they offer an RSS (Rich Site Summary) feed of their latest news, subscribe to it. Just imagine the impression you'll make with clients when you can inform them about the latest industry developments as soon as they're made available.

For information specific to client companies, visit both their websites and their social media pages. Many companies handle their customer service questions via social media. If you see that Company A has customer's talking about a specific challenge that your product can resolve — what power that gives you when contacting them! Companies also often make announcements about new products, business developments, and changes in leadership via social media. When a client company is important to your future sales success, you'll be wise to follow them everywhere they exist online but especially through their social media channels.

When using social media, invest a little time in understanding *hashtags* — words or phrases that begin with #. Those tags are searchable for additional information or posts related to that topic.

It's direct word of mouth

You can experience for yourself how your competition handles business by submitting a request for information on your competitor's website or by reading existing customer comments on their social media pages. If you're on their website, look for something under the heading "Customer Service," "Technical Support," or "Contact Us." Find out exactly how accessible they are to clients. (Do the same with your own site every now and then to be sure your service is better than that of your competition.)

Many companies handle customer service issues via social media. Due to the social aspect, negative comments or unresolved challenges can and are shared. This can create a ripple effect of negative public relations or at least put a dent in your company's goodwill. The closer you monitor social media messages about your company, and the faster you respond with gratitude for positive comments and resolutions to the negative, the more positively it will impact your bottom line.

You can also review websites to find out how your product ranks compared to the competition. Then you can pass those links or the information on to your potential clients. (Chances are that they've already been checking up on you anyway.) Showing your prospects that you're on top of things helps them to recognize your high level of competence, thus inspiring trust in your advice.

It eliminates guesswork

Social media allows you and your company to capture very specific information on customer needs and respond to them effectively. It allows your clients to receive answers to their concerns faster than ever before, which increases their confidence in you and your company's ability to serve their needs. And it allows your satisfied clients a quick and easy means to tell others how great you are!

The data-mining industry is one of the fastest growing in the world at the time of this writing. Nearly every interaction you have online can be captured and analyzed in such a way that companies who think you're an ideal client for them can get their ad placed where you go. Did you think it was coincidental that, as an example, you searched on Amazon for a new coffee maker then coffee maker ads popped up when you were on Facebook? How about the fact that ads for businesses right down the street from you have started showing up in some of the sidebars on your social media sites?

If your business is social media-ready, take advantage and implement as many of these tools as possible to grow it. If your company already collects such in-depth information, gain access to it. The more you know about all your clients, the better you can handle each one's individual needs and the more easily you'll identify ideal new candidates for your service. If your clients don't make purchases online, this technology may not be for you, but it's still a good lesson on the power of today's marketing strategies.

Never assume that your clients have only one area of need. If your company offers a variety of products, always try to get your clients happily involved with as wide a range as possible.

Using Social Media during your Selling Cycle

Selling is all about serving your clients' needs, and the Internet doesn't change that. But the Internet *does* allow you to help your clients in new and exciting ways, whether your clients are right next door or across the planet. In this section, I offer some suggestions for ways to put the Internet to work for you in your daily selling life — especially by using social media.

Several For Dummies books published by Wiley can help you get the most out of social media:

- ✔ *Facebook Marketing For Dummies* by Paul Dunay and Richard Krueger
- ✔ *LinkedIn For Dummies*, 3rd Edition by Joel Elad
- ✔ *Twitter Marketing For Dummies*, 2nd Edition by Kyle Lacy

Prospecting online with LinkedIn

LinkedIn (www.linkedin.com) can be a great source for finding potential clients. It's a networking tool you can use to help other professionals find you . . . and for you to find new potential clients. LinkedIn is more business oriented than some of the other social media platforms. Here are some great methods for prospecting on LinkedIn (see Chapter 7 for general prospecting pointers):

- ✔ If you sell products in a particular company or industry, conduct searches for those industry profiles, and you'll find whom to contact and maybe even find a photo and profile of Mr. or Ms. Decision Maker.

✔ You can look for people who work for XYZ Company all over the world. Who knows, the person living three doors down from you may work there or have worked there in the recent past. Put your relationship-building skills to work, and soon you'll find yourself connected with someone who can make a decision about your product or service.

✔ Look for LinkedIn groups with topics related to your industry and join them. By participating in some of the posted discussions, you demonstrate your expertise . . . and get familiar with the expertise of others. LinkedIn is a great tool for sharing industry information.

✔ If you belong to an organization related to your industry, it may have a LinkedIn profile listing the other members and how to contact them. Other members may be a big help in reaching decision makers who may be excellent potential clients.

Offering to give to the other person first (before asking for something from him) makes for good networking. Sometimes, all you need do is ask, "What can I do for you?" The other person often feels obliged to make the same offer — and you get what you wanted in the first place.

Tweeting from the rooftops

Twitter (www.twitter.com) is what is called a microblogging site that people use to provide quick updates on whatever is of interest at the moment. Twitter is an interesting tool in that it was initially used mostly by celebrities and groups of friends to keep in touch. Then, the business world discovered its power to connect with clients and potential clients with product announcements and contests, and now companies use it even for handling customer service challenges.

The key element of Twitter is that the messages are brief. And in today's world, brief is good. A *tweet* (a single message posted in Twitter) is limited to 140 characters. Please note that it's *characters* not *words*. A *character* is a letter, number, or symbol. Spaces in the message also count as characters. This limitation forces you to really think about how to quickly build curiosity or impart value in a concise manner.

A benefit of Twitter is that you can include a link (the link also counts as characters) to a website such as a landing page for your product or another information site you refer clients and potential clients to. Think of Twitter as a great place to raise a question, then point to the answer.

Presenting and selling online

Ideally, your company's website effectively presents your message to create enough trust that potential clients view or read about your product or service and choose to get happily involved — maybe even placing an online order. Selling online is how thousands of small companies become very, very profitable. In the following sections, I describe online tools for making a presentation from afar and explain how to walk a potential client through your company's website via the phone; check out Chapter 10 for an introduction to making presentations.

Not only does your online presence need to put forth the image and message that you desire, but the living, breathing people who actually fulfill the orders need to do what your site promises. Keep in mind the old selling adage to "under promise and over deliver" in order to please your clients.

Be careful of how much dazzle and showmanship you put into your Web presentations. Not everyone has an Internet connection at the maximum speed, so your presentation should be developed to dazzle the low-end connections. Make it easy for the potential client to navigate around the presentation and make their purchases or risk losing them to frustration.

Presenting from afar

If you can't be with your potential client, but he needs information right away, you can use your website to get him the information he needs. Knowing your company's website inside and out is definitely a necessity if you want to succeed in using it to your advantage. So start by locating the exact URL (web address) for each piece of information your buyers need to see. Then send those URLs to the prospect in the order in which you recommend he view those pages, and explain that in your email. For example, your instructions to your client may be as follows:

> Start with our home page at `www.mycompanyhomepage.com`. Then go to `www.mycompany.com/theparticularproductyoureinterestedin`. Here, you can see a photo of the item and read a description of what it will do for you. Next go to `www.mycompany.com/testimonial fortheparticularproductyoureinterestedin`. Here, you'll see how much others have enjoyed and benefited from owning the product. You may want to follow that by going to `www.mycompany.com/ howtoordertheparticularproductyoureinterestedin`. Here you can place an order and receive a confirmation-of-delivery date.

If you have to work with clients this way, *always* follow up your instructions with a personal phone call to answer any questions they may have about ownership, delivery, installation, and so on. Your clients may have questions that can't be answered by your website — and that's what you're there for.

For more sophisticated products or services, or when a more in-depth online presentation is needed, you can also take advantage of an online service such as WebEx (www.webex.com), which allows you to take buyers through your own customized slide deck presentation, such as PowerPoint, from afar.

In addition to giving a slide presentation over the Internet, you can take advantage of *webcasting* in your sales as well. Webcasting is not unlike telecasting, which is what your local news station does several times each day. Instead, webcasting is done over the Internet. If your company uses webcasting, you can attend your national sales meeting from your desk. Your client can view the latest news on products and services if they are webcast. And webcasting is a wonderful method for getting consistent, firsthand, high-quality video or slide messages to your clients. You can also use webcasting for real-time communication. A chat session can be included with the webcast so you can interact with and answer questions from the audience, even if you're not in the room with them.

Telemarketing with the best of them

If you do a lot of long-distance selling or if you're in telephone sales (where you rarely meet your client in person), you can use your website to enhance your prospective client's satisfaction. How? By directing him through the site while you're on the phone with him. Walking through the site together is the next best thing to sitting at a table with your prospect and demonstrating your product or brochures. You may use the same links discussed in the preceding section, or you can follow an entirely different path, dictated by the client's questions and concerns. The key here is to absolutely, positively know what's on your site and what may be missing. You don't want to get caught off-guard by a client's question.

Never direct a client to an area of the site that you haven't been to recently. It may have changed, and you can end up with egg on your face and look less than competent.

Staying in touch with your clients

Another great use of the Internet is in staying connected with your clients, building those long-term relationships, and inspiring loyalty (as introduced in Chapter 14). Sounds like a lot of reward from just a few keystrokes, doesn't it?

If you find an article online about a client's particular industry or a client's competition, you may want to print it out and send it to him along with a short "I'm thinking of you" note. Or just drop him an email with the link attached.

If your client's company stock has a great day, send a congratulatory note. How will you know about that great day? Check the company's listing on the stock exchange. It's as simple as visiting the websites of the New York Stock Exchange (www.nyse.com) or Nasdaq (www.nasdaq.com) and entering the company's symbols to see today's activities and news releases.

You can even make a personal connection to a client; for example, if John BigBoss is your largest client and his interests involve fishing, use some of your 30 minutes a day to seek out new websites on fishing and pass those URLs along to old John — just to let him know you're thinking about him and want him to enjoy his hobbies. Why? When John enjoys his hobbies, he's happy. And if he's happy because of something you did for him, he'll want to stay connected to you.

Using Social Media Well

As a salesperson and sales trainer, I have made the subject of selling my life-long hobby. Even as a young man I often wondered why two people selling the same product could have totally different results. It seemed to me at first that they were saying the same thing. Yet one was rubbing people the wrong way while the other seemed to sell so smoothly.

As my study of the art and science of selling developed, I noticed and tested hundreds of nuances to determine which ones worked . . . and why. After learning a lot about what not to do when trying to sell myself or my products, it became natural for me to evaluate every selling situation I encountered.

I'm the first to admit that technology often baffles me, but if I'm going to participate in the online community, I want to understand it. Although social media platforms are incredibly helpful tools for sales and business professionals, it bothers me to see so few use them well. There's certainly some etiquette that needs to be applied throughout these applications.

First and foremost, please note that it's not a race to see how quickly you can accumulate connections. Making connections via social media is a sales process. Those who do it well are sincere in their requests for connections. They mention a common ground they have with you and suggest a valid reason for connecting.

Smart users of this technology also have their profiles complete. When I'm asked to connect with someone who doesn't have a completed (or mostly completed) profile I wonder why. What aren't they telling me about themselves? Why are they in such a hurry to connect that they don't allow me to see who they are?

One of my long-time students connected with me recently. After I accepted his connection, he sent me this very short but to-the-point message: "Just a quick thank you for connecting with me on LinkedIn. I hope I can bring value to you through our connection. If I can help connect you to someone in my network, please don't hesitate to let me know."

How does that make me feel? Better than I feel about the hundreds who have connected but never reached out to me other than to tell me about their product, their listing, or to ask me to endorse them.

Social media has created the opportunity to connect with people you may otherwise have a tough time getting through to. Demonstrate the same level of professionalism with it as you would if you had the opportunity to make these connections in person.

Steering Clear of the Technology Trap and Avoiding Personal Burnout

With today's technology, you can easily be available to your clients 24 hours a day, 7 days a week, 365 days a year. Isn't that great? You can live your life entirely for your clients. Unfortunately, many salespeople try to do this — and they lose in the long run. Why? Because they lose their personal relationships and, even worse, they often lose their health.

Top people in the field of selling manage their lives to stay in balance with both business and personal needs. In order to do this, yet maintain a high level of service to your clients, you have to put in place systems to ensure that everything goes as smoothly as possible all the time.

Do you know the best thing about having all this technology to help you take care of business? All of it has an "off" setting — and you should take advantage of that to rest and recreate. If you don't take care of yourself, you won't be able to do a good job of taking care of anyone else. Champion salespeople know when to forward everything to someone else and let that person take care of it so they can have a break.

Although most salespeople like to think of themselves as being indispensable — and they actually may be the only people in the world who can serve their clients best — everyone requires balance. To achieve and maintain balance, you need to determine how many of the 86,400 seconds of your day you'll devote to clients, how many to your personal development, how many to your loved ones, how many to rest, and so on.

Don't become so much of a Techno-Joe (or Jo) that you lose sight of what's really important — the service you provide to your clients and the personal relationships that fulfill your life. I'm sure you've heard the saying that no one on his deathbed ever said, "I wish I'd spent more time at work" (or, in this case, "more time learning that software"). Your computer and cell phone won't show up at your funeral, so don't allow them to take over your life. They're just tools for you to master to live your life to the fullest.

Chapter 16

Planning Your Time Efficiently

● ●

In This Chapter

▶ Paying attention to how you use your time

▶ Setting aside time every day to plan

▶ Keeping interruptions to a minimum

▶ Organizing your workspace for maximum productivity

▶ Jumping over the common pitfalls of time management

● ●

*T*ime is your most valuable resource, and until you realize that, you'll always be wondering where all your time goes. Time is more valuable than money and more important to master than selling skills themselves. The greatest challenge with time is that there isn't a source to gain more of it. Everyone has the same number of seconds, minutes, and hours in a day. You can always get more money. You can even learn more and better selling skills. But you can't get more time.

Ask a dozen people to name one thing that would make their lives easier, and the overwhelming response will be *more time*. When you have more time to do the things you *need* to do, you can usually generate more income to do the things you *want* to do. As my dear friend and fellow trainer Zig Ziglar said, "When you do what you need to do when you need to do it, you will soon have the time to do what you want to do when you want to do it."

In this chapter, I give you some great tips for staying on top of your time so that you have more time to do the things you *want* to do instead of only being able to do the things you *need* to do. (For more great tips on managing time, turn to *Successful Time Management For Dummies* by Dirk Zeller [Wiley].)

Investing Your Time Rather Than Spending It

Average salespeople often spend their time foolishly doing unproductive busywork — and then they wonder where their day went, why they accomplished so little, and why they never seem to have time for the fun stuff they'd really like to do. The key word here is *spend:* They *spent* their time instead of *investing* it. And that makes all the difference.

The words *spending* and *investing* connote very different ideas. When you spend money, depending upon what it's spent for, you may think of the loss of that money rather than the benefits you enjoy from what you got in exchange for it. On the other hand, the word *invest* signifies a payment from which you will derive a return; you don't focus on the momentary loss of money, but rather on the gain of the product or service that you will receive. Similarly, when you spend your time instead of investing it, you focus on lost time rather than on personal gain.

If you've never put a dollar value on your time before, do it now. To determine what your time is worth, take your hourly rate and follow this simple equation:

Gross Income ÷ Total Annual Working Hours = Hourly Rate

To help you see the value of this equation, suppose that your annual income is $40,000, and you work 40 hours a week for 50 weeks a year (allowing 2 weeks off for vacation). That means that the value of each hour in your workweek is $20. In straight-commission sales, if you spend just one hour each day of each workweek on unproductive activity, you spend about $5,000 a year on nothing. And that's exactly what you have to show for your wasted time, too — nothing. When you choose not to manage your time, you may end up wasting 12 percent of your annual income or more. And this amount doesn't even account for all the future business you lost because you spent time instead of investing it. If you're a regular, full-time employee, that $5,000 is money your employer may as well drop off the roof for all the productivity she gets for it.

In sales or persuasion situations, you often don't see immediate financial payoff from the time you invest. The selling business requires patience and wise money management practices as well. When I was selling real estate, for example, I invested my time in prospecting, demonstrating property, and getting agreements approved, but I saw no return until the transaction was completed and my broker had the check. The final transaction commonly occurred weeks, and in some cases months, after my actual investment of time. During the period between my invested time and my financial reward, I sometimes lost sight of my goals — but that's normal in selling. The longer the period between selling and payoff, the harder it is to stay focused on investing your time wisely. When you invest time in the people you're trying to persuade, thinking of the returns on your investment is normal. I don't know of any new salesperson who doesn't take out her calculator and figure the percentage she gets on a sale as soon as she's out of sight of the client. After all, helping others is a career choice that pays very well when done correctly.

Managing yourself to get a handle on your time

Time management is really all about managing yourself. Don't believe me? Stop and think about it for a minute. When did you last control time? Can you stop time or even slow it down? No way. Can you negotiate with time? If you've figured out how, then you should be writing a book instead of reading one. No one has more time to invest than you do, and you don't have any more time than anyone else, yet some people succeed more often than others, and they do it without controlling time. They do it by disciplining themselves to make the most of every minute.

For example, if you have a healthy dose of road time in your selling life, you can choose to use that time to listen to motivational or educational content. In doing so, you turn your required expenditures of time into investments in your professional education.

Another way to manage yourself when you have to spend time traveling is to cluster your meetings. By organizing your presentations or customer service appointments by geographical area, you can save a lot of travel time — and if you live in a rather large metropolitan area,

you're saving time sitting in traffic as well. If your travel time is primarily within major cities, you may want to schedule it so you don't get stuck in rush-hour traffic. Besides, taking side streets and back roads may lead you to new opportunities if you keep your eyes open and remain aware of your surroundings.

Tip: If you can't put your fingers on the contact information for all your clients within a matter of minutes, consider investing some time in good contact management software. With today's technology, the only reason a client or prospective client's information won't be at your fingertips is because you didn't invest the time to input it correctly as soon as you received it. Entering the information only takes a few minutes, and then it's there forever.

If you think that people who practice time-management strategies are fanatical workaholics who leave no time for personal relaxation, you're mistaken. Just the opposite is the case. In operating more efficiently, they create *more* time for personal endeavors. Invest time in planning your time, and you'll think of dozens of ways to manage yourself more efficiently.

Recognizing the Activities You Must Plan

People who don't practice effective time management often complain that they don't have time to plan their time. But if you don't make time for planning and self-improvement, you may as well plan to earn the same income that you earn today for the rest of your life. It's a fact: By taking the time to plan, you save as much as 20 to 30 times the amount of time that you expend in the planning process.

When you plan your time, divide the things on which you choose to invest time into four categories:

- ✔ **Immediate activities:** These are the tasks you *must* complete today.
- ✔ **Secondary activities:** These tasks are close to immediate, but not quite. You probably need to complete them this week instead of today, for example.
- ✔ **Relatively unimportant activities:** These tasks don't need to be completed by a specific deadline. You can work them in when you have a spare moment.
- ✔ **Emergencies:** Although they're rare, you need to build time into your schedule to handle emergencies so you're not totally in a bind with your other tasks when they happen.

In the following sections, I go into more detail on each of these four categories.

Immediate activities

Immediate activities are *only* those activities that you must complete today. If you clutter your mind with things that should be secondary activities (the things you don't have to do today), you can end up neglecting your immediate activities or not giving them the full, focused attention they require.

Ask yourself these questions to determine the immediacy of your activities and prioritize them by either the amount of relief you'll feel in getting them done or the amount of goodwill or income they'll generate:

- ✔ If I can achieve only three or four activities today, which ones should they be? What if I can only accomplish one?
- ✔ Which activities will yield the largest rewards?

✔ Which activities will complicate my day tomorrow if I do not accomplish them today?

✔ Which of these activities can I delegate to someone else in order to leave myself more time to generate more business or enhance my personal relationships?

✔ Which activities, if I postpone them, will damage my relationships with others?

Have your immediate activities in front of you at all times. If you can't see what you need to accomplish today because you've buried your immediate activities under other less-important work, those activities can get lost in the shuffle — and you can lose sight of your goals.

Enter your immediate activities into your calendar, and set them so that you're reminded about them automatically. If the task is a large one, break it down into smaller pieces so you can accomplish those pieces in a realistic time frame and get them off that list. Accomplishing those smaller pieces of the project will leave you with a very satisfying feeling — and when you're feeling good, you're more productive.

Secondary activities

Identifying your secondary group of activities is usually easier than identifying immediate ones. Some secondary activities may be almost-but-not-quite immediate, so put them at the top of your secondary activity list. As you do for immediate activities, prioritize your secondary list so you finish what's most important first.

Put any paperwork related to those secondary activities in a desk drawer or a letter tray that you can move to your desk or even put on the floor if necessary. Don't let yourself get preoccupied with piles of paperwork. Paperwork overload causes stress and confuses you about what really needs immediate attention. (See the sidebar "Staying on top of your paperwork" for additional advice on dealing with paperwork.)

Staying on top of your paperwork

Paperwork, which includes computer-generated or online reports that your company requires, can crop up in any task, but it's often associated with secondary activities. Depending on your own personality, your best bet for dealing with paperwork may be to do it in the first hour of each day when you're fresh — unless, of course, that's your prime selling time. For some sales pros, the last hour of the day is best for doing paperwork — when the details of what generated that paperwork is still fresh in their minds. Either way, pick up paperwork only once, decide its importance, and deal with it by passing it on or filing it. Don't read it and put it in a pile to be looked at again later. After all, when the paperwork's done, you're free to move on to something more productive toward generating new business. If you do file it, add a tickler note in your calendar to circle back around to it in your future planning.

If you dread doing paperwork, do it as you go through your day. Don't leave it for the end of the day if you can help it because f something unexpected comes up, you won't get to your reports, and the next day you'll just have twice as much to do. This buildup, in turn, causes you even more anxiety because now you have a *really* big task ahead of you.

Relatively unimportant activities

Identifying which tasks fall into the "relatively unimportant" category is difficult: You may think everything needs your attention (if it didn't, it wouldn't come your way, right?). But such thinking simply isn't true. Other people pass many unimportant activities to you to take care of — activities that have a funny habit of working themselves out if you just ignore them for a while. By putting those activities in your "relatively unimportant" category, you may be able to avoid spending time on these chores when you should be investing time on your immediate activities.

So what do I mean by *relatively unimportant activities?* Think about the number of times an associate has come to you for help with a challenge, only to reveal that it wasn't your assistance she wanted after all? She just wanted you to take on the problem as your own. What begins as a favor thus ends up being a real chore. Her worries become your worries — and she's off having a relaxed two-hour lunch, knowing you'll take care of it.

I'm not suggesting that you never help an associate, but I *am* cautioning you about taking on work that should be someone else's responsibility. If you help an associate, make sure that you get compensated, either financially or by an exchange of help on one of your projects. And always get *your* work done first. Establish reasonable rules with your peers about work-related assistance. Doing so helps prevent hard feelings later.

Emergencies

Planning your time efficiently can prevent some emergencies from happening in the first place, but you should always have an alternate approach to your most important activities just in case an emergency arises. Planning ahead and being prepared like good little Boy and Girl Scouts keeps you from panicking and completely trashing your schedule, and that of others, when emergencies do arise.

If you have children, you know that they get sick or hurt from time to time, or they forget to tell you about vital events you need to attend. If you have a whole day of report writing to get done and you get one of those "Mrs. Slack, Mary Beth has just thrown up at school. How soon can you pick her up?" calls, do you have a backup person, such as a grandparent, willing to care for your daughter at least until you can get there yourself? If not, see what you can do about getting that backup in place. Then notify the people at work that you're leaving in 15 minutes so they can get what they absolutely need from you. Save all your report data onto a flash drive, grab your laptop, and head for the door. Or, if you use email, send the file to yourself at home so it's waiting for you when you can sit back down to work while your child rests.

Technology being what it is, don't count on every piece of information being *where* it should be *when* it should be 100 percent of the time. Transferring important information to an external drive is a good idea.

Have backup plans in place for transportation as well. Is there someone else at work who lives near you with whom you can hitch a ride on those mornings when your car won't start? Or if there's a bus route close by, do you have a schedule handy or have the app on your phone? Is there a taxicab number in your contact list?

If you travel long distances by car, it's a good idea to subscribe to a service you can call to get roadside assistance immediately. Also, some apps for smart phones allow you to unlock your car if you lock your keys inside. *Remember:* You can always turn the phone off when proper etiquette requires your full attention to be given elsewhere.

Knowing When and Where to Plan

If you want to manage your time wisely, you need a planning device of some sort. Whether you prefer the pen-and-paper route or the high-tech one, find an option that works well for you. Also, look for contact management software that includes a calendar section so you have both your contact information and meeting schedule all in one place. (Turn to Chapter 6 for more information on contact management software.)

On the first day of every month, set aside 15 minutes at your desk or with your briefcase, laptop, tablet, or smartphone (wherever you keep all your pertinent information) to enter the important things you must do that month. Take a few moments to review all unfinished business from the previous month and plan how and when you'll get it done. Commit to everything you want to accomplish that month. Be realistic and be very specific.

Include any family or social events you're committed to attend. Add any important dates: family, friend, and client birthdays; your wedding anniversary, if it's this month; your child's school play; your spouse's company picnic; and so on. Then note the company meetings you must attend for the month. Add any projects you're working on, their estimated completion dates, and reminders to follow up on them. If you're working on a large project, break it down into smaller pieces that you can accomplish each week. Taking large projects a week at a time helps you see your progress, and the one big project won't seem so oppressive. As you work with your calendar on a daily basis throughout the month, you'll be better prepared to schedule the smaller events and commitments effectively.

In daily time planning, keep track of all activities as you go. Don't wait until 4 p.m. to try to remember what you did at 9:30 a.m. Be truthful. Don't play around with numbers or fake anything just so you can check it off. On the other hand, don't overwhelm yourself with writing down every detail of your workday. You're not trying to write a book. Just note the key events and any information you simply don't want to forget.

I strongly recommend that you do your daily planning where you conduct your business. If you wait until you get home, you won't have that phone number or other detail you need to record and you'll only half plan. If that means you sit in your car to plan, so be it. You may need triggers to remember everything you need to plan, and those triggers will be most available to you at your place of business.

Organizing Your Workspace

One of the main causes of wasted time and lost income is disorganized office space. Believe it or not, clearing your desk also helps to clear your mind. When your mind is clear, you're more able to focus on one task at a time. And all you can accomplish is one thing at a time, anyway, so why try to do more.

So where do you start? Try the tips in the following sections.

Keep only immediate activities on your desk

Keep everything but your most pressing tasks out of sight. And keep everything you need for accomplishing the immediate tasks somewhere nearby (in a place you'll remember), so you don't waste time running hither and yon looking for what you need.

Be proactive with your time

If you suffer innumerable interruptions, close your door. If you don't have a door, try earplugs or a headset to isolate yourself. Maybe your company will allow you to post a sign on your door or cubicle saying something like this: "Unless you are a client with a large need or have a fantastic lead for me, please let me do what I need to do to find those people." As a last resort, consider posting a snarling Doberman near your desk!

Develop your ability to focus on your work. Let your co-workers or family know that sometimes they simply cannot interrupt you. Don't answer your telephone — let voice mail be your receptionist for a while. In many cases, it can be very effective to check voice mail and email only four times each day rather than allowing interruptions to come at you willy-nilly.

Make yourself less accessible to non-clients. If you need to, set up a specific time of day for your associates to freely walk into your office; make all other times off-limits. If an associate drops by at a bad time, don't be afraid to look at your watch and say, "I'd love to catch up with you, but let's do it at 3:00." If what she has to tell you is important enough, she'll be happy to return then. If it's not that important, she'll beg off, and you will have saved yourself from spending time listening to her.

Handle phone calls and email wisely

If the phone is not a necessary tool of your immediate business, remove it from your desk. Put it on a table behind you or even on the floor if you must — but get it out of your sight.

Not every phone call is an emergency. When the other party gets off the subject, or when the other party stays on the subject but is long-winded, try these techniques:

- ✔ **If you initiate the call, tell the person, "I have three things to cover with you."** If she starts to get sidetracked, you have the right to bring her back to one of your three topics.

- ✔ **If the other party initiates the call and you don't have a lot of time to give her, let her know her call is important, but that you were just heading out the door.** She doesn't need to know it was to get a glass of water. Get the basic information she needs to tell you and make an appointment to call her back. Unless it's an irate customer who has a total stoppage of an assembly line because of your equipment, most people are willing to accept a callback. If she can't wait, it's an emergency, and you'll have to handle it on the spot.

- ✔ **Call a long-winded person just before lunchtime or just before she goes home for the day.** If that's not possible, start your call by saying, "I'm really pressed for time, but I just wanted to let you know something," or, "I'm on my way to an appointment, but I wanted to touch base with you."

Treat email similarly. Unless you're expecting urgent information, don't check your email every time you receive a new message. Studies show that it takes a minimum of ten minutes to refocus on a task after an interruption.

With email, you get to choose when and how to handle it. Many professionals include in their email signature line something like this, "Please note that email is checked periodically throughout the day. I will respond as quickly as possible." Others are even more specific, "I check email at 8 a.m., noon, and 4 p.m. daily. If your message is urgent, please call me instead at 555-5555."

The key is not to let phones and email messages run your day unless your job is solely to handle them. They are tools to help you — not devices to control you.

If you don't take control in nonemergency situations, you'll forever be at the mercy of others. And they hardly ever have your best interest in mind.

Avoiding the Most Common Time Traps

You probably know some people who have raised time wasting to an art form. They have mastered the ability to fall into every time trap they encounter. Not surprisingly, these folks aren't the people who get things done, help the most people, or earn the biggest incomes in selling. If you want to get more yeses in your life, knowing — and avoiding — the following common time traps is a great place to start.

Desperately seeking what shouldn't be lost

A sure way to waste valuable time is to keep looking for something you desperately need because you were careless when you "put it away." Looking for lost items is the single biggest time waster for everyone. How many hours have you wasted looking for the scrap of paper you wrote an important phone number on or for the folder with all the referrals that your new client gave you? How about your sunglasses or your car keys? Ring any bells? Those few minutes here and there can really add up, so designate a specific place for every item you use regularly, and then make sure you always use it. If you always hang your keys on a hook by the door, you won't spend precious time searching for them.

Failing to do the job right the first time

Because of the demands salespeople place on themselves, they tend to rush through their paperwork and their planning of presentations without carefully checking or rechecking details. Get out of that habit right away. If you don't have time to do it right the first time, how will you find time to do it again? Consider how much less time you need to do something right the first time than you need if you have to go back and do it over. Don't risk angering others with costly delays or mistakes caused by carelessly written paperwork. Champions double-check everything for accuracy and clarity.

Procrastinating

Procrastination can kill your career. Don't feel alone on this one; everyone procrastinates. Most people procrastinate because of fear. They fear making a mistake, so instead they do nothing. They fear something will take much longer than they anticipate or require much more effort than they're willing to give it. So, again, they do nothing. The trouble with doing nothing, though, is this: Doing nothing can only *produce* nothing. Mistakes can and will happen. Champions accept their mistakes and learn from their experiences.

If a client phones to report a problem with the product or service she acquired from a salesperson, what do most salespeople do? They try to put off facing the challenge until tomorrow. By then, though, when they do call to apologize and solve the problem, the client may be furious and vow never to do business with the salesperson's company again. So the salesperson has to work doubly hard and spend even more time with the client, just to diffuse her anger.

Always call an angry client immediately. The longer you wait, the more the situation worsens. Perhaps you've heard the saying that "a professional is someone who does things even when she doesn't want to." How true.

Making unnecessary or unnecessarily long phone calls

The telephone can be your greatest ally or your greatest enemy, especially when it comes to time management. Here are some ideas to help you deal with wasted time on the phone:

- ✔ **Set aside specific time each day to take and make phone calls.** The time of day is up to you. Choose whatever time is best for you to serve your clients well.

- ✔ **Set a time limit for your calls.** If you're prospecting, the calls probably won't be very long. If you're making a presentation, they may need to be longer. By paying attention to the length of time you're on a call, you'll be more efficient in getting your message across.

- ✔ **Write down your objective for the phone call and focus on it.** Having a focused objective keeps you from straying off topic. Chatting about things that aren't pertinent to business is a big time waster.

- ✔ **Have all your materials and information within reach before you pick up the phone.** Expect to invest more time in preparation than you expect to spend on the call itself. The more prepared you are, the more professional you come across.

- ✔ **Find polite but effective exit lines to help you get off the phone without interrupting the other person or abruptly ending the conversation.** For example, try saying, "Barbara, just one more thing before I hang up. . . ." Such a statement lets the person know that you're coming to the end of the call.

- ✔ **Let all your customers know exactly when you're available for them to call you.** This information should be printed on your business card and become a part of your email signature information.

- ✔ **If you do business with someone who chatters and won't let you off the phone, whenever she calls, tell her you're in the middle of something extremely urgent and that you will call her back.** Call her just before the time when she leaves for the day. You'll be surprised how brief conversations with such people can become.

- ✔ **If you spend great amounts of time on the phone, or if you're in telemarketing, invest in a high-quality headset.** Using a headset allows you to keep both hands free so you can attend to the details while you're on the phone.

If you think of the phone as a business tool, not unlike your computer, you'll be able to form new habits for using it that should keep you out of that common time trap.

Holding unnecessary or unnecessarily long meetings

Attending too many nonproductive meetings can be a major time waster. If you're in management and you think you waste a great deal of your time in meetings, maybe you should reevaluate how often you need to meet with your people and what you need to accomplish when you do get together. Is a daily or weekly meeting really necessary? Or can more effective communications within the company eliminate the need for such meetings? Don't hold a $1,000 meeting to solve a $50 problem.

Many people have found that holding meetings standing up is highly productive. When people don't settle into comfortable chairs for the duration, they finish their business much more quickly. This strategy can be effective for both in-house meetings and those with clients. If your meetings don't require a laptop or large presentation materials, give this method a try. Your clients who sit at desks all day may appreciate a walking or standing meeting if it's brief.

Attending client lunches that last for two or more hours

As with the phone, when you're out for lunch with clients, you need to develop ways to let them know that you've finished your business for today and that you must move on. For example, when you sit down for lunch at noon with a notorious "friendly afternoon waster," you can say something to the effect of "This works out great. I don't have another commitment until 1:30, so I have plenty of time to talk." They'll get the message that you don't have all afternoon.

Getting lost online

Have you ever gone online to look for a piece of information and not paid attention to the time? Next thing you know it's 30 minutes later and you're looking at your screen wondering "how did I ever get onto this subject?" It happens way more often than most people admit. Rather than risking a time-wasting venture into the cloud, if what you are seeking isn't critical to what you're working on at the moment, jot it down for later. Then, when the critical work is finished for the day, invest 20 or 30 minutes in looking up all the little bits and bytes of information you wondered about throughout the day.

Another suggestion is to set a timer for yourself when you venture online. Set it for the amount of time you expect it to take for you to locate that bit of information. If you still haven't located it when the alarm sounds, ask someone else if they know where to find the information. And, if you're exploring some completely different topic when the alarm sounds, use the sound as a prod to get back to business.

Engaging in negative thinking

Negative thoughts that produce negative talk are another big waste of time for salespeople. If you dwell on life's negatives, what do you think you can accomplish? I'm positive (ahem) that you will accomplish very little. Push negative thoughts from your mind. No one who was a negative thinker ever became a success in selling.

Instead of focusing on things you don't like or can't do, think about the positive things you *can* do. And by all means surround yourself with positive thinkers — their positive energy will rub off on you.

Not using driving time wisely

Most people in professional selling spend a lot of time in their cars driving from appointment to appointment. The average salesperson drives 25,000 miles a year for her job. That works out to about 500 hours a year, or about 16 weeks — your basic college semester.

So how can you make the best use of this time? Hundreds of educational programs are available in audio format. Publishing companies produce audiobooks because people don't always have time to read a book. You can use this driving time to listen to programs on sales training, motivation, self-esteem, financial planning, small business strategies, foreign languages, classic literature, history, as well as a growing number of how-to programs and the latest popular novels. That way you're getting where you need to go, both literally and figuratively.

Neglecting to confirm appointments

I'm always amazed at how many people do not confirm meetings before they leave the office or their previous client. Why do salespeople fail to confirm appointments? The old standby: fear. Some salespeople fear that, if they call, the person may say, "Oh, I can't make it today, let's reschedule."

Such salespeople would rather drive all the way to a client's office and have the receptionist tell them that the person they were supposed to meet with got called out of town for the day. How silly is that?

A quick phone call before you leave not only can save you valuable selling time, it also tells the prospect that you're a professional with something valuable to say. If you handle it properly, your brief call to confirm may keep your appointment from being the one that gets canceled if your customer needs to change her schedule. When you call to confirm an appointment, do it this way:

> Hi, Jamila. I've spent a lot of time preparing for our meeting, and I just thought I'd call to let you know that I'll be there right at two o'clock. I think you'll be excited about what I have to show you.

Never say, "I'm just calling to confirm." When you let the decision maker know how much time and effort you've put into preparing for this meeting, she'll feel guilty about canceling and be more likely to find a way to keep the appointment. And another benefit: Even if the decision maker does have to cancel, you have her on the phone to immediately schedule another appointment. If for some reason you can't get to the person you have the appointment with, tell the person taking the message that you're on your way and you'll be on time. Ask the message taker to convey your message to the client you're meeting with in plenty of time for her to be ready for you.

Always take the time to confirm your appointments. The time you save will be well worth the time you invest because it frees up your time to prospect for new business or to take care of something else on your to-do list.

Watching television mindlessly

My experience with high achievers says that they do not waste time watching television. Television watching is probably the single least-productive activity in the American lifestyle. I'm not going to preach to you about the mindlessness of most of what's on television these days, but I will say this: Television should be used properly. Some examples of how to use your television are

- ✔ For improving your personal or business skills.
- ✔ For gaining new knowledge that is valuable in your communications with clients.
- ✔ For winding down from a productive day by enjoying a quality program with your loved ones.

What part of the word *no* can't you say?

Many people just can't say no when others want a chunk of their time. But it's better to say no to someone and get the job done than it is to say yes and not get the job done. Sometimes you're not even the most capable person to do the job.

Professionals recognize their limitations. And when they bump into their limitations, they delegate requests for work that's outside their scope to colleagues who are more capable and more likely to complete the job efficiently.

If you explain, with warmth and care, the fact that others are better suited to getting the job done properly, the people who ask you for favors will appreciate your honesty and your ability to refer them to someone trustworthy to do the job. As you become more successful, your time becomes more valuable, making it all the more important for you to learn when (and how) to say no.

Short of these reasons, I can't think of many others that are worth spending your valuable time watching television. Only you know how much you really watch, so the next time an hour in front of the television turns into three, stop and ask yourself what else you could've been doing with your time instead. Then, plan your time better for the future.

Handling Physical Interruptions

Expect part of your day to be spent working with people, supporting your co-workers, or helping the company problem solve. But you also need to allow yourself some solo time, both at work and in your personal life. *Solo time* is time for whatever you need to do. It can be your time for emotional and physical health in your private life, as well as your most productive work time.

During your solo work time, if someone asks, "Do you have a minute?" just answer, "Not right now. Can it wait until 11:00?" By that time, most people who were looking for your help have solved the problem themselves, or they realized that their problem wasn't all that important anyway.

Here are some tips for handling physical interruptions to your solo time:

> ✔ **Arrange your office so that your desk is out of the line of sight from people who walk down the hallway.** If people don't see you as they're walking down the hall, they're less likely to stop in to chat.

✔ **Remove extra chairs from your office.** Position any necessary chairs as far away from your desk as possible. This way, people won't be tempted to sit down for long periods of time.

✔ **Place a large clock where you and any visitors can see it clearly.** A clock helps you — and your visitors — keep track of how much of your time they're taking up.

✔ **Don't look up when someone walks into your office.** This habit is hard to get into, but if you appear to be extremely busy and the potential interruption is nothing serious, most people will simply walk away. This advice may sound cold, but if you can't get your work done, your inefficiency will cause your clients to receive less service, and it will cause you to earn a lower income.

To get started on minimizing interruptions, keep an interruption log just for one day. In it, record the following:

✔ Who interrupted you

✔ How much time you wasted

✔ What you can do about it

If the same person is interrupting you all the time or the same type of challenge is continually presenting itself, taking a bit of time to train that person or to institute a new procedure can save you a lot of time in the long run.

When an occasional crisis comes up, deal with it quickly and then go right back to your original schedule. You don't have to become antisocial around the office, but you may be surprised at how much more efficient you can be when you start taking back stray minutes here and there. Time flies … and you never hear the rustle of its gossamer wings.

Part V
You Can't Win 'Em All: Keeping the Faith in Sales

Five Steps to Fulfilling Your Goals

1. Set goals that you want more than anything.
2. Vividly imagine your goals, and create a clear picture of them in your mind.
3. Put your goals in writing.
4. Commit to your goals sincerely and completely.
5. Review your goals daily and take the necessary action steps you have chosen.

For more on how to get what you desire by setting achievable goals: www.dummies.com/extras/selling.

In this part ...

- ✔ Stay positive and upbeat and remember what it is that motivates you and what de-motivates you.

- ✔ Face challenging times in your industry and when you suffer disappointment or failure, learn how to overcome negative feelings.

- ✔ Understand different types of goals and learn how to set realistic ones for yourself.

Chapter 17

Staying Upbeat When You Don't Succeed

*Y*ou're *bound* to experience rejection — it's as inevitable as death and taxes. What separates you from all those who let themselves get sidetracked by rejection is your attitude toward it.

So what's the best weapon to use when fighting those inadequate feelings created by failure and rejection? *Enthusiasm!* That one little word, a word you've heard so many times, can make the difference between being a highly successful champion in sales and an ineffective struggler. If you're just going through the motions of selling but doing so with little or no enthusiasm for the job, you'll be terribly disappointed with your results on payday. (After all, your income in selling is in direct proportion to the amount of service you give others. Little service = little income; lots of service = lots of income.)

Dwindling enthusiasm isn't the only concern of professional persuaders, but it is the forerunner of other difficulties that may short-circuit your career. If people knew the secret of why enthusiasm wanes and depression creeps through the back door, they would easily see the enemy approach and prepare for its descent upon their livelihoods. The hard part about battling the depression experienced because of failure and rejection is that it sneaks in, and you don't recognize depression for what it is: a total thief of your motivation to succeed. Instead of focusing on why depression happens, in this chapter I focus on how to overcome such feelings. Keep reading, and you'll see what motivates people and what you can do to increase your own levels of enthusiasm in your selling career and beyond.

Finding Out What Motivates You

Why do you do what you do? Philosophers, psychologists, and psychiatrists have had a field day with that question for thousands of years. And they came up with a list of the most common reasons people give for doing whatever it is they do. Review the following sections so you can determine what your primary motivator is and then use that knowledge to spur yourself on to even greater success.

Money

Many professional salespeople admit to being motivated to sell because they enjoy lighting up the faces of the people they help to benefit from their offering. Few but the candid and outspoken, however, say that money motivates them to sell.

Give yourself permission right now to admit that money is a big motivator. Being money conscious is okay — as long as the money you make is in direct proportion to the service you give your clients. If that's not the case (if you're raking in the dough but providing poor service), your money will soon disappear — as will your motivation to strive toward greater achievements in sales.

Money can be one of your motivators, or even your primary motivator, but it cannot be the be-all and end-all of all your sales transactions. Many top producers look at the amount of money they make as a reflection of the excellent service and high sales standards they develop over the years in their industries. When champion salespeople notice a decline in income, they look to improve service and product knowledge instead of wasting time being depressed about how a drop in income could have happened to them.

Security

Many people say they work to have security. It's something that's wise to aspire to as it relates to protecting and supporting your family and living comfortably in your retirement years.

However, security can be a false motivator because there are no guarantees in life, much less in sales. In fact, you are only as secure as your ability to handle insecurity.

That statement is so important that it bears repeating: You are only as secure as your ability to handle insecurity.

No matter who you are, you've never been totally secure. I don't care how successful you are — you've experienced fear and want somewhere along the way. Fear and want can even motivate you to achieve. So it isn't the state of being free of these feelings that contributes to security, but rather how you deal with the insecurities that confront you.

The key to getting what you want may be the ability to give up what you have. If you're bound and determined that you will never take a chance to further your career, you may as well get out of sales right now because taking risks is what selling is all about. If you can't give up what you have, then keep it; but resign yourself to the knowledge that you will never go much farther up the ladder of success.

Most famous and powerful people who have acquired a great deal of security have also lost as much (if not more) than they have made. What sets these people apart from the average worker is that they were willing to take the chance in order to become all that they could be, whereas the average worker is not willing to take the necessary risks.

Great salespeople follow the same pattern. Be willing to give up what you have for what you can attain. Be a risk taker. You may wonder how you ever find security if you're constantly taking risks. With whatever semblance of security you ever find will come the knowledge that you create your own destiny. Your success and security are determined primarily by your ability to overcome the setbacks that your career in sales hands you. And, believe me, in sales you'll have plenty of time to test your ability to be a risk taker.

Achievement

Everyone wants to achieve something. Some people strive only for modest goals, whereas others shoot for the moon — but all are in gear to achieve. In fact, few people are born who wander aimlessly through life without, at the very least, the desire to achieve the basic needs of food and shelter.

All people believe that they should get what they deserve, and unfortunately, many of them feel they're deserving of greatness, whether they work for it or not. In those moments when you're brutally honest with yourself, you probably realize that the results you're getting are equal to the effort you expend.

Achievement isn't always measured monetarily. In sales, achievement is measured by sales quotas (meeting or beating them) and being given larger territories or levels of responsibility, such as being asked to train or mentor others. In your personal life, you can measure it by the influence and power you wield or by the humanitarian efforts you make for those in need. Achievement means different things to different people — but it's usually a great motivator.

Recognition

For most people, the need for recognition begins in childhood. Think about it: When you were five or six years old, you probably stood on your head, played dress-up, or did other clever little-kid things that adults thought were adorable, just so you would get attention. Some children have even been known to eat bugs or destroy things, all for the sake of recognition. Salespeople receive recognition when they win company-sponsored contests or annual sales awards. There's nothing like standing on the stage at the annual company meeting, listening to the applause of your peers and the other company team members because you did something spectacular for the company.

Not only do people have a need for recognition, but they also like to be the ones to do the recognizing. Look at much of the media today. Whether the recognition is negative or positive, the results are similar. Think about how most people recognize the evil but well-publicized face of Osama Bin Laden more quickly than they do the face of someone who has *positively* changed history, someone like Thomas Edison, for example.

Acceptance from others

Relying on acceptance from others as motivation can be a dangerous thing. The day you rise above the masses as a top producer is the same day that others stop trying to climb up to your level. So what do they do instead? They try to pull you down. The old adage "It's lonely at the top" is true.

When was the last time you heard people say or do things to bring a person down who is already down in the dumps? It just doesn't happen that way. You can always find someone to tell you, "Oh that won't work!" or to say, "Well, that may have worked for him, but do you really believe that you can pull it off?"

Try to surround yourself with positive people who support you in your efforts toward a successful career. Why not make it your philosophy to keep company with people who have similar goals and desires as yours? Try to get the acceptance of the people you know are good for you — and try to get the dismissal of the people who are not. When you think about it, how many people in your lifetime have you accepted advice from who are more messed up than you? Stay away from the negative people: They only pull your opportunities down the tubes with them.

Self-acceptance

When you accept yourself and are happy with the person you are, you experience a freedom you may never have thought possible. Achieving self-acceptance is critical to overall success in both sales and in life. When you have it, you are free to do things your own way or not to do them at all. You are free to enjoy life and all the wonders it has to offer. You are free of the damaging effects of rejection and failure. After you achieve this motivator, there's no going back. You are your own person. You know what you want and how to get it, and you go after it with all of your heart.

Most people measure their success by how much money they have, so, as a motivator, self-acceptance can run neck and neck with the amount of money you accumulate. When you truly accept yourself, you can do what you *want* to do and not what you think you *should* do. Life is much sweeter when you accept yourself — and wonderful things and people seem to gravitate toward you.

Just remember that many motivators work together:

- ✔ You cannot get recognition if you have achieved nothing.
- ✔ You cannot attempt the things you want to achieve without first having a sense of security in your ability to do so.
- ✔ You cannot earn money without giving service. In fact, in sales, money is a scoreboard reflection of the amount of service you give.

The very picture of diligent research

I know of a guy — I'll call him Sam — who went so deep into his study of his competition that he got to know the personal habits of the salesman who covered the same territory he did. Because the two directly competed for the same business, Sam had a chance to research his competitor just by talking with the prospects they shared. Sam learned his competitor's name, his method of operation, and his presentation style. What was the result? Because of Sam's detailed efforts, his company was number one in the territory. Seldom does someone take the process that far, but doing so paid off big for Sam and his company.

And just how far did Sam's knowledge of his competition go? He once showed me a photograph of that competing salesman from a piece of literature put out by that salesman's company. Sam carried that photo with him every day. And he said whenever he felt like quitting early or taking a shortcut, he would pull out that photo and remind himself that this guy would be the next one to talk with the customer if Sam didn't give his prospects 100 percent of his effort every time.

Knowing What De-Motivates You

If motivators are what make people move forward toward successful sales careers and de-motivators cause them to stop dead in their tracks or even go backward, why doesn't everyone just do the things that motivate them? Believe it or not, it's because the average human being is more de-motivated than motivated. Negativity is kind of like gravity — a powerful force that can hold you back and requires tremendous effort to overcome.

Just as you need to know what motivates you to succeed, you also need to recognize the danger signals that will bring your career to a halt. The next sections discuss four of the most powerful de-motivators that stop people from achieving.

Loss of security

A big de-motivator for many people is the fear of losing their security — financially or otherwise. Some are nervous about being in a commission-only arrangement in sales where if they don't sell, they don't get paid. This continues to be nerve wracking only to those who don't invest their time in developing their selling skills like you are doing by reading this book. When you begin a career in sales, what really happens is that you take control of your income. Your income is no longer dictated by someone in upper management who believes someone in your position is worth a certain salary and nothing more.

Self-doubt

Self-doubt is a big de-motivator in selling. I can hear what some of your family members probably said the day you told them you were going into sales: "What? Are you crazy?" or, "Selling … it's feast or famine!" or, "Can you get me stuff wholesale?" They have yet to discover what you and I already know: Selling is one of the few careers left that offers great security — when you overcome self-doubts and learn the strategies of selling, that is.

Most beginners in sales busy themselves with the unnecessary question of "What did I do wrong?" when they do not succeed in their selling attempts. The difference between champions and novices is that champions ask themselves a different question: "What did I do *right?*" When the champion examines what was right about the sale, he can easily keep doing what was right over and over again. The champion in sales has realized that the only way you ever learn what to do right in selling is by doing it wrong, keeping your enthusiasm, figuring out what to do, and overcoming that pain. Just keep on keeping on!

The only way to overcome self-doubts is to face them, look them in the eye, and stare them down by doing the exact opposite of what they make you feel like doing. Don't give in to your self-doubts. Develop strong habits such as well-honed sales skills, post-sales analyses, and keeping good notes for yourself.

Fear of failure

A great many people are so afraid of failing that they just quit trying. Now there's a surefire way never to experience failure — never attempt anything in the first place! Of course, you won't experience any successes, either, so you throw out the baby with the bathwater if you let this de-motivator get the better of you. If you never meet the client, you'll never close the sale.

I recommend that you live by this principle: Do what you fear the most — and you control your fear.

If you're afraid of one of the required aspects of selling, such as phoning for appointments, you're going to need to face it down if you truly want to succeed in sales. Almost anything you do that you once feared doing turns out to be much easier to do than you thought. The process gets easier each time you make yourself do what you fear until, one day, you forget how badly you feared what you feared so much only a few months before. (Did you follow that?)

Control your fears, and you will receive such gratification that soon you will burn with anticipation to do what you once dreaded. Bungee jumping, anyone?

Change

Change is a fierce opponent of progress. You've probably often heard statements such as these: "We've always done it this way," "You'll get used to it — it's just my way of doing things," or "We prefer to stay with the standard procedure." Workers really don't favor the old ways, though. Instead, what they really favor is resisting the pain in change. If they only knew for certain that the potential benefits in making change far outweigh the pains, their resistance would quickly dissipate.

The hardest thing for most salespeople to do is to prospect. Wouldn't hanging around the lobby or the office and waiting for people to come through the doors begging for your product be wonderful? Dream on!

If you can push yourself to make your calls, get out of the office, meet with the people who need to hear about your offering, and call back the difficult clients you sometimes wish you'd never heard of, you're on the road to sales success. You don't have to depend on or blame your company when business is bad. You are responsible for your own success or failure, whatever the case may be — so take charge.

By the way, doing what you don't want to do is what you are paid the most to do. You really have to *want* to change. Being satisfied with yourself today is still crucial, but if you want more tomorrow, then you must be willing to put up with the pain of change. According to Dr. Maxwell Maltz, former plastic surgeon and developer of psycho-cybernetics, it takes 21 days to effect change. So you'll need about 21 days of concentrating and studying the material in this book for this material to become a part of you. No pain, no gain.

The champion salesperson's anti-failure formula

What's the first word your mother and father taught you when you were a baby? *No.* Ah, those were the days, now weren't they? And why do you suppose *no* was the first word you learned? Because your parents wanted to protect you from painful experiences.

But all you knew as a child was that *no* kept you from getting what you wanted. So, as you grew older and kept hearing *no,* you didn't give up quite as easily as when you were a baby. You caught on to this persuasion stuff early on when you realized that *no* doesn't necessarily mean "No! Absolutely not! Never! No way!" and you tried to cajole your parents to see things differently — even if it involved holding your breath and turning several lovely shades of blue.

The same thing happens in your selling career. When you begin in sales and you hear *no,* you think it's the end of the discussion. Some beginning salespeople even relate stories of how they never got completely through their prepared presentation because the moment the client said *no* the salespeople slid out the door quicker than a pat of butter on hot pancakes.

As they matured in sales, though, their stories changed. *No* took on different meanings. *No* came to mean many things besides a plain-old, final, everyday *No.* These salespeople began to realize that *No* could mean, "Slow down," "Explain that part a little more," "You haven't presented the feature I'm most interested in yet," "You need to ask more questions about my likes and dislikes," or, "I don't want to part with that much money right now." These salespeople realized — as one of their first steps toward professionalism — that they could overcome *all* those things instead of having to slip out the back door with their tails tucked between their legs.

Use the following champion's anti-failure formula only when you know you have no chance to get to *Yes* during your meeting. If you follow this formula, you will be able to look at every *No* you receive as money in your pocket. Here's the formula:

> Suppose that you earn $100 for closing a sale. So 1 sale = $100. For the sake of this formula, imagine that, for every 10 contacts you make, you receive 1 sale. So 10 contacts = 1 sale. So every contact, whether it results in a *Yes* or a *No,* is worth $10. Every rejection you get brings you that much closer to that $100.

So what does that knowledge do for you? If you concentrate on it, you see every *No* as a moneymaker instead of getting down on yourself when the prospect gives you a *No.* Instead of getting angry or feeling as though you've wasted an hour of your day, think of a *No* as being handed $10 and moving you one step closer to your goal.

Here's another way to look at it: If you work with a client who has said *No* many times, but you persist in your attempts for a *Yes,* then you may sit through $200 to $300 dollars' worth of *Nos* in that one meeting when it results in a long-term sales relationship. Just keep asking. Don't fear rejection. Welcome the admiration the client will have for you when he realizes that you hung in there 'til the end.

Surveying Strategies for Overcoming Failure

As a salesperson (especially if you're new to sales) you'll experience nonsuccess (another word for failure) at least once or twice a day. How you handle that experience determines how far and how fast you'll start seeing sales or persuasion success. In the following sections, I recommend five strategies for overcoming failure. Think of them as specific attitudes to adopt to help you look at failure in a new light.

View failure as a learning experience

When you demonstrate your product to a disinterested party, when you are rejected by a prospect, or when you thought you had your offering sold and the transaction falls through, you can react in one of two ways: You can get angry and be unproductive, or you can investigate the reasons for the failure. I recommend the second of these two options, because when you discover what went wrong, you can prevent those pitfalls from happening again.

Look at the tremendous negatives Thomas Edison overcame in developing the light bulb. Edison performed more than 1,000 failed experiments before he succeeded. But because of his persistence, today we have the light bulb, an invention that has changed humankind's quality of life. Can you imagine receiving a big fat *No* to what you want to achieve more than 1,000 times — and still persisting? What fortitude! The priceless part of the story of the light bulb, though, is Edison's comments in response to questions about how he felt after experiencing all that failure: "I have not failed. I've just found 10,000 ways that won't work." You see? It's all in the way you look at things.

Think of failure as the feedback you need to change direction

Negative feedback (also known as rejection) is really just the information you need to get on course again. What a delightful way to look at rejection! When a client never gives you any negative feedback and loves everything presented in your offering yet still decides not to own, you have nowhere to turn. But when a client tells you what he doesn't like, you have a place to start selling the benefits he should want to own.

Think of yourself as a rocket locked on to a moving target. As the target moves, the rocket constantly makes adjustments to achieve its designated goal and stay out of the danger zone. If the target veers to the left, the rocket receives that feedback and adjusts course. This may happen several times during the course of the rocket's flight.

But what if the rocket's feelings were hurt from all this negative input, and it entered its danger zone? What are the two things that occur when you enter into *your* danger zone? Withdrawal or hostility. So what would happen if the rocket decided it couldn't take any more rejection? Would it return home to explode? Or what if the rocket took the rejection personally and decided to take it out on the closest target? An innocent victim gets hurt.

If you take negatives personally, not only will you not reach your destination, but others around you will be hurt by your untimely explosions. That's why some salespeople lose it right in the midst of their colleagues and why some just stop showing up at the office and stay in bed all day feeling sorry for themselves. When the rocket hits the wrong target, everybody loses!

See failure as an opportunity to develop your sense of humor

Can you remember having an absolutely disastrous meeting with a prospect? At the time, you probably wanted to crawl in a hole and never see daylight again. But what did you find yourself doing about two weeks down the road? Sure enough, after a little time to heal, you told the story to your peers, embellishing it to provide special effects, and everyone — including you — got a good laugh.

When you're facing failure, you have to learn to laugh sooner rather than later. Laughter is a powerful tool in healing hurt feelings and wounded pride. As a matter of fact, when you share your humorous stories with other salespeople, you find out that similar things have happened to them. Misery loves company, you know!

Look at failure as a chance to practice techniques and perfect your performance

What happens when you do everything you were supposed to do and the client *still* doesn't decide to own your offering? What has he given you? That's right! He's given you an opportunity to practice and perfect your selling skills. You don't really want to practice on qualified buyers, but if this person doesn't buy after you give your exceptionally professional presentation, perhaps he wasn't really qualified after all. (Chapter 9 fills you in on how to qualify clients.) In those cases, look at the experience as an opportunity to practice.

View failure as the game you must play to win

Selling is a percentages game — a game of numbers. The person who sees more people and faces more rejection also makes more money. So, even if you haven't gambled before, you begin to do just that when you get into the game of sales. With every *No* you hear, you're one step closer to hearing a *Yes*.

In life, it's not the number of times you fail that count, but the number of times you succeed. It's no different in selling. Keep this mantra, what I like to call the *Champion's Creed,* in mind: I'm not judged by the number of times I fail but by the number of times I succeed, and the number of times I succeed is in direct proportion to the number of times I can fail and keep trying.

Doing the Opposite of What Average Salespeople Do

Did you know that there's not a whole lot of difference between the activities of an average salesperson and a great one? They both work to find potential clients. They each qualify clients, present information and products, handle concerns, and close sales. The main difference is the point where they give up when the going gets tough. Successful people keep going at the point where failures or average people stop. Top sales pros may not take *hours* longer to close a sale. It may just take them one more closing attempt than the average salesperson tried.

Another way successful salespeople differ from their average counterparts is in time management. Average salespeople don't plan their time effectively. They don't invest time in themselves to improve their skills. Some even work their sales job like it's a clerical position. They don't ever see the incredible opportunities that lie before them. Successful salespeople know what time of day is best for selling. That's when they sell instead of doing paperwork.

They keep the details of pending sales organized and readily accessible because they understand that opportunities to close sales can show up randomly. They also schedule time for reflection, to review of strategies and training. Go to Chapter 16 for more details on efficient time management.

A final point of difference is that average salespeople just don't want to work very hard, whereas successful salespeople know the harder they work, the more they earn. One of my favorite phrases from my own mentor, J. Douglas Edwards, is this: "Selling is the highest-paid hard work and the lowest-paid easy work there is." Average salespeople are average simply because they're not motivated enough to work just a little harder.

Keeping Your Personal Life Out of Your Professional Life

When you're meeting with a potential client, always keep your personal life to yourself. After all, it doesn't matter to a potential client if you have anything other than his needs to tend to. Your need to pick up your kids after school and drive them through rush hour traffic in time for soccer practice has no bearing on your client's situation, your presentation, and whether or not he becomes a long-term client. Knowing that you have to close three more sales this week to meet your goals should not affect how you relate to the person you're sitting in front of.

Try thinking of yourself as a servant (because that's effectively what you are). You serve the needs of both your company and your clients so your income can serve the needs of you and your loved ones. Think about servants you've seen in movies or read about in books. Do you ever find out much about their personal lives? Rarely. I'm not saying you should be a man or woman of mystery. Just keep your personal life personal.

Before every client contact, do yourself and your potential and current clients the biggest favor of all. Clear your mind of any distractions. Take a deep breath if you must. Shift your body physically if that helps. Do whatever it takes to focus only on the matter at hand — the serving of this person or company's needs. Doing so will make the outcome of the meeting more pleasurable and positive for everyone involved. You'll close more sales, have more happy and satisfied clients, and earn a better income.

Facing Challenging Times in Your Industry

It doesn't matter what your product or service is. Sooner or later you'll hit a bump in the road. A competitor may release something that's a way better product shortly after your latest release. Your industry can get some bad press because of poor service provided by someone else in your field half a world away. It doesn't matter exactly what happens — what matters is how you react to whatever *it* is.

The first thing is not to panic.

The second thing to do is to gather as much information as possible about what has happened so you can prepare your answers for your clients' questions. Make a list of everything you *can* do along with what you cannot because of the challenge.

The final thing to do is to reach out to your best clients before they contact you. Being proactive is essential to keeping their business through a rough stretch.

Note: If the challenge you're facing looks like it may take awhile to overcome, and you don't have enough financial resources to wait it out, you may need to consider moving on and marketing a different product. That decision depends upon your commitment to your clients and your company (and your company's commitment to weather out the storm).

True professionals never abandon ship when challenging times arise. They do what's best for their clients first. Even if it means suggesting they take their business to another company if yours may be going out of business. Handling yourself ethically and professionally during the tough times will benefit you in the long run no matter where you end up.

Chapter 18

Setting Goals to Stay Focused

· ·

In This Chapter

▶ Creating balance in the goals you set

▶ Managing activities for goal achievement

▶ Writing down goals to make them real

▶ Starting all over by setting new goals

· ·

Success should be something you don't just kinda-sorta want to reach; success, as you define it, should be something you feel you *must* reach. Those who achieve the most usually burn with a *have-to* attitude, not a *want-to* attitude.

If you have no concrete goals and you've been succeeding in spite of yourself, just think of how much *more* success you could enjoy if you set your sights on a definite path and have a specific time frame in which you expect to reach your destination. If you're a newcomer to sales and you think you don't need to set goals — think again. The sooner you map a course for success, the more likely you are to achieve what you want.

Even though you don't need to set goals to reach some level of selling success, most professionals who fail to set goals reach a peak in their selling skills and lack either the motivation or the direction to go beyond it. They never move upward to a higher selling status. What they don't know — and what you *need to* know — is that goals give you three distinct benefits that help you succeed:

✔ They keep you motivated.

✔ They help you stay focused.

✔ They tell you when to celebrate.

And, if nothing else, goals let others know what they can expect from you. In this chapter, I give you the information you need to make goal setting a part of your daily life.

Setting Realistic and Effective Goals

When you first considered a career in sales, you probably had some vague notions of success in mind — mostly related to your income. Now it's time to turn those notions into specific, vivid pictures of your soon-to-be reality. The pictures will inspire you when you feel like packing it all in and running away to a deserted isle somewhere in the South Pacific to lie on the beach watching your toenails grow.

When you're setting goals, give yourself the time and privacy you need in order to think about what would make you happy, what would motivate you to sell with the big boys and girls. Goal setting should be fun. Don't make it so complicated that you end up setting no goals at all out of fear that the goals you set will be wrong. So what if they are? Are the goals police going to come to your front door and ask to do an audit of your goals? Probably not. Goals are maps you create for your journey to success — and sometimes with growth and development maps change. Road maps include unfinished roads or roads that you need to detour around while improvement is underway. The road map you create for yourself is no different.

When you're in the beginning stages of goal setting, keep the following rules in mind to help yourself form and stay committed to what's important in your life:

- ✔ **The goal must be better than your best — but believable.** Don't set a goal that you don't truly believe you can reach. The trick to setting goals is to make them high enough to push you to strong levels of performance, yet reasonable enough that you can envision reaching them. If you set goals you don't think you can reach, you most likely won't be willing to pay the price to reach for them when the going gets tough. Even worse, you'll be setting yourself up for failure. Who would do that to themselves on purpose?

- ✔ **Set goals based on productivity, not just on production.** If you set goals based only on the money you want to make, you're setting yourself up for failure. It's better to set productivity goals; they'll give you a guideline for how many people you must contact in a week or how many calls you must make. Productivity precedes production anyway, so you're jumping the gun if you set production goals. Actively pursue your productivity goals, and increased production will result. For example, you're productive if you make 20 phone calls today. Even if you only speak with three people, you've still been productive. You're productive if you sent information and thank-you notes to those three people, even if you didn't generate a sale from those contacts — yet.

Breaking Your Goals into Smaller Pieces

When you're setting goals, always begin with long-term goals and work backward to medium-range and short-term goals. Your long-term goals can be the hardest to set, so if you set those first, you accomplish the tough stuff right up front. Besides, you develop your medium-range and short-term goals from your long-term ones. The next sections help you set all three kinds of goals.

Long-term goals

Long-term goals should be 20-year projections. Granted, if you're 75, your 20-year goal may be just to be healthy enough to plant both feet on the ground each morning. No matter how young or old you are, picturing what you want your life to be like 20 years from today is difficult. But try to anyway — keeping in mind that your goals may change.

Three areas you may want to consider when you set your long-term goals are for personal accomplishments, including health, lifestyle, and net worth. When you set long-term goals, be specific. Instead of saying, "In 20 years, I want to live in a large house and be financially independent," write something like this:

> In 20 years, by the first of June, I will live in a 3,200-square-foot beach-front house by the Pacific Ocean. I will own this home free and clear and will live off the interest generated by the $5 million I have in the bank. I will walk on the beach every day as part of my health regimen and be a regular, committed volunteer in the community.

Get the picture? Your long-range goals don't have to be this grand, but they do need to be this specific.

Medium-range goals

When you finish setting your long-term goals, cut them in half and set medium-range goals for about ten years down the road. Compare your 10-year goals to your 20-year goals and then determine the activity you need to keep to make those goals a reality. Then divide your ten-year goals into five-year goals.

Your medium-range goals are your largest and perhaps fuzziest area, the goals you'll probably have to adjust the most frequently. This is why I stress the importance of not casting your goals in stone, rather allowing them to be flexible and dynamic. In looking at the long-term example, the medium-range goal you might draw from that could be that in ten years you will have

$2 million dollars in the bank and know the specific area of beach where you plan to own your home.

Short-term goals

Always set your short-term goals last. These are the goals that demand most of your attention. For the best results with short-term goals, never set them for any longer than 90 days. Short-term goals for anything longer than 90 days aren't immediate enough to create a sense of urgency.

Immediately after you set short-term goals, you need to start taking steps to achieve them. That way they take root as real, not-to-be-denied entities in your mind — not tomorrow, not next week, but as soon as you make them. Your 90-day goals should then be broken down into 60-day goals, 30-day goals, and eventually, the steps you can put in your calendar to take today to achieve them.

For example, if one of your short-term goals is to improve your health, start a walking program now. It may take you awhile to make it a daily habit. And, you'll quickly find out just how dedicated you really are to this as a long-term goal.

Looking at Particular Types of Goals

You can and should consider setting goals in all areas of your life. For the examples here, two business categories are covered rather than personal goals. The sections that follow offer insight into setting both types of goals.

Sales-specific goals

Selling is both an art and a science. Knowing the numbers you plan to achieve and how they break down is critical to the science side of selling. This is where you develop your own personal measurements to help you know if you're on track to your chosen achievements. Sales newbies may need a little extra help in setting goals for their selling lives.

Your sales manager can probably assist you, but be aware that any goals she helps you set may look more like company quotas. You see, every manager has a certain sales revenue amount she needs to meet for the overall company goals. Most managers spread that quota out among the various members of the sales team. Usually this is based on the manager's belief in the abilities of each salesperson to produce. Unless you have an incredibly savvy manager, her quotas are not likely to consider what you want or believe you can achieve.

So take a look at the various activities required to generate income before setting your sales goals or agreeing to any quota your manager may try to put on you:

1. **Determine what you believe you can have as an annual income goal.**

2. **Divide the amount from Step 1 by 12 to find your monthly income goal.**

3. **Divide the amount from Step 2 by 4 (the number of weeks in a month) to find your weekly goal.**

4. **Divide the amount from Step 3 by the number of days you work each week at making sales.**

   Now you have the numbers clearly before you of how much income you need to generate each day in order to reach your annual goal.

5. **Take the average amount you earn from each sale and divide it into the money amounts for annual, monthly, weekly, and daily goals from Steps 1 through 4. This tells you how many sales you need to make each day, week, and month to achieve your annual income goal.**

6. **Consider how many presentations you need to make to get the number of sales you came up with in Step 5 and figure your presentation-to-sales ratio.**

   For example, if you typically close one sale for every three presentations, your sales conversion ratio is 1:3. So, you multiply the numbers in Step 5 by 3 to get the number of presentations you need to make.

7. **Take your sales conversion ratio from Step 6 and figure out how many contacts you need to make to get the necessary number of presentations to make the sales and earn the income.**

8. **Decide whether these numbers are realistic.**

Table 18-1 is a chart you can use to fill in the numbers from the preceding steps. Use pencil on it or make several copies of it as you work through your sales goals. When you start improving your ratios, it's fun to fill in new numbers and re-do the math. You may see that you'll beat your income goal. Or, you may see that you can achieve the goal while working less.

Table 18-1	Sales Goal-Setting Chart			
	Annual	*Monthly*	*Weekly*	*Daily*
Income				
Number of sales				
Number of presentations				
Number of contacts				

Grab a calculator and play with the numbers until you set sales goals that feel just right. They should be a bit of a stretch for you above and beyond where you are now, but they must be believable!

If any of the numbers you compute along the way in this exercise cause you to doubt your belief that you can achieve the goal, stop. Think about solutions you could implement to make the goal a reality. Do you need to sharpen your skills to improve your ratio? Are you setting your expectations unrealistically high as to the number of people you need to contact *every* day based on your current level of productivity? Are you willing to make the changes necessary to achieve these goals?

Personal goals

Setting personal as well as career goals is important to keep your life well balanced. If all your goals are business goals, you'll have trouble taking time out for family and friends — who are your true support system — because you'll always be pushing toward the next career goal.

Although I encourage you to pursue your business goals with fervor, I also encourage you not to pursue them at the expense of family, friends, or time out for yourself. If you do, you risk becoming so single-minded that you eliminate the human qualities you need in order to succeed in sales. Nobody wants to do business with someone who is too busy to understand and care about her needs.

As a way to make sure that your goals are well balanced, let your family help you set them. If you do, they'll be more understanding when you have to spend a late night working or invest in a multiday training seminar away from home. Your family will be more willing to share in your sacrifices if you let them share in the celebration of achieving your goals such as a fun family vacation.

Other areas of personal goal setting include

- ✔ Making time to develop your spiritual life.
- ✔ Exercising so you'll be in great physical condition to enjoy the fruits of your labors.
- ✔ Setting goals for continued education outside of sales — such as learning more about your favorite hobby.

Another benefit from involving the family is that they hold you accountable for your part of the goal and will do what it takes to motivate you. Have you ever thought that sleeping an extra few hours is just what you needed, only to have your spouse encourage you to get up and get busy earning your share of that special weekend trip that you both set as a mutual short-term goal? You knew you should get up, but your immediate desire for sleep clouded your judgment. How do you think you'd feel, and what message would you send to your spouse, by showing him that sleeping is more important to you than working to achieve shared goals?

Fulfilling Your Goals

Follow these five steps for achieving your goals and you'll be on the straight-and-narrow road to reaching them because you'll be focused both consciously and subconsciously on seeking out the means to your chosen ends:

1. **Set goals that you want more than anything.**

2. **Vividly imagine your goals, and create a clear picture of them in your mind.**

3. **Put your goals in writing.**

4. **Commit to your goals sincerely and completely.**

5. **Review your goals daily and take the necessary action steps you have chosen.**

Although all five of these tasks are important, two take precedence: writing down your goals and committing to them fully. The following sections focus on these two important actions.

Putting it in writing

After you set your goals, you need to make your final commitment to them by putting them in writing. This step is the single, most vital one in goal setting. Writing down your goals makes them something you can grab onto. The day you write down your goals is the day you commit yourself to reaching them. Until they're in writing, they're merely wishes and dreams. After you write them down, your mind starts seeking out whatever it takes to make those goals a reality.

Writing down your goals helps you do what I call *in-your-face goals viewing*, a process that's great if you need a tangible reminder of how far you've come toward achieving your goals. What's better, in-your-face goals viewing encourages you to put forth the amount effort your goals require. No matter how tough the going gets, you don't want to put your foot on a banana peel when you're right at the brink of reaching your goals.

To achieve the maximum effect of in-your-face goals viewing, put your list of goals where you see them often, such as on your bathroom mirror, in your wallet, and in your car. When you'd rather take a break, remind yourself of the importance of doing what you know you have to do to succeed. Each time you accomplish a step toward achievement, visibly check off that step. That's the basic formula for proper in-your-face goals viewing.

Committing completely

If you want your life to change, *you* have to change it — or you'll stay pretty much the same as you are. So set some goals that turn you on and get your life into gear. All you have to do is make the effort to do it. You can change and become or do anything you want. Just want it, then plan it out with your goals!

The harder you work toward a goal, the sweeter the taste of success. If you doubt that, ask any Olympic medal winner. Don't think for a second that your road to success won't be painful at times. If you don't experience at least a little bit of stretching to achieve your goals, you probably haven't set them high enough to challenge you. And if your goals *aren't* high enough, they may be holding you back, making you content to remain at levels that are no big deal for you. So when the road gets rocky, dig in your heels and let nothing distract you from your goals. The people who persevere today produce tomorrow. Giving up immediate gratification or postponing what would satisfy you for today just for a promise of greater things down the road isn't natural. In today's instant-gratification society, long-term gains are almost unheard of. But don't sell yourself short by settling for what you know will bring you only temporary satisfaction. If you settle for less than your goals, that's exactly what you end up with — less.

If you're determined and enthusiastic about your goals, you won't settle or waver. Your resolve helps you keep a vivid picture in your mind of what you want to happen and how you will make it happen. If your imagination isn't vivid enough, cut out pictures or write detailed descriptions of your goals so you can refer to them when you get distracted. The more reminders you bump into, the more determined you are — and the more determined you are, the more goals you will achieve.

Signing an agreement with yourself

An effective tool to help you reach your goals is a binding agreement in which you commit to reaching your goals. Such agreements are hard to recognize in the wild, but if you see something that looks like this, you're probably face-to-face with a real one. Feel free to use this one to make a commitment to yourself — and be sure to hold yourself to it. If you're afraid of the temptation to waiver when the going gets tough, share your goals with someone else who will help to hold you accountable.

Date: _____ 20_____

Name: _____

The undersigned proposes to furnish all materials and perform all labor necessary to complete the following goal:

_____

_____

_____

_____

_____

_____

_____

_____

I hereby swear to start today to reach out and do more with my life and achieve the greatness that I know lies within me, which is waiting to be brought out.

From this day forward, I will not deny myself any longer. Today is the day when I finally get the guts to do what I know I must do and quit taking the easy way out. I will invest the time and effort necessary to reach this goal because I know the pain of not fulfilling myself is greater than the pain of doing any job, no matter how hard the job may be.

I understand that I will reach my life's plan by reaching one goal at a time, each smaller goal putting me one step closer to my greater future. I understand that each agreement I fulfill always puts me one step closer to what I want out of life, and I will not have to settle for what others give me or for just earning a living. I have the power to change my life.

_____

Signature

As I endorse this agreement, I understand that my future is in my hands only and I can look to no one else for its fulfillment.

(continued)

(continued)

Acceptance

Upon the completion of this goal, I congratulate myself for proving that I can do anything that I want and be anything that I want. I also can get anything I want as long as I know what it is.

I have taken one more step toward being the person I dream of. I take pride in knowing that I have the backbone to plan and reach a goal.

I am now one step closer to my major goal. Major goals are just a string of successful small goals that lead me to the top.

_____

Signature

Date Fulfilled: _____ 20_____

Terms and Conditions

1. Any goal I ever include in this agreement, no matter how small, must be treated with great respect, because the achievement of goals builds my character and self-image.

2. This agreement must be filled out in full and dated with starting and completion dates.

3. My goal must be precise and explicit. It must paint a very clear picture of what I want and when I want it.

4. In front of the mirror every day, I must read all of my agreement that I have not completed, and I must read them with great conviction so as to embed my goals into my subconscious mind.

5. When I reach a goal, I must endorse the agreement and then write, in large red letters on the face of the agreement, "This agreement fulfilled." I must save all fulfilled agreement and keep them in order by date completed, so that I may see a pattern of growth.

6. Each goal in my plan, no matter how small, must become part of my larger plan; when it does, it may then help me to turn my beautiful dreams into a fantastic, rewarding life. I can be as great as anyone as long as I have a plan.

7. I will not make conflicting goals, such as "I will spend more time at home" and "I will double my sales," because they may not work together and may cause frustration in my life.

8. My goals will entice me so intensely that they ignite my soul and make me burn with enthusiasm.

9. I cannot reach a destination if I do not know how to get there. Each goal becomes a stopping point or starting point on the road map of my life, which in turn becomes the blueprint for my every success. With the blueprint I choose, I build the life of my dreams.

What to Do When You Achieve Goals

The funny thing about achieving your goals is that, as you get close to achieving them and you look back, the struggle to achieve them doesn't seem as difficult as you had originally thought. Time has a way of blurring the gory details of the daily grind. For example, think back now to what you were doing five years ago. Now think forward five years. Which seems longer? If you're like most people, the future always seems to loom out there longer because you don't know everything that will happen and how your life will take shape.

But when you get in the habit of setting goals, you'll find yourself looking toward the next set of goals before you close on those you're about to achieve — and that's a good thing to do. You don't want to wait to set new goals until you're done with the ones you have today. Keeping your eyes on the future and the opportunities it can bring your way has many advantages. Soon you get so caught up in the goal-setting process that achieving your goals becomes reward enough.

When you achieve your goals, one of the first things you want to do is celebrate your success. When you celebrate, keep these suggestions in mind:

- ✔ **Include in your celebration everyone you involved in setting and accomplishing your goals.** They were there with you in the beginning, and they'll be eager to rejoice with you in your successes.

- ✔ **Celebrate in proportion to your achievement.** For example, don't give yourself a trip to Hawaii for calling 100 people in a month. A good reward for this accomplishment may be a dinner at a special restaurant, or a new suit.

- ✔ **Ready yourself for a letdown after you achieve a difficult goal.** Indulging the natural tendency for a letdown is okay, but don't allow the letdown to run too long. The longer you remain inactive, the harder it is to get revved up again. Play a while, but then head back to work. After all, if you sell something that you enjoy, your work is just an extension of your hobbies anyway.

After you celebrate, start working on the new goals you set. Keep records of all your successes. When they start piling up, you'll want to do whatever it takes to add to that pile. Remember the difficulties you overcame while you accomplished each preceding goal; mentally reward yourself for your successes. When you do set the next goal, push yourself just a tad more. Always stretch yourself; that's what keeps you growing in sales. If everything's too easy, you get bored — and selling stops being a hobby and looks more and more like a job.

The harder the goal is to achieve, the more value you find in its achievement. Don't wait until you fully achieve one goal before you set your next one. Have your new goal already in place so that you're ready to start the necessary steps to gain even greater success.

The Law of Expectation

Most people have experienced the phenomenon of fulfilled expectations, but they tend to shrug off fulfilled expectations as coincidences rather than planned, envisioned events.

The Law of Expectation states otherwise:

> **When you think something will happen, and you feel strongly about it, you bring about its happening.**

I think this is where the phrase "Mind over matter" came from. The Law of Expectation works with simple things, as well as with matters as complicated as achieving your 20-year goals.

For example, one evening a friend of mine left home to take a walk. All she took with her were the keys to her apartment (and, of course, the clothes on her back and the shoes on her feet). She had been out for about an hour and was returning home right around dark when she felt a grate beneath her feet. No sooner did she feel the grate than the thought crossed her mind that if she dropped her keys into the grate she would not be able to get back into her apartment because her husband was away on a three-day business trip. What do you suppose happened? You got it! The keys fell into the grate and left my friend with the dilemma of finding the best way to break into her own apartment.

Now because my friend learns from every situation, even the negative ones, after the whole ordeal she sat down to record what her experience had taught her. One of the things she learned was the power of her thoughts. But she learned something else just as important. When she finally broke into her apartment, she realized just how easy the task really was. The next day she went to the hardware store and bought various goodies that, after she installed them, made breaking in difficult if not impossible. She avoided a dangerous situation (a possible burglary) by being open to learning from what began as a negative experience.

So be your own fortune-teller. Predict your own success by making your goals happen. The more you believe in your own success, the more you will do to turn your goals into realities. Success is no accident! You plan it, you work on it, you monitor it, and you adjust it to enable yourself to enjoy a productive and prosperous life. People may look at the success you've spent years accomplishing and see you as an overnight wonder. They may even try to tell you how lucky you are to have the things you have. Well, I say you create your own luck. You control your own destiny. Lady Luck has little to do with your success, and she shouldn't get the credit for your achievements.

Part VI
The Part of Tens

For ten tips on how to master the art of selling, head to a bonus chapter at www.dummies.com/extras/customerexperience.

In this part . . .

✔ Discover ten ways to avoid mistakes that cost you sales.

✔ Find ways to keep a positive attitude.

✔ Read about ten little ways you can keep your clients satisfied and improve your selling skills.

Chapter 19

The Ten Biggest Sales Mistakes to Avoid

In This Chapter

▶ Finding ways to serve your clients better

▶ Keeping your attitude positive

*E*veryone makes mistakes in life. And you should expect to make some when you're trying something new. In this chapter, I share with you the ten most common mistakes others who have gone before you have made so your journey to success in sales can be shorter and much more enjoyable.

Misunderstanding Selling

In some cases, the primary contact a business has with the outside world is through its sales and service people — and the only reason those companies have salespeople is for them to sell the product or service. Stronger companies realize that selling is much more than that. Selling is done through the gathering and sharing of information via professional skills. Those skills help the prospective client make decisions that move him to making the final ownership decision . . . and move companies to develop new and better products.

How this is evolving with technology is that *everyone* in the company is involved in selling the brand and its products. Everyone who does anything that touches buyers is technically in sales. Everyone needs to know the demographic audience for the company's product and work to understand what they really want and need — not necessarily new features, but the benefits derived from those features.

You can't know too much about why people do and don't buy your product or service — and gaining that knowledge is a function of selling. It helps you not only succeed now, but also come up with new products and services to continue to grow your business for the future.

Professional selling doesn't involve becoming pushy or aggressive in any way. Professional salespeople or persuaders are low key, service-oriented relationship builders. An attitude of servitude will take you far.

Thinking You're a Sales Natural

Sales skills are not a gift of birth. They are learned skills that anyone can master with a little study and work. Start watching others in persuasive situations wherever you go. Ask yourself why some persuaders are good and why some are bad. You will find that identifying why they are bad is much easier — when persuaders are bad, you can usually tell that they're incompetent, that they don't know what they're talking about, or that they're just making mistakes in general. But when salespeople are well trained and highly skilled, things seem to move forward so smoothly that spotting the sale happening is almost impossible. That's why you tend to think of these people as naturals. Even though they may be naturally comfortable talking with others, the actual skill of persuading must be learned, just as the ins and outs of the product or service must be learned in order to succeed.

Talking Too Much and Not Listening Enough

Most people think that you have to be a good talker in order to persuade others. A typical "good talker" thinks that he can tell the customer enough about the product that he will automatically buy it. But the truth is just the opposite. When you're talking, you're only telling what you already know. You're learning little about the buyer. Ask questions, and you discover what your potential clients want to own. Then, you can start selling them on the benefits of your product.

A good salesperson is just like a great detective: He asks questions, takes notes, and listens intently to the customer's spoken words, as well as to his body language.

In most cases, people who talk too much want to control the conversation and are more likely to be perceived as aggressive and pushy. Professional sales training involves more questioning and listening techniques than it does speaking skills. It's knowing the proper questions to ask, not just talking, that leads to closed sales. A salesperson who has been trained to ask questions *leads* the buyer down the path to the sale. He doesn't *push* him down that path.

Using Words That Kill Sales

In any presentation you make, your words paint pictures. And a few wrong word pictures can ruin the entire portrait you're trying to paint.

How many presentations do you suppose are made daily that don't succeed just because of the sales-killing pictures that the presenter's words paint, like referring to a "contract" someone has to "sign" to have a product installed? Both of those terms can bring to mind negative images. *Contracts* are legally binding and should be avoided by the average person unless he has the advice of his attorney. Mom and Dad always warned you not to *sign* anything without thoroughly reading and understanding it. By using the wrong words, salespeople create negative pictures in the minds of the people they strive to serve — giving them more reasons not to go ahead than to get involved. To master the words that are more conducive to generating sales, head to Chapter 4.

Not Knowing When to Close the Sale

Most customers who leave a place of business without owning a product or service are shrugged off by untrained salespeople as being "just lookers." or "be-backs," or any number of other euphemisms that hide the basic fact that the salesperson did not do the job as well as it could have been done. A professional salesperson, however, prefers to see such customers as what they really are: lost sales.

Ask for your prospect's decision when you recognize his *buying signs,* such as asking more questions the answers to which he needs to know when he owns it or using language that shows an attitude of ownership, such as, "Yessir, that Van Gogh original certainly will enhance our living room." A key word to look for from the customer is the word *will* — as opposed to something more hesitant such as *might* or *would.* Buying signs also include asking for more details, wanting to see the instructions for how to operate your product, and asking financing questions. Your prospect may ask questions that refer to delivery, such as "Is it in stock?" or "Is there a delivery charge?" When you see such signs, *yes* is usually right around the corner. (Chapter 12 talks about recognizing closing signs.)

If you don't close a sale when you recognize the buying signs, the prospect could very well cool off and give the purchase second thoughts that include not making a decision today.

Not Knowing How to Close the Sale

In many cases, all you have to do to close the sale is ask. If a customer asks, "Do you have it in red?" and you say, "I believe I do have a red one," what do you gain? Nothing.

Why not ask this instead:

> If I have the red one, do you want to take it with you today, or shall I ship it?

Or this:

> Let me check on our color selection. By the way, would you like it gift-wrapped?

In other words, ask a question that moves the prospect into a position of having to make an either/or decision about ownership. Learn even more simple yet powerful closes in Chapter 12.

Being Insincere

If you're trying to persuade someone else to adopt your point of view, to own your product, or to start an account with your service, you must first help him to see that you're talking with him for his benefit, not yours.

Never let greed get in the way of doing what's right. If you don't sincerely believe that what you have to offer is good for the other party, yet you still try to convince him to own, one of two things will happen:

- ✔ He'll recognize your insincerity, not get involved with you, and tell at least 11 other people how terrible his experience with you was, thus ruining your reputation.

- ✔ He'll be persuaded even though what you're selling isn't good for him, perceive you as nothing more than a con artist, and take every measure possible to see that you're punished as one.

When you're professionally selling or persuading others, it must be your sincere desire to serve others and help them get involved in something that's truly beneficial for them. You have to truly believe in your product and what it can do for others before you can sell with sincerity. Honesty and integrity are the key elements to every successful selling career.

Failing to Pay Attention to Details

When you wing it on your presentations, skim over details, and ignore important cues from others, you also skim over big potential wins for yourself. Lost or misplaced information and orders, correspondence with typographical errors, and missed appointments or delivery dates all ruin your credibility with your clients. They also take away from the high level of competence professionals strive so hard to display. If your clients don't have the impression that you're doing your best for them, they'll find someone who will — maybe even someone else in your own office. Ooh, that would hurt, wouldn't it?

Letting Yourself Slump

Getting out of a slump takes a lot out of you, both mentally and physically. Why put yourself through hard times when with a little bit of diligence you can keep things on an even keel instead?

 Most people have patterns to their selling cycles and efforts. Try charting your daily activities, productivity, and winning presentations on a graph or chart for not less than 30 days, preferably for 90. If you watch your cycles carefully, you'll see a slump coming long before it hits and be able to correct the errors of your ways to even out your successes.

Neglecting to Keep in Touch

Most people who switch from your product, service, or idea to another do so because you're being apathetic and someone else is paying them more attention. Someone else is keeping in contact on a regular basis and making them feel important. When all it takes is a bit of regular contact to keep people doing business with you, why would you ever get so lazy as to let them go?

All you need to do is schedule two or three quick phone calls to say, "Diane, this is Tom from ABC Company. I'm just calling to see if you're still enjoying the increased productivity and cost savings with your new software. If all is well, I won't keep you. I just wanted to touch base with you and thank you once again for your business." These words take about 12 seconds to say, and that 12-second investment is well worth it if it keeps a client happy.

Chapter 20

Ten (Plus One!) Ways to Master the Art of Selling

In This Chapter

▶ Taking your selling skills up a notch

▶ Committing yourself to continual improvement

*I*n this chapter, you have eleven choice bits of selling wisdom to return to as your career progresses. Use this chapter as your road map to mastering the art of selling, as your eleven easy steps to becoming a champion in all your future selling endeavors.

Develop Your Curiosity

Before you enter into any new sales experience, make sure you bring with you an attitude of positive anticipation and enthusiasm. Anticipate learning something new — whether it's about your potential client or about the product itself. Be enthusiastic about learning experiences in your daily life, and keep your mind open as to what experiences might apply in future selling situations. What you gain from this book will be directly proportionate to the amount of time you invest studying and practicing the techniques and suggestions offered in its pages. As a result of what you discover, your income will grow right along with the maturity of your knowledge in sales. (Go to Chapter 3 for more information on having the right attitude for a career in sales.)

If you want to be a master of persuasion and selling, keep in mind that all masters were first excellent students. In addition to that general advice, I can give you three specific hints to make your learning experience more productive:

- ✔ **Discover your best learning environment.** Figure out where and how you can most effectively focus on learning. For some, sitting in the family room with the family as they watch football may be the appropriate place, whereas others require silence and isolation to best comprehend what they read. Whatever your personal needs, if you plan to study, memorize, and adopt the sales techniques in this book, you need to make the most of the time you set aside for that purpose.

- ✔ **Study at a pace that fits you.** Some people learn better when they read little bits of information and give themselves a chance to internalize what they've learned. Others like to take big clumps of information at one sitting so they can see the bigger picture and understand the full concept of what is being presented.

- ✔ **Limit your interruptions.** Set up a regular time to study, and let your family and friends know that you will be unavailable during this time. This may be a good time to let your calls go to voice mail and to turn off your computer. If your concentration skills are anywhere near average, you need eight to ten minutes after being interrupted to regain the concentration level you were at before the interruption. That's why staying in the study mode when people interrupt you is so hard. Getting 30 minutes of uninterrupted reading and studying is better than patching together four or five interrupted periods to equal an hour of study time. If you can't hide out for a long period of time, cut your time or break it into two sessions in order to maximize your learning.

By analyzing your optimum learning patterns and working with them, your attitude about the material being studied will be positive. You'll be more relaxed and definitely learn at a faster pace.

Have Realistic Expectations

Reading this book won't automatically turn you into a sales champion. It gives you the tools and knowledge to succeed, but your application of the strategies may be awkward at first. This may limit your effectiveness. That's to be expected. So have realistic expectations for yourself. Practice, drill, and rehearse the strategies until they become a natural part of your speech. Continue to study sales and test new tactics all the time.

Allow yourself time to adapt some of this material to your own style in order to create a genuine presentation and communicate naturally with the customer.

Be patient with yourself. Don't expect to be a winner 100 percent of the time. On the other hand, be honest with yourself and recognize times when inadequate knowledge or an inaccurate application of new selling techniques kept you from giving your best performance.

Know your limitations, but don't be bound by them. Do what you know you should do, do it the best way you know how, and always stay on the lookout for ways to improve your selling skills.

Keep an Open Mind and Welcome Change

You are changing the way you think about and possibly the way you behave in selling situations just by reading this book. Wanting to return to your cocoon when things get tough is only natural, especially if you experienced a degree of success through your old methods. Nobody ever said that change would be easy. Think what those poor little caterpillars have to go through to become butterflies. If you have a difficult time with change, adopting some of the techniques in this book may require a supreme effort on your part. Most of the time, changing your old selling habits is harder than trying new ones.

One thing you can do to better accommodate change is to select just a couple of things to change at first. No matter how many things you need to work on, you'll be too distracted and fragmented if you try to change everything at once. Changing all your selling skills at once is like going on a diet, starting an exercise program, and giving up smoking — all at the same time. It's certainly doable, but why put yourself in such a stressful situation if you don't need to? For best results, choose two things to change that would significantly increase your sales. Work on those aspects of your performance until they become normal parts of your routine. When that happens, choose two more new selling skills to learn or change.

During this period of change and improvement, you'll have normal feelings of anxiety and confusion. Sometimes your presentation may be awkward or rough around the edges. But think of yourself as a diamond in the rough. As soon as you get some polish and put yourself in the proper setting, you'll outshine them all.

As you become a more effective salesperson, you'll find yourself applying what you've discovered to your personal relationships as well. But there's lag time between the practice and the perfection, so allow yourself and others time to adjust to the new and improved version of you. For example, if your goal requires you to work many more hours than you've ever worked, share this with your family and friends and ask them to help you to be your most productive self. Recognize that they may have as much difficulty adjusting to your changes as you have making them. Keep reminding yourself and others of the future value of this time of change.

If you stay open-minded and flexible, you'll be able to welcome the changes necessary for a successful career in sales.

Rehearse, Perform, and Critique Your New Skills

After you internalize some of your new selling techniques, you need to practice them. At first, go over them by yourself until you feel confident enough to practice them in front of your loved ones or peers who can give you valuable feedback.

When you get advice from people you respect, listen! On the other hand, if you get unsolicited advice from people you don't respect, don't let them share in your learning experience: Their responses may damage your delicate psyche.

When you've rehearsed so much that the words are permanently etched on your brain, it's time for your opening night performance. Performing new selling skills and concepts in front of strangers who may recognize your twitching eye and sweaty palms as lack of polish is scary. Give yourself permission to be a rookie, but be sure to follow the rookie rules:

- ✔ Give yourself many, many opportunities to perfect your new selling techniques.

- ✔ When you look back, feed the positive — celebrate all the things you did right.

- ✔ Hold on to your rookie enthusiasm even when you become a polished sales professional.

Honestly critique your performance of your new skills. At this point, you need to look with a critical but fair eye. You'll be able to do this only after you have performed your new skills for at least three weeks and are able to see measurable increases in your sales.

You need to have a tool by which to measure your success. For example, if you've been in sales for a while but haven't been able to reach the level of success you'd hoped for, you may want to jot down your sales ratios and compare the old with the new as you move forward. Seeing positive results gives you something tangible to encourage a continued pattern of improvement.

If a specific stumbling block keeps inhibiting your sales growth, ask another sales professional whom you respect for some advice. Sometimes taking such a person along on a presentation or recording a meeting and critiquing it together can be a big help. In fact, you may be surprised to review a recorded presentation and discover all the things you could have done differently. Critiquing a recorded presentation gives you some distance from the excitement and anxiety of the actual meeting and allows you to analyze your perfor-mance more objectively. Some of your recordings will hold great entertainment value. You'll be amazed at how many things you don't remember and how many things you'd swear you never did or said — it's a real eye-opener and a great learning opportunity.

Personalize Your New Sales Skills

When you memorize concepts and specific words — and sometimes you must memorize word for word — look for ways to make the words you memorize reflect your personality. Practice how you will say them. Think about how you will carry yourself, how you will stand or sit when you utter those words. Use your sense of humor, your previous knowledge, and your natural speech and mannerisms to make your new selling skills sound spontaneous.

The worst thing you can do is memorize phrases and then shut off your personality and resort to a robot imitation whenever you get desperate. The thing to remember as you sell is to be genuine and personable. Being yourself is almost impossible to do if you haven't made the concepts you've learned uniquely yours by wrapping them in your own words and actions. The last thing you want your clients to feel is that they're being given a canned presentation.

Be Disciplined

If you crave the financial and personal freedom that a successful sales career can provide, you have to be willing to go the extra mile. If that means working on a Friday night when all your friends are at happy hour, then so be it. If that means getting up hours earlier each morning until you master your new skills, then that's what you must do. If that means no more two-hour lunches or lazy afternoons for a while, then make the sacrifice. The sacrifice you make today will pale in comparison to the reward you'll enjoy later.

Be a self-disciplined self-starter, and eventually you'll reap rewards.

One of the greatest pitfalls of great success in a short period of time is a failure to *continue* to hustle. People have a tendency to want to rest on their laurels when they have had a good run. Slowing down after achieving success quickly is a dangerous mistake. The fact that you've tasted some success doesn't mean that you can stop hustling and fall back into the same old methods that crippled your sales career.

Stay on your feet and run the race to the finish. Don't allow yourself the luxury of self-doubts or overconfidence. They are production killers. The real trick is to remain balanced during your successes. Don't let increased sales go to your head or repeated rejection beat you down. Although it can seem almost impossible at times, always strive to keep your activities and attitudes balanced.

Evaluate Your Results

Accurately evaluating the results you're getting with your newfound selling skills is difficult if you don't know what your sales results were before you changed. Sure, you'll have a hunch about how things are going, but often you can't trust these feelings. For example, when you're discouraged, you tend to view your accomplishments unfavorably. During such times, your successes diminish, and you can easily feed the negative until it grows into an unconquerable monster. On the other hand, on days when you're overly optimistic, you may conveniently blame a bungled presentation or the lack of knowledge on the client's disinterest and fail to take the necessary steps for self-improvement.

When you evaluate the results of your efforts, avoid comparing your progress to someone else's. Even if another salesperson has received the same training and has read the same books as you, everyone learns at different speeds. Some learn more quickly than others yet can't retain the information for long.

Others learn slowly and give the appearance of having fallen behind, when actually they've internalized the information and will receive longer-lasting rewards for their efforts.

Keep a Success Journal

Keep what I call a *success journal* to monitor your performance. By recording specific instances and details of when you successfully used new selling techniques, you not only immediately reinforce the benefits to your career, but more important, when you need encouragement you can review your journal and relive a positive selling experience. Do it. You'll be surprised at what a great motivational tool a success journal can be. (You can find apps for everything, including success journals, so keep an electronic journal if you like.)

When you review your success journal, compare what you did right in a given situation to what you did when you did not get the sale. When you make such a comparison, the reasons for not getting the more recent sale should become obvious to you. By comparing an unsuccessful experience to a successful one, you see what you left out or skimmed over and why you failed to convince the client of the benefits of your offering.

When such negatives occur, you need to adjust your presentation or sales techniques. And the only way you can accurately make adjustments is to write down your achievements and recognize a good model for a successful sale. After you have contemplated what you need to do to improve your selling, the next step is to just do it.

If you're going to play the "if only" game, then be a finisher. It's okay to ponder what could have been (for example, "If only I had asked more questions . . ." or "If only I had been able to answer the client's objections with more skill . . ."). The trouble with playing "if only," though, is that many times you're defeated before you finish.

After you think about all of the *if onlys,* you must envision yourself as that master of sales and then act on your visions. "If only" is a game of recognizing areas that need improvement. After you recognize those areas, you need to take action and turn your *If only* into *Because I:*

- ✔ "If only I had asked more questions" becomes "Because I asked more questions, I closed the sale."

- ✔ "If only I had been able to answer the client's objections with more skill" becomes "Because I successfully answered the client's objections, he was able to benefit by owning my offering."

By monitoring and adjusting your new selling skills with the help of your success journal, you continue to increase your sales ratios. Be diligent and persistent in your self-evaluation, though. Don't just look at your sales once a year and make bold promises about how you'll do things differently at some unspecified future date. Be consistent and meticulous in your search for excellence and be specific in your plans for improvement.

How effective can a statement like "Next year I want to do a bigger volume of business" really be? Wouldn't the following be much clearer and more productive?

> Beginning January 1, I will spend two hours more a day prospecting and increase my face-to-face selling by 20 percent. In the process, I will increase my sales volume by 5 percent.

This revised statement gives you a more distinct monthly, weekly, and daily activity schedule to follow in order for you to improve. It gets easier to achieve a goal when you know exactly what you're going after. (Check out Chapter 18 for more details on setting goals for yourself.)

Learn from Every Selling Situation around You

You'll be surprised at how many unexpected selling situations you notice when you keep your eyes and ears open. You'll soon see in almost every situation where two people come together an opportunity for someone to sell something. Not only will you be alert to the selling situation, but you'll also start to critique the selling skills used in situations that surround you on a daily basis. When you witness a good job of selling, make a note of it in your success journal (I describe this tool earlier in this chapter). When a master sells you on something, jot down in your journal the superior job he did in selling you his offering. Make specific notes of things he did that especially impressed or influenced you.

To observe all this selling going on around you, you have to stop, listen, and take time to reflect on the situation. If you're not a party to the sale, being an observer is, of course, easier. Not being a party to the sale gives you the distance to recognize some of the familiar selling techniques being used. But that distance also enables you to observe the expressions and actions of the other party as a result of these selling methods being used.

You may see a salesperson use a common technique with a personal twist — and you realize that the strategy you previously thought would not work for you most certainly will if you give it your own personal twist. Creativity is the name of the game in many selling situations. Don't let yourself become trapped into one single mode of thinking or one way of looking at things. If you can be flexible, almost anything is possible.

And if you're one who learns by experience, isn't it better to learn from others' mistakes than to make them all on your own? Their loss becomes your gain. And the experience you observe doesn't always have to be positive in order to have a positive effect on your selling career. Sometimes the negative lessons have a stronger impact than those that look smooth and effortless.

Make a Commitment to Lifelong Learning

Think of every technique you read in this book as one link in the chain of your success in sales. If you have weak links in your chain, then you may need to review a chapter or two to build, say, your prospecting or presentation skills (see Chapters 7 and 10, respectively). If you don't go back and make the weak link stronger, your career chain will never carry the weight it needs to carry in order to haul you up to top-producer status. So, stay committed to the education you aspired to gain when you first opened the pages of this book.

When you find yourself in the fortunate position of top dog, champion salesperson, you'll probably get asked to share some of what you know to others. In fact, you may be asked to train at a sales meeting. The class you teach may be a training class for newcomers to your office. It can be a back-to-the-basics program for seasoned salespeople who have allowed their focus to blur. It may be as simple as helping your children know what gets results and what doesn't when communicating with others.

If you don't already know it, you'll relearn one *big* lesson every time you teach: When you teach, you learn. By teaching your techniques to others, you clarify your own skills and reinforce your knowledge of what makes an effective salesperson. Teachers are students, too. If you can remain flexible — sometimes the teacher, sometimes the student — the opportunity to learn in diverse situations will constantly present itself, and you'll be prepared to learn from the experience.

Put Your Clients First

This business of getting what you want cannot be a totally selfish act. Your selling success increases at a significantly faster pace when your intention to serve your clients and satisfy their needs is number one on your list. Even though you want to make more profit and more sales, you're most apt to accomplish these goals only when you put your customers first.

When your clients know that you're not concerned with being the star, but that you are putting their needs before your own, they forgive some awkwardness or lack of product knowledge. When they can recognize your integrity and honesty, most clients are happy to go the extra mile with you to make your meetings mutually beneficial. People are the key to your sales success.

At the risk of sounding repetitious, let me say that again: *People are the key to your sales success.* Treat your clients with great sensitivity and unflagging respect. Remember this fundamental principle, and before you know it, all the techniques you've mastered will naturally improve your ability to sell with the best of the best.

Chapter 21

Ten Alternative Closes

After you master the closing strategies in Chapter 12 and are ready to move ahead, try these ten additional closes that have proven successful for myself and for others in sales.

The Wish-Ida Close

When you know what you're offering is truly good for your prospective client, and your prospect has agreed but just doesn't seem to want to make a decision, the Wish-Ida close is perfect. It's lighthearted, yet it makes a valid point:

> Everyone's a member of the Wish-Ida Club. Wish Ida stayed in my first house and paid it off. Wish Ida invested in gold 20 years ago so I'd be rich today. Wish Ida grabbed a chance to gain an exclusive advantage. Wouldn't it be great to get rid of at least one Wish Ida by saying yes to something you really want?

The Business-Productivity Close

When you're marketing products or services to businesses, the business's main concern is always going to be the bottom line and whether your product or service makes or saves them money. If your product does not clearly fall into one of those categories, the business-productivity close helps the prospect view the decision from a different perspective — that of having happier employees:

> What I am offering is not just a product/service. It's a boost in employee morale. Haven't you noticed that anything new increases job interest and excitement in your employees? Excitement increases morale. Morale increases productivity, and what is productivity worth?

The Best-Things-in-Life Close

Everyone wants to have the best things in life. Everyone wants to believe that she made some of her best decisions when considering major purchases or investments. The best-things-in-life close gets the prospect's mind off the money objection and onto the enjoyment of benefits, which is what ownership is really all about:

> Isn't it true that the only time you have ever really benefited from anything in your life has been when you said yes instead of no? You said yes to your marriage. (*Optional:* And I can see how happy you are.) You said yes to your job, your home, your car — all the things that I'm sure you enjoy. You see, when you say yes to me, it's not really me you're saying yes to, but all the benefits that we offer, and those are the things you really want for your family, don't you agree?

The No Close

When you've given your best presentation and your buyer still says "No," you have little to lose by saying the following words and putting your shoes on your prospect's feet. The following example is for life insurance, but it works for any type of product.

> Johanna, there are many salespeople in the world, and they all have opportunities that they're confident are good for you. And they have persuasive reasons for you to invest with them, haven't they? You, of course, can say no to any or all of them, can't you? You see, as a professional with ABC Company, my experience has taught me an over-whelming truth. No one can say no to me. All she can say no to is herself and her own peace of mind knowing that her family will be taken care of financially should

something unforeseen happen to her. Tell me, how can I accept this kind of no? In fact, if you were me, would you let Johanna say no to anything so critical to her family's future?

You must speak the preceding words with sincerity and empathy for your prospect's situation.

The My-Dear-Old-Mother Close

I first learned about the my-dear-old-mother close from my good friend and fellow trainer, the great Zig Ziglar. I would never tell you to tell your prospects anything that's untrue, so the next time you talk to your mother or grandmother or someone else's mother, ask her if she's ever been in a situation in which silence means consent. If she has, ask her to say those words to you. Now you can honestly use that line as a close. If she hasn't heard of such a situation, simply ask if she believes it can happen.

This technique can be your salvation when you find yourself involved in a series of silences as you roll from close to close with the same prospect. How, you ask? If you have a clever way to break tension, pressure turns into humor — explosive laughter sometimes. Lots of people can handle pressure, but laughter will pop them wide open. So when the pressure has been on for several seconds after your last close, and it's getting heavy in the room, suddenly grin from ear to ear and say, "My dear old mother once said, 'Silence means consent.' Was she right?"

The Law-of-Ten Close

The law-of-ten close works especially well for intangibles such as financial services, insurance, or education. It's also useful for large-ticket items such as real estate or stocks — items where the expectation is that the offering will appreciate in value. If the person is not totally a Wish-Ida person (covered earlier in this chapter), something in her life has appreciated in value. Here's how to use it:

Ms. Garcia, I've found over the years that a good test of the value of something is to determine whether it will stand the test of ten-times. For example, you may have invested in a home, car, clothes, jewelry, or something that gave you great pleasure. But, after you owned it for a while, could you answer this question positively: "Would I now be willing to pay ten times more for it than I did?" In other words, has it given you that much pleasure, increased your satisfaction, or income?

If you paid for some advice that greatly improved your health, it was probably worth more than you paid for it. If you received some information that allowed you to have a life-changing experience or increase in income or self-image, it was worth more than you paid for it. There are a lot of things in our lives that I think you would have paid ten times more for, considering what they've done for you.

Ms. Garcia, step with me into the future. Ten years from now, will today's investment be worth more or less to you than you'll be investing in it today?

The Buyer's-Remorse Close

When people are making major decisions, you can expect them to have second thoughts about things after those decisions are made. That's why so many contractual agreements for large-ticket items have a 72-hour clause that allows buyers to change their minds. Champions understand this and figure out how to address the issue before they leave a new client with these words (fill in the blank with the name of your product or service):

> Juan, Maria, I feel good about the decision you made tonight to get involved with _____. I can tell you're both excited and somewhat relieved. From time to time, I have had people just like you who were positive about the decision they made until they shared it with a friend or relative. The well-meaning friend or relative, not understanding all the facts and maybe even being a little envious, would discourage them from their decision for one reason or another. Juan, Maria, please don't let this happen to you. In fact, if you think you may change your mind, please tell me now.

The It's-Not-in-the-Budget Close

Business people say, "it's not in the budget" as a standard line to get rid of average salespeople. Why? Because that line *works* with average salespeople. Professionals are businesspeople themselves, and they understand the value of having and managing a budget. They also know that the budget is little more than a tool and that it's not carved in stone. But if the product or service you're offering has enough value, most companies can find a way to loosen up that budget or take steps to own it. The following words often cause the business owner to give you the real reason she isn't going ahead with your product or service — and then you can continue your selling cycle in the appropriate manner.

> I can understand that, Ms. Jones. That's why I contacted you in the first place. I'm fully aware of the fact that every well-managed business controls the flow of its money with a carefully planned budget. The budget is a necessary tool for every company to give direction to its goals; however, the tool itself doesn't dictate how the company is run. It must be flexible. You, as the controller of that budget, retain for yourself the right to flex that budget in the best interest of the company's financial present and competitive future, don't you? What we have been examining here today is a system that will allow your company an immediate and continuing competitive edge. Tell me, under these conditions, will your budget flex or will it dictate your actions?

The Take-It-Away Close

Some people won't want to make a decision about ownership of your product or service simply because they feel they can make the decision at any time. And that may be the case, unless you're working on a special offer or limited quantity of product.

No one wants to be thought of as not good enough for something. As a child, if you knew you could play ball, but someone said you may not be good enough for the team, you probably wanted to be on the team more than ever. By subtly inferring that you have to see if your prospect qualifies before she can own the product, she may try awfully hard to get it. This close works especially well on products that involve financing or insurance (which may require the client to meet a certain health standard).

> Well, Ms. Franklin, I understand your concerns about going ahead with this new equipment. Before we can place an order with our supplier abroad, however, we need to go through the financial process to be certain your company can qualify for such a large investment. Let's proceed with that aspect of the purchase first, shall we?

The Lost-Sale Close

If you've done everything and your prospect still doesn't go ahead, admit defeat. Pack up your visual aids and prepare to head for the door. Then, use the lost-sale close. More often than not, it reopens conversation enough that your prospect gives you something to grasp onto to tell you if she may say yes.

> Pardon me, Ms. Johnson. Before I leave, may I apologize for not doing my job today? You see, if I had been a bit more eloquent, I might have said the things necessary to convince you of the value of my product. Because I didn't, you and your company will not be enjoying the benefits of our product and service and, believe me, I am truly sorry. Ms. Johnson, I believe in my product and earn a living helping people own it. So that I don't make the same mistake again, will you please tell me what I did wrong?

Index

About the Author

Tom Hopkins is the epitome of sales success. A millionaire by the time he reached the age of 27, he is now chairman of Tom Hopkins International, one of the most prestigious sales-training organizations in the world.

In his late teens and early 20s, Tom considered himself a failure. He dropped out of college after 90 days, and for the next 18 months he carried steel on construction sites to earn a living. Desirous of a career less backbreaking and on the advice of a trusted relative, he went into sales — and ran into the worst period of his life. For six months, Tom earned an average of $42 a month and slid deep into debt and despair. Using his last few dollars of savings, he invested in a five-day sales-training seminar that turned his life around. In the next six months, Tom sold more than $1 million worth of $25,000 homes. At age 21, he won the Los Angeles Sales and Marketing Institute's coveted SAMMY Award and began setting records in sales performance that remained unbroken until this century.

Because of his unique ability to share his enthusiasm for the profession of selling and the successful selling techniques he developed through his personal experience, Tom began holding seminars in 1974. Training as many as 10,000 salespeople a month, he quickly became known as the world's leading sales trainer. Today, he presents approximately 30 seminars a year to more than 7,200 salespeople throughout the world.

Tom was a pioneer in producing high-quality audio and video programs for those who could not attend his seminars or who wanted further reinforcement after the training was over. Recognized as the most effective sales-training programs ever produced, they are now being utilized by more than 1 million people.

Tom has also written 17 other books, including *Sales Prospecting For Dummies* and *Sales Closing For Dummies* (both published by Wiley) as well as the best-selling *How to Master the Art of Selling* (published by Business Plus), which has sold more than 1.7 million copies and has been translated into 8 languages and offered in 27 countries.

Tom is a member of the National Speakers Association and one of a select few to receive its Council of Peers Award for Excellence. He is often the keynote speaker for annual conventions and is a frequent guest on radio talk shows.

Dedication

This book is dedicated to all my teachers and my students. Some of you have been both to me. Thank you for your loyalty and for sharing your successes with me. You are the reason why my life has been so filled with love, laughter, and abundance.

Author's Acknowledgments

I thank Judy Slack of Tom Hopkins International for writing and managing my content for so long. I also thank the rest of my team. You all work hard to make my life easy, allowing me to do what I do best — teach.

I thank the team at Wiley for the book and for putting together a team of wonderful, excited people who are dedicated to making *Selling For Dummies* a continued winner for all its readers. Special thanks go to Stacy Kennedy, acquisitions editor; Tracy Brown Hamilton, senior project editor; and Kathleen Dobie, copy editor, for keeping the book true to *For Dummies* form and on schedule.

Special thanks go to Barry Moltz of Business Insanity Talk Radio, the technical editor, for the time, effort, and sincerity he brought to this essential position.

Publisher's Acknowledgments

Acquisitions Editor: Stacy Kennedy

Project Editor: Tracy Brown Hamilton

Copy Editor: Kathleen Dobie

Technical Editor: Barry Moltz

Cover Image: